ROYAL HISTORICAL SOCIETY
STUDIES IN HISTORY 61

FREEWILL OR PREDESTINATION

FREEWILL
OR
PREDESTINATION

THE BATTLE OVER SAVING GRACE
IN MID-TUDOR ENGLAND

D. Andrew Penny

THE ROYAL HISTORICAL SOCIETY
THE BOYDELL PRESS

BT
809
. P45
1990

First published 1990

A Royal Historical Society publication
Published by The Boydell Press
. an imprint of Boydell & Brewer Ltd
PO Box 9, Woodbridge, Suffolk IP12 3DF
and of Boydell & Brewer Inc.
PO Box 41026, Rochester, NY 14604, USA

ISBN 0 86193 219 6

ISSN 0269-2244

British Library Cataloguing in Publication Data
Penny, D. Andrew
    Freewill or predestination : the battle over saving grace in mid-
    Tudor England. — Royal Historical Society studies in history ;
    v. 61)
    1. Christian doctrine. Free will & predestination
    I. Title   II. Series
    234.9
    ISBN 0-86193-219-6

Library of Congress Cataloging-in-Publication Data
Penny, D. Andrew, 1952-
    Freewill or predestination : the battle over saving grace in mid-
    tudor England / D. Andrew Penny.
        p.   cm. — (Royal Historical Society studies in history ;
    no. 61)
    Includes bibliographical references and index.
    ISBN 0-86193-219-6 (alk. paper)
    1. Freedom (Theology)—History of doctrines—16th century.
    2. Predestination—History of doctrines—16th century.
    3. Christian sects—England. 4. England—Church history—16th
    century.
    I. Title.   II. Series.
    BT809.P45   1990
    234'.9'094209031—dc20   90-44729

This publication is printed on acid-free paper

Printed and bound in Great Britain by
Woolnough Bookbinding Ltd, Irthlingborough, Northants

The ordinary respectable Englishman is often a Pelagian at heart, though he has never heard of Pelagius. Partly he has very little idea of God's intense holiness and the absolute consecration and self-sacrifice that God requires of him. He confuses the standard of Christ with the standard of decent society. Virtues such as meekness and patience lie entirely outside his vision. He does not even desire to acquire them. Those qualities that he most admires, courage, fair play, truthfulness, he supposes that he can achieve by himself, if he will only make the effort to do so. As soon as a man awakens to a sense of the meaning of holiness as opposed to respectability, he learns his need of God's help and ceases to be a Pelagian — E. J. Bicknell, *A Theological Introduction to the Thirty-nine Articles of the Church of England*, p. 196

Here were the essentials of the great doctrine of salvation by the election of grace alone, and on these points there was and continued to be substantial agreement among all English exiles and reformers, whether they held by the English or the Genevan settlement of church worship and government. When doctrinal deviation or dispute occurred, as it usually did wherever Calvin's systematic formulation of these ideas penetrated, it was over the question, who and how many were called, and on what terms. On this matter the English, while they were all Calvinists up to a point, were seldom Calvinists in a strict Genevan sense. Many of them had imbibed the doctrine of grace not directly from Calvin, but in modified form from Bucer at Cambridge and Peter Martyr at Oxford. They had followed the latter back to Strasbourg, and some of them had gone on to listen to Zwingli's disciple Bullinger at Zurich, with whom they were to keep in frequent communication after their return to England.

Under these influences they learned to hedge in some degree on the rigorous form of predestined election worked out by Calvin in a situation very different from their own. The situation which awaited them on their return from exile would be one in which they would have to preach and go on preaching for, so to speak, their very lives. Under these conditions while not faltering as to the all-sufficiency of grace, they would naturally preach it as though there were something the people they were trying to convert could do to participate in the process of their own redemption. Vocation was still essential, and still God's doing. But the elect were called to co-operate with the Lord as though they were indeed His chosen agents, confident that His purposes could not fail and that He would never let them down unless they let Him down first. Far from suggesting to the subjects of Elizabeth that they might safely sit back and leave everything to the Lord's determination the effect was to encourage them to suppose that, whatever they might choose to undertake, the Lord's hand would be in it. — William Haller, *Foxe's Book of Martyrs and the Elect Nation*, pp. 74 – 5.

Contents

The Society records its gratitude to the following whose generosity made possible the initiation of this series: The British Academy; The Pilgrim Trust; The Twenty-Seven Foundation; The United States Embassy's Bicentennial funds; The Wolfson Trust; several private donors.

Preface

I wish to acknowledge my especial indebtedness to a number of people who have provided invaluable assistance of one sort or another in the production of this book: firstly, to Dr Kenneth R. Davis, for awakening (and to a large degree creating) my interest in intellectual and ecclesiastical history while at the University of Waterloo; to Dr W. Stanford Reid, for suggesting that I investigate radical activities in the south-east of England during the Reformation era, and for ably supervising my doctoral dissertation at the University of Guelph; to Mrs Diana Burnett of Oakville, Ontario, and Miss Derryan Paul, Lecturer in Palaeography and Archive Administration, College of Librarianship, Dyfed, Wales, for a stellar job in transcribing and translating key Latin sources; to Dr Vaden House, my colleague at The King's College, and James Dykstra, former student and recent project aide, for indispensable technical assistance; to Professor Sir Geoffrey Elton for his constant encouragement, indefatigable correspondence, and amazing vision in helping to resuscitate and reshape this project, and see it through to its now happy conclusion; and lastly, but by no means least, to my wife, Hazel, sometime research assistant, travel companion and valued critic, for incredible patience and enthusiasm which have permitted her to enter fully into the spirit and purpose of this study. To all, my heartfelt thanks and deepest appreciation.

D. Andrew Penny
7 March 1989

Abbreviations

AC	*Archaeologia Cantiana*
APC	*Acts of the Privy Council of England*
CPR	*Calendar of the Patent Rolls*
DNB	*Dictionary of National Biography*, eds. Leslie Stephen and Sidney Lee
EM	*Ecclesiastical Memorials*, John Strype
L&P	*Letters and Papers, Foreign and Domestic of the Reign of Henry VIII*, eds. J. Gairdner and R. H. Brodie
LCC	*The Library of Christian Classics*
MQR	*The Mennonite Quarterly Review*
NIDCC	*The New International Dictionary of the Christian Church*, gen. ed. J. D. Douglas
RSTC	*A Short-Title Catalogue*, 2nd ed. (Revised)
SAW	*Spiritual and Anabaptist Writers*, eds. G. H. Williams and A. M. Mergal
VCH	*The Victoria History of the County of Kent*, ed. William Page

1

Introductory Considerations

We have as yet failed to produce the definitive monograph on the Tudor sects. This task can hardly be done for us by American visitors or even by Englishmen primarily concerned with theology. It can only be done properly by researchers steeped in our local history and archives − A. G. Dickens, 'Past and Present', 1964

Professor Dickens's words of almost a quarter of a century ago retain much of their validity today. There is no doubt that in the intervening years efforts have been profitably expended upon the sectaries of the early Reformation era in England; yet no one would claim to have attained sufficient mastery of the topic to attempt a comprehensive chronicle along the lines of G. H. Williams's magisterial work on the nature of sixteenth-century heresy and radicalism, especially that pertaining to the Anabaptist-Mennonite tradition.

Nor does the present study, have any such aspirations. It is simply offered as a helpful exercise aimed at greater comprehension and synthesis − not encompassing the entire gamut of Tudor sectarianism, but as a necessary contribution towards clarifying one significant aspect thereof: the role of freewill thought in the early English Reformation. In keeping with Professor Dickens's perspective, the use of local sources will form an integral part of the examination of the freewill community, whose members have thus far successfully evaded the eye of county record enthusiasts.

The question of approach

The subject under consideration could be logically approached in at least two ways. One might choose to focus upon the individuals or characters who were prominently engaged in the spread of freewill ideas or one could dwell primarily upon the ideology involved and describe how this appeared to have been carried along at times by a movement of sorts. If we used the former approach, we should wish to think in terms of the Bocking-Faversham conventiclers of the

1

Edwardian years whose most distinguished member was the now almost-celebrated Henry Harte of Kent, and whose progress throughout the Marian reaction involves the intricacies and intrigues of the King's Bench prison dispute. In this instance, then, we should be concentrating on the freewill radicals of the mid-Tudor years — a reconstruction involving the actual people at the centre of the episode under consideration.

The latter approach would lead to an examination of the overall role of freewill doctrine in the early Reformation in England. Stated negatively, we would examine the opposition or reaction to the Reformed doctrine of the unconditional election of individuals to salvation.

A third possibility would be to combine the two approaches as they relate to the sources, allowing the flow of the record to determine the focus at any given moment. Thus, at certain points the sources appear to emphasize the identity of the participants, while at others the information calls for a change of pace. This, by far the most natural course, will be the path generally adopted throughout the study.

Before proceeding, a word of warning and explanation is perhaps in order: rigid classification of the subjects under consideration has been avoided at the outset in order to assist the spirit of inquiry and avoid begging a question which is fundamental to this study; to treat the subject from the perspective of, say, freewill sectarians or separatists is both a risky and a presumptuous exercise, since it is by no means clear that the radicals in question can be legitimately classified according to designations such as 'sectarian'[1] or 'separatist', at least as the terms are usually used (nor even that they were genuinely 'radical' in the pejorative sense). Furthermore, it is debatable whether the freewill exponents themselves would accept any such labels, since it will be shown that the decisive bond which drew the Kent-Essex network together was their firm opposition to what may be referred to as rigid predestinarian thought,[2] along with the conviction that individual believers committed to a godly lifestyle could interpret the English Bible for themselves — views and positions which may or may not be considered radical depending upon one's terms of reference. As far as the individuals themselves were concerned, they were nothing if not loyal Englishmen.

[1] The application of the term 'sectarianism' is adequately discussed by David Loades in 'Anabaptism and English Sectarianism in the Mid-Sixteenth Century' in *Reform and Reformation: England and the Continent c1500 – c1750*, ed. Derek Baker (Oxford: The Ecclesiastical History Society, 1979), pp. 59 – 70.
[2] See pp. 25 – 6, 213 below regarding the freewill men and the questions of sectarianism and separatism.

Historiography and definitions

Whatever else one might say, there is no doubt that the freewillers are becoming popular. In addition to several short examinations which focus specifically on the group itself,[3] it is scarcely possible to find a recent treatment of popular religion in sixteenth-century England which fails to give them at least a mention.[4] This is invariably accompanied by an attempt to invest them with the appropriate label or designation.

To Williams, Henry Harte was an 'influential leader of English Anabaptism'.[5] Williams somewhat superficially accepted that Harte's 'people were "the first that made separation from the reformed church in England" ', although he conceded that 'much of English Anabaptism up to and during Edward's reign appears to have been nonseparatist in aspiration, possibly because of the precedent set by Lollardy'. M. M. Knappen had earlier referred to these subjects as 'a group of English sectaries who may be called halfway Anabaptists.' They 'denounced the doctrine of predestination, and refused to have their children baptized by Roman Catholic clergy, though they did not object to infant baptism as such, or hold many of the other Anabaptist principles of which they were accused'.[6]

Knappen's interest in these 'freewillers' or 'liberals' stemmed more from their commitment to a puritan or ascetic lifestyle than to their opposition to the reformed version of the doctrines of sin and grace *per se*. He also appeared to waver somewhat in assessing the possible connection between these 'primitive Arminians' and later puritanism, commenting that 'it is tempting to see in their activities

---

[3] For example, see J. W. Martin, 'English Protestant Separatism at its Beginnings: Henry Hart and the Free-Will Men', *The Sixteenth Century Journal*, VII, 2 (1976), 55 – 74, and 'The First that Made Separation from the Reformed Church of England', *Archiv fur Reformationsgeschichte*, LXXVII, (1986), 281 – 312. Also, see O. T. Hargrave, 'The Freewillers in the English Reformation', *Church History*, XXXVII, 3 (1968), 271 – 80, and 'The Predestinarian Controversy Among The Marian Protestant Prisoners', *Historical Magazine of the Protestant Episcopal Church*, XLVII (1978), 131 – 51.

[4] One could cite numerous examples, such as Claire Cross, *Church and People, 1450 – 1660* (Atlantic Highlands, N. J.: Humanities Press, 1976), pp. 98 – 9, 114 – 17, and Patrick Collinson, 'Voluntary Religion: Its Forms and Tendencies' in *The Religion of Protestants: The Church in English Society, 1559 – 1625* (Oxford: Clarendon Press, 1982), pp. 252 – 4. For further historiographical data, see my 'The Freewill Movement in the Southeast of England, 1550 – 1558: Its relationship to English Anabaptism and the English Reformation' (unpublished Ph.D. thesis, University of Guelph, 1980). See especially the first chapter.

[5] G. H. Williams, *The Radical Reformation* (Philadelphia: The Westminster Press, 1962), p. 780.

[6] Marshall Knappen, *Tudor Puritanism* (Gloucester, Mass.: Peter Smith, 1963; orig. pub. 1939), pp. 149 – 50.

some of the preliminary stirrings of the later English separatist movements' — this despite his overall conviction that 'no direct connection can be traced between Puritanism and Anabaptism.'[7] Knappen thus reached the likely conclusion 'that this semi-Anabaptist movement was overwhelmed by the waves of predestinarian orthodoxy which rolled in from the continent in the early years of Elizabeth's reign'.

Subsequently, the freewillers of Kent and Essex have continued to draw varied commentary from English, continental and North American scholars. A. G. Dickens spoke at one point of 'Tracts by known English Anabaptists' in the early Edwardian years, and, within this context, referred to Henry Harte as 'a leader of the Kentish sectaries'.[8] He also noted that one of the aforesaid tracts attributed to Harte, *A godly new short treatise*, contained 'passages which the Calvinists would have regarded as Pelagian'. In another place, Dickens continued in this vein by describing the early conventiclers as 'Pelagian dissenters' whose history 'suggests a subdued and anglicized type of Anabaptism'.[9] Irvin Horst, who adopted an extremely broad (and controversial) definition of Anabaptism for his study, *The Radical Brethren*, pointed to a similarity in outlook involving Harte, the continental Anabaptists, and Erasmus of Rotterdam on the subject of the freedom of the will. He openly wondered whether Harte had actually read any of Erasmus's works. J. W. Martin's research drew attention to Harte as the most articulate spokesman of a lay group whose members' lives had been radically influenced and even redirected through an intensive encounter with the recently-published English Bible. He also tended to downplay the significance of the question of predestination, claiming that this was simply the topic which kept surfacing in their deliberation during at least one phase in their development.[10]

Drawing in part upon Martin's work, Dewey Wallace saw Harte as a leader of 'a group of independent Protestant laymen' whose roots were to be found 'in an unofficial lay Protestantism that can be detected much earlier in the English Reformation'.[11] He criticized

---

[7] *Ibid.*, p. 151.
[8] A. G. Dickens, 'Religious Toleration and Liberalism in Tudor England,' in *Reformation Studies* (London: The Hambledon Press, 1982), p. 436.
[9] A. G. Dickens, *The English Reformation* (New York, N. Y.: Shocken Books, 1964), p. 238.
[10] Irvin B. Horst, *The Radical Brethren* (Nieuwkoop: B. de Graff, 1972), p. 133; Martin, 'The First that Made Separation', 291, 302.
[11] Dewey D. Wallace, Jr., *Puritans and Predestination: Grace in English Protestant Theology, 1525–1695* (Chapel Hill, N. C.: University of North Carolina Press, 1982), pp. 20–1.

O. T. Hargrave for depicting 'these freewillers as forerunners of later English Arminianism', as Hargrave had in fact agreed with Knappen that they 'might quite accurately be labeled Arminians "avant la lettre" '.[12] And, while Hargrave concluded that the freewillers 'initiated an anti-predestinarian tradition in England which came to full fruition only later in the developments at the turn of the century', Wallace asserted that 'they were far closer to the Lollards, certain representatives of the continental Radical Reformation, and later English "freewilling" Separatists than to seventeenth-century Laudians'.[13]

Thus, in even a brief introductory survey of opinion, one notes a relatively wide spectrum of perspectives regarding the precise nature of the freewill movement and its relationship to early modern English religious history as a whole. Given this diversity, the question of definition would seem crucial before any attempt can be made to actually unravel the complexities referred to above by means of a renewed examination of the record itself. Terms such as Anabaptism (with specific reference to the English context), Arminianism and Pelagianism, Lollardy and even 'freewill sectarianism', require some investigative analysis before proceeding further. In addition, since we are involved with a classical theological argument in a peculiar historical setting, some attention to definition in connexion with the opposing world of thought is required. For example, should one speak of the Reformed view of predestination in Edwardian England, or the Calvinist, or simply that of mainstream Protestantism? Should we refer to these antagonists in the controversy as the 'Gospellers', the 'Predestinators', or the 'orthodox Protestants'?[14] As always, it will prove somewhat easier to define the relevant terms more or less precisely than it will be to apply them rigidly to the appropriate *dramatis personae*. Nevertheless, such a discussion will prove indispensable in the process of identifying bench marks during the crossing of admittedly difficult terrain. If possible, we shall also wish to identify the most likely sources of influence and avenues of transmission (both native and foreign) in connection with the evolution of freewill thought in this chapter of early modern English history. But these questions cannot be answered in a single chapter, and will be pursued

---

[12] Hargrave, 'The Freewillers', 280.

[13] Wallace, p. 21

[14] 'Orthodox Protestants' appears to be the term preferred by Martin in his studies. See 'The First that Made Separation', 287. For use of the term 'Predestinators', see John Foxe, *The Acts and Monuments*, ed. Josiah Pratt. 8 vols. (London: Religious Tract Society, 1977), VIII, 384. The term 'Gospellers' is employed by Peter Heylin in *Ecclesia restaurata: or the history of the reformation of the Church of England* (London, 1661), p. 73.

throughout the course of the investigation. At this point, a brief examination of possible native sources of freewill ideas – surely the most obvious place to begin – is offered for consideration.

Lollardy

the association of the vernacular with clerical suspicion was not new in lollardy. The Waldensians much earlier on the continent had fallen under suspicion for exactly the same matter: an insistence upon the native language, a preoccupation with vernacular scriptures and, the apparently inevitable consequence, lay preaching . . .. There is then a sense in which it may not be unreasonable to claim lollardy is the heresy of the vernacular, the English heresy. – Anne Hudson, 'Lollardy: The English Heresy?', p. 163.

The point of departure for any discussion of dissent, or even popular religion, in early sixteenth-century England, must be the question of Lollardy. This is particularly true when one is concerned about the question of antecedents and avenues of ideological transference.

As is well known, a veritable renaissance in Lollard studies has ensued since the publication of Professor Dickens's *Lollards and Protestants in the Diocese of York* in 1959. Whether one prefers to think in terms of Lollard survival or revival,[15] (or perhaps better, a combination of some sort), it is perhaps sufficient to state that no serious scholar in the field of the early English Reformation would today question the existence of significant Lollard forces and influences during the Henrician era, in fact, well before the royal divorce and the proceedings of the Reformation Parliament. What specifically happened to these forces with the advent of continental Protestantism is still problematic, although once again Professor Dickens may be articulating something of a consensus when he repeatedly asserts that the Lollard residuum eventually merged with the newer strains as time went on.[16]

[15] See Margaret Aston, 'Lollardy and the Reformation: Survival or Revival?' in *Lollards and Reformers: Images and Literacy in Late Medieval Religion* (London: The Hambledon Press, 1984), pp. 219 – 42.

[16] A. G. Dickens, 'Heresy and the Origins of English Protestantism', in *Reformation Studies*, pp. 364 – 5; cf. his comments in Norman Cantor, *Perspectives on the European Past: Conversations with Historians* (New York, N. Y.: Macmillan Company, 1971), pp. 270 – 2.

As a result of recent scholarship, it is likely that agreement on the essentials or distinctives of Lollardy as the Reformation dawned is closer, although cases of substantial disagreement undoubtedly remain. It has been suggested, for example, that Lollardy was losing some of its religious character by 1509, having become something of 'an underground revolt with home-made weapons'.[17] This may be reflected in the fact that Lollards did not preoccupy themselves with Paulinian justificatory ideas in the continental sense at all. One must also bear in mind with Margaret Aston, however, the possibility that Lollard theology may have actually suffered 'debasement' and significant alteration during the reformation period itself.[18] At the same time, one wonders with J. A. F. Thomson whether 'the reception of other ideas by the Lollards may have actually preceded the Reformation'.[19] Thus, although the idea of change appears to be generally acknowledged, the timing and degree of that intellectual shift are very much open to question.

In terms of the sources of Lollard ideas, one need look no further than to the reading of the scriptures by these underground laymen who anticipated the continental movement in their reliance upon the vernacular. This does not assume universal or even widespread literacy in Lollard ranks, of course, since illiteracy in this era did not at all preclude considerable doctrinal and scriptural knowledge.[20] Learning favourite biblical passages by heart was certainly one way of getting around the problem of not being able to read, although it is undeniable that along with their zeal for truth, they also derived plenty of errors during their study and discussions.[21] We are assured by the experts, however, that despite the cranks and fringe lunatics whom underground cells appear to foster there was still 'a certain coherence of tone and tenor' among the Lollards;[22] and that although we may be hard pressed to come up with 'a set of consistently worked out doctrines', we can at least count on finding 'a set of more or less consistent attitudes'.[23] As for the inevitable discrepancies in evidence among various Lollards, this may be traced to either the prevalence of ignorance in certain Lollard circles or to a combination and blending with other traditions.[24]

---

[17] Dickens, 'Heresy', p. 379.
[18] Aston, p. 219.
[19] John A. F. Thomson, *The Later Lollards, 1414 – 1520* (London: Oxford University Press, 1965), p. 252.
[20] Dickens, *English Reformation*, p. 30.
[21] Aston, p. 11.
[22] Dickens, 'Heresy', p. 364.
[23] Thomson, p. 239.
[24] *Ibid.*, pp. 239 – 40.

Lollard distinctives

How adaptable late medieval Lollardy could be emerges in the appearance of incarnational deviations during the reigns of the early Tudors. As G. R. Elton has observed, heresies associated with the Incarnation were always regarded as the ultimate by the Church,[25] and it is not surprising to see considerable attention devoted to detecting them. An indication of the kind of questions being asked in this regard is provided by a case in 1491, where a carpenter from the diocese of Bath and Wells confessed not only to denying the doctrine of transubstantiation and other common opinions, but also objecting to the concept of 'damnation for sin, "for then Criste must nedis dampne his owne flessh and blode that he toke of the Virgin Mary" '.[26] The concern in this case was clearly over the nature of the Incarnation, or more specifically, how to arrive at a common-sense understanding of the union of divinity and humanity in one Person, thus preserving the relationship between Christ's unique conception and His act of atonement. This man's solution apparently lay in doing away with the penalty for Adamic disobedience altogether. As seen below, another option in rationally surmounting the difficulties posed by the Incarnation came to be known as the celestial flesh doctrine, and related speculations in this direction were popular in Kent in the first half of the sixteenth century in areas such as Waldershare and Lenham.[27] The answers given and ideas displayed in these latter cases were in fact similar to those propounded somewhat later on the continent by Clement Ziegler and Melchior Hoffmann, and are often laid claim to by Anabaptist scholars in terms which suggest they are being viewed as the particular preserve of that branch of radicalism.[28] Thus, a possible Lollard connexion with early Tudor heresy is apparently overlooked in the eagerness to establish continental linkages.

Some twentieth-century scholarship has served to highlight the close relationship between Christology and the eucharist in early Reformational thought.[29] This connexion has been recently

[25] G. R. Elton, *Reform and Reformation: England, 1509 – 1558* (Cambridge, Mass.: Harvard University Press, 1977), p. 362.
[26] C. Jenkins, *Studies presented to A. F. Pollard*, pp. 46 – 50, as quoted in A. G. Dickens, *Lollards and Protestants in the Diocese of York, 1509 – 1558* (London: Oxford University Press, 1959), p. 9.
[27] See pp. 38 – 9 below for a fuller discussion of these cases.
[28] See for example Williams, pp. 328 – 9, 332; also Horst, p. 83.
[29] See Williams, pp. 329 – 30 regarding the views of Hoffmann.

reinforced by J. F. Davis, whose research demonstrates the centrality of eucharistic doctrine to the entire question of Lollard survival. Indeed, Davis considers sacramentarianism to be the foremost distinctive of Lollardy, with its most common belief 'that material bread remained in the host' throughout the mass.[30] Lollards were convinced that, since 'Christ is in heaven', He could not be physically present in the elements.[31] Davis concluded that this 'old Lollard argument . . . was taken over by the Protestants'. At the same time, it is extremely difficult to deduce precisely how far Lollards had moved away from traditional dogma in this area; for although it appears likely that some Lollards developed an appreciation for the commemorative aspect of the eucharist,[32] one would probably be wise to resist the temptation to equate this with the full Zwinglian or signification sense.[33]

If Davis is correct in focussing on the eucharist as the most prominent feature of late medieval Lollardy, it must be conceded that several related postures vie for attention at the secondary level. The denial of special powers to the priesthood in the process of transubstantiation confirms the anticlerical and antisacerdotal mould which Professors Elton and Dickens have stressed.[34] This, along with the denunciation of such practices as prayers to and worship of the saints, and the preoccupation with pilgrimages and relics, surely relates to the Christocentric focus which is at least strongly implicit in Lollardy. Thus, direct confession to God in an Erasmian sense becomes more crucial than the reliance upon practices and doctrines which are considered highly suspect. One might also include the rejection of images as a fundamental principle following along these lines, particularly since it helps in some measure to distinguish Lollardy from its continental counterparts (especially Lutheranism).[35]

As has been often observed, Lollardy can be described as an essentially negative creed.[36] More attention has perhaps been devoted

[30] J. F. Davis, *Heresy and Reformation in the South-East of England, 1520 – 1559* (London: The Royal Historical Society, 1983), pp. 27 – 8, and also 'Lollardy and the Reformation in England', *Archiv für Reformationsgeschichte*, LXIII, (1982), 220 – 1.
[31] Davis, *Heresy*, p. 109.
[32] Thomson, p. 247.
[33] Dickens, *English Reformation*, p. 34. The Zwinglian interpretation would be essentially acceptable to the continental Anabaptists as well.
[34] Thomson, p. 248; Dickens, 'Heresy', pp. 377 – 9; G. R. Elton, 'England and the Continent in the Sixteenth Century' in *Reform and Reformation: England and the Continent, c1500 – c1750*, ed. Derek Baker (Oxford: The Ecclesiastical History Society, 1979) p. 13.
[35] Davis, *Heresy*, p. 109. I am indebted to Professor Elton for his comments in these areas during the course of correspondence.
[36] Dickens, 'Heresy', pp. 377 – 9; Thomson, pp. 249 – 50.

to what it opposed rather than what it stood for in positive terms. In an attempt to address this traditional imbalance, A. G. Dickens and J. A. F. Thomson each attempted to come up with two positives of Lollardy. For Dickens, the conviction that clerics should stress the role of preaching over the place of the sacraments was one obvious choice.[37] The second was most predictable — the sanctioning of the vernacular Bible in the hands of the laity. Thomson's choices appear to be two sides of the same coin: the existence of a 'scriptural fundamentalism' alongside a 'common-sense rationalism'.[38] It is significant that each of these points draws attention to the scriptures in the English language in one way or another (that is, either explicitly or implicitly), together with the privilege and responsibility of Englishmen to discern their depths before God. As seen above,[39] these beliefs and practices were not without their disturbing consequences, though the existence of a 'fringe of cranks' seems to have been far less disturbing to the Lollards than to the spiritual and temporal authorities.[40] Nevertheless, the presence of extremist beliefs underscores the need to avoid stressing only the 'scriptural basis' and soundness of Lollard beliefs,[41] and helps demonstrate that the radicals of the mid-Tudor years were the heirs of a deeply-entrenched native tradition which had its excesses. At the same time, one is struck by the moderation of Lollardy in respect to apocalyptic expectations and fervor. Although there were evidently some Lollard millenarians — along with those who displayed considerable interest in the Apocalypse itself[42] — the Lollard heritage appears, in at least some respects, more akin to the quietist than the chiliast.

In terms of organization and numbers, it has been estimated that, on the eve of the English Reformation, Lollardy could claim at best only a few thousand genuine adherents meeting in regularized cells.[43] Areas of concentration are readily identified, however, particularly in the south-east where well-developed traditions tended to be found in textile-producing regions with relatively high population densities and sophisticated trading relationships — northern Essex, the Kentish Weald, and north-west London.[44] More problematic is the question of Lollardy's relationship with church and state. Did it constitute a genuine sect and was it treated as such by the authorities

[37] Dickens, *English Reformation*, p. 24.
[38] Thomson, p. 244.
[39] See pp. 7 – 8 above.
[40] The phrase belongs to Dickens. See *English Reformation*, pp. 24 – 5.
[41] Thomson, p. 245.
[42] *Ibid.*, p. 240; Dickens, *English Reformation*, p. 30.
[43] Dickens, 'The Reformation in England' in *Reformation Studies*, p. 445.
[44] Davis, *Heresy*, p. 2.

(as Thomson affirms), or were the Lollards merely adept at the art of occasional conformity (as held by David Loades)?[45]

The existence of Lollards in Essex who appear to have 'advocated adult baptism' (to quote Christopher Hill),[46] suggests serious intentions in a separatist direction, as does the refusal to salute or greet those not of like principles.[47] We are not helped in our inquiry by the understandable desire of our subjects to cover all traces of their footprints in order to avoid detection, nor by the obvious tendency to recant (perhaps to the point of betraying others of the same fellowship), yet to remain of the same belief afterward.[48] And, although the Marxist in our midst would like to find unmistakeable connexions abounding between religious ideals and social discontent, we must in the end agree with Thomson that the Lollard program cannot be seriously interpreted as an indicator of social unrest.[49]

Lollardy and the winds of change

It is by now clear enough both that the survival of Lollardy helped to give a home outside academic circles to the newer heterodoxy, and that the Protestant Reformation, even in its early days, added some reviving strength to the beliefs of those secret gatherings of husbandmen and craftsmen in London, Kent, the Chilterns and the Cotswolds where English bibles and Wycliffite tracts, battered and thumbed manuscripts, hidden with care from curate and archdeacon, were reverently read aloud after the day's work was done. – G. R. Elton, *Reform and Reformation: England, 1509 – 1558*, p. 74

The relationship between late Lollardy and the strains of continental Protestantism which swept over England during the latter half of the reign of Henry VIII naturally depended somewhat upon the strength of these two forces relative to one another. Perhaps then, one should

---

[45] Thomson, p. 239; Loades, p. 64.
[46] Christopher Hill, 'From Lollards to Levellers' in *Rebels and Their Causess: Essays in Honour of A. L. Morton*, ed. Maurice Cornforth (London: Lawrence and Wishart, 1978), p. 58. Hill, of course, should be speaking of believers' baptism, not adult. This point about Lollard interest in this form of baptism does not come across in Thomson's work at all. See *The Later Lollards*, pp. 239 – 50.
[47] Davis, *Heresy*, p. 127.
[48] Hill, pp. 49, 55; Dickens, 'Heresy', p. 366.
[49] Thomson, p. 249. There is some evidence of tithes resistance, however, as mentioned by Thomson, p. 247.

expect to find considerable variation in the interaction between the forces at work from region to region, rather than a straightforward, homogeneous pattern. If, as suggested by Professor Rupp, Lollards were in poor shape in terms of both leadership and theology during the early Reformation,[50] one might conceivably expect that newer doctrines and influences would enter relatively unmolested and establish distinctly different standards. This does not appear to have been the case in any general way, even though we may certainly go at least part of the distance with Professor Rupp in stating that things could have been better within the Lollard ranks at the time. Coupled with indications of decline, however, were 'signs of reviving', so that plenty of confusion still exists regarding 'old Lollardy or new Lutheransim'.[51] Indeed, some heresies detected in 1536 show traces of Lutheran origin, while others were obviously Lollard. Still others could belong to either camp, and one must not forget that the introduction of Anabaptist ideas provided further possibilities for confusion.[52] A simple denial of transubstantiation tells us little about origins, since the position was shared by Lollard, Lutheran and Anabaptist. Undoubtedly, Lollardy provided (in at least some areas) 'an extensive platform of critical dissent upon which the various newer movements could build'.[53] Thus the ground was prepared for the reception of new ideas, even though Lollardy itself may have been somewhat close to losing its recognizable profile. The possibility of revivification under foreign contact cannot be ruled out either, although Davis was struck in his work by the 'total lack of Lutheran influence' upon the Lollards in Essex.[54] This might suggest that the survival of Lollardy in certain parts could in fact serve as more of a hindrance than a help to incoming Lutheranism (or even Anabaptism), since the existence of a healthy dissenting tradition at the popular level could lessen the sense of need for new perspectives.[55] This would leave the field for continental Reformed doctrines open largely only to intellectual circles where 'more sophisticated' approaches could expect to receive a warmer welcome.

Such considerations eventually raise the spectre of the Christian Brethren and their status relative to both the Lollard movement and Lutheranism – yet another problem of identification and definition.

[50] E. G. Rupp, *Studies in the Making of the English Protestant Tradition* (Cambridge: University Press, 1966), p. 5.

[51] Elton, *Reform*, pp. 11, 128.

[52] Dickens, *Lollards*, p. 13.

[53] *Ibid.*, p. 245.

[54] Davis, *Heresy*, p. 64; cf. Dickens, *Lollards*, p. 243.

[55] R. J. Knecht, 'The Early Reformation in England and France: A Comparison', *History*, LVII, 189 (1972), 7.

Once again a variety of opinions are in evidence. Davis, for example, tends to refer to the Brethren as 'that organized wing of Lollardy' in some instances, while at another time he appears to equate them with the 'known men'. Further blurring is noted when the Lollards and 'known men' of Essex are evidently regarded as one and the same.[56] Although such a tendency is understandable given the complexity of the case, it is certainly not overly helpful. Even the assertion that the organization of the Christian Brethren depended heavily upon literacy does nothing to differentiate their programme from that of Lollardy itself.[57] More prevalent, and perhaps more reliable, is the opinion of Professor Rupp. Christian Brethrenism is seen not as being more or less interchangeable with Lollardy, but as becoming virtually interchangeable with continental reform. Members of the Brethren showed a particular interest in book-making, and were often associated with the wool and cloth trades.[58] Also, similar to Lollardy, men of various callings and opinions were attracted to their ranks.[59] Their distinctiveness, however, lies in their commitment to Reformational principles emanating from the continent.

Despite some improvement, even this attempt at clarification leaves much to be desired; for, as already noted,[60] even Lollardy and Lutheranism are not readily distinguishable in certain key areas of thought. A. G. Dickens attempts to shed light on this distinction by stating that men of Lollard persuasion were involved with the Brethren, and that these Brethren were the allies of the Cambridge intellectuals who adopted Lutheran and Zwinglian ideas. Lollardy and Lutheranism, within this context, were still relatively distinct, nevertheless, owing to differences in doctrine and social ethos. Thus, the Cambridge men, despite being connected in some way to those of Lollard persuasion, owed very little to Lollardy in concrete terms.[61]

Some assistance in sorting out these complexities is available by recalling the approach of G. R. Elton, who sees the Brethren as a combination of Lollardy with adapting Lutheranism. The clearest point of delineation is theological and concerns the doctrine of the real presence. While this tenet is acceptable to Lutheran exponents, the Christian Brethren adopt a sceptical stance, and gravitate toward the Swiss sacramentarian approach as exemplified in Zwingli. Even so, native English influences remain strong.[62] Fortunately, one thing

---

[56] J. F. Davis, 'Joan of Kent, Lollardy and the English Reformation', *Journal of Ecclesiastical History*, XXXIII, 2 (1982), 228; 'Lollardy', 227; *Heresy*, pp. 54, 60.
[57] Davis, *Heresy*, p. 28.
[58] Rupp, p. 8.
[59] *Ibid.*, p. 14.
[60] See above pp. 11 – 12
[61] Dickens, *Lollards*, p. 10.
[62] Elton, 'England and the Continent', p. 12.

emerges abundantly clear in all of this: there is virtually no room at all for confusing the Christian Brethren with either the Henrician Anabaptists or the Edwardian freewillers.

Tyndale

At this juncture, one might also legitimately inquire about the place of Tyndale in this search for native sources which could possibly have had an influence upon the development of freewill thought in England. What was his relationship to the old and the new in the early Reformation? To begin with, we can rest assured that his New Testament was warmly received in circles coloured by residual Lollardy, willingly supplied by men such as Robert Barnes.[63] As to its popularity and potential influence, the existence of some 64,000 copies among a population of approximately three and a half million persons suggests high scores in both categories.[64] In terms of doctrinal affinities, we know that Tyndale drew heavily upon the thought and writings of Martin Luther; in fact, so much so, that one writer has concluded that predestinarian theology in sixteenth-century England actually 'preceded Calvin's influence by a good number of years.'[65] At the same time, Protestant intellectuals (including Luther) were quick to see the value of using Lollard writings as part of their Reformation propaganda efforts,[66] thus indicating something of the two-way street prevalent in the 1530s.

The question of predestinarian origins in England is understandably crucial to an examination of freewill or anti-predestinarian thought. One is accustomed to designating themes such as total depravity, divine sovereignty and unconditional election as Calvinist with reference to the Elizabethan era in particular, when the full effects of Calvin's assumption of Luther's basic doctrines are felt.[67] We must remember, however, that Calvin's writings were still on the list of prohibited books in England as late as 1542,[68] although Catherine Parr appears to have shown considerable interest in what

---

[63] Dickens, *English Reformation*, p. 34.
[64] Davis, 'Lollardy', 230.
[65] R. T. Kendall, 'The Puritan Modification of Calvin's Theology' in *John Calvin: His Influence in the Modern World*, ed. W. S. Reid (Grand Rapids: Zondervan Publishing House, 1982), p. 199.
[66] Dickens, *English Reformation*, p. 37.
[67] Cf. *ibid.*, p. 199.
[68] Dickens, *Lollards*, p. 8.

was becoming fashionable Protestantism at the court of the day — justification by faith in combination with a predestinarian outlook.[69] The role of Tyndale in fostering interest along these lines and in preparing the ground for the more thoroughgoing revolution of the Edwardian years is certainly far from clear, since his stress upon the notion of covenant appears to weaken the forensic approach to grace and faith matters so pronounced and one-sided in Luther and Calvin.[70]

Perhaps the most helpful presentation of Tyndale's position is contained in the preface of the 1534 edition of his New Testament. Here he expounds as follows:

> The generall covenaunt wherin all other are comprehended and included, is this. If we meke oureselves to god, to kepe all his lawes, after the ensample of Christ: then God hath bounde him selfe unto us to kepe and make good all the mercies promysed in Christ, thorowout all the scripture.[71]

Tyndale goes on to make the conditional aspect of God's dealings with men uppermost, asserting that 'all the promyses of the mercie and grace that Christ hath purchased for us, are made upon the condicion that we kepe the lawe'. He adds that he is spelling out the responsibilities on the human side to his reader, 'least thou shuldest be deceaved, and shuldest not onlye reade the scriptures in vayne and to no proffit, but also unto thy greater damnacion'.[72]

As for predestination itself, Tyndale considered this to be a subject not at all suitable for novices in the faith. Only believers who knew something of the depths of adversity, temptation and desperation could begin to appreciate its complexities and see that God is both 'righteous and just'. Only then can the 'secret wrath and grudging inwardly' of men be overcome.[73]

Tyndale's somewhat tentative approach to the subject of predestination is indeed remarkable when compared to the unmistakable convictions of a Luther or a Calvin, and bears little resemblance to the proclamation of the 'decretum horribile'. In fact, it could be

---

[69] Davis, *Heresy*, p. 35.
[70] Elton, 'England and the Continent', p. 13.
[71] *The New Testament*, trans. William Tyndale (1534 ed.) ed. N. Hardy Wallis (Cambridge: University Press, 1938), p. 4. I have generally followed the original spelling when quoting from old works, except that I have tried to change v's to u's and i's to j's when in keeping with modern form.
[72] *Ibid.*, p. 5.
[73] William Tyndale, 'A Prologue Upon the Epistle of St Paul to the Romans' in *The Works of William Tyndale*, ed. G. E. Duffield, The Courtenay Library of Reformation Classics, I (Appleford: Sutton Courtenay Press, 1964), p. 141.

argued that Tyndale's position is rather typically English, given the somewhat ambivalent attitude on the subject found in Wycliffe himself. This may come as a shock to historians acquainted only superficially with the fine points of theological argumentation, but should be obvious enough to those who approach the history of Christian doctrine with some concern for precision and detail. Moreover, there appears to have been little prominence given to the matter of election and predestination in Lollard circles themselves, and, as already observed, Lollards did not in any complete sense anticipate the full continental perspective on justification by faith.[74]

Wycliffe

It is true that Wycliffe is traditionally seen in Augustinian terms, owing for the most part to his view of the Christian church as the body of the predestined.[75] It has even been suggested that Wycliffe's deterministic outlook may have helped seal his condemnation.[76] According to Vaughan, Wycliffe did indeed tend to see a law of necessity operative in all things, yet at the same time he was aware of the perplexities in his own position.[77] After examining Wycliffe's teaching regarding election and foreknowledge, Lechler reached the conclusion that 'Wycliffe has by no means succeeded . . . in solving all of the difficulties which confront his view of election and the fore-ordination of God'.[78] Lechler postulates that either man emerges as a truly free moral agent whose choices determine his eternal destiny, or one is left to conclude that human responsibility is completely undermined by the over-arching and stifling determinism of God.

Wycliffe's 'double-sided assertion of doctrine' is perhaps reflected in the text of the tract, *Speculum de Antichristo*, where the availability of grace to all men is openly propounded within the context of a defence of preaching.[79] Although 'trewe men' acknowledge that 'god hath

---

[74] See above p. 7; cf. Dickens, *English Reformation*, pp. 22 – 3.

[75] Dickens, *English Reformation*, p. 22.

[76] *English Wycliffite Writings*, ed. Anne Hudson (London: Cambridge University Press, 1978), p. 5.

[77] Robert Vaughan, *The Life and Opinions of John de Wycliffe, D. D.* (London: Holdsworth and Ball, 1831; rep. AMS Press, 1973), p. 320.

[78] G. V. Lechler, *John Wycliffe and His English Precursors* (London: Religious Tract Society, 1904), p. 318.

[79] 'Speculum de Antichristo' in *The English Works of Wyclif*, ed. F. D. Matthew (London: Early English Text Society by Trubner & Co., 1880), p. 108.

ordeyned goode men to blisse',[80] this does not contradict the truth
that he also 'geveth to eche man a free wille to chese good or evyl &
god is redi to geve hem grace gif thei wolen resceyven it'.[81] In a
similar vein, the destiny of men is evidently related to their capacity
to choose:

> And who knoweth the mesure of goddis mercy, to whom herynge
> of goddis word schal thus profite. eche man schal hope to come to
> hevene & enforce hym to here & fulfille goddis word, for sith eche
> man hath a free wille & chesyng of good & evyl, no man schal be
> savyd but he that willefully hereth and endeles kepith goddis
> hestis, and no man schal be dampnyd but he that wilfully &
> endeles brekith goddis comaundementis, & foraskith thus &
> blasphemeth god. & herynge of goddis word & grace to kepen it,
> frely govyn of god to man but gif he wilfully dispise it, is right weie
> to askape this peril & come to endeles blisse.[82]

The point which is worthy of note in all of this, of course, is not that
Wycliffe and his following failed neatly to resolve a theological and
philosophical issue to the satisfaction of all, but that a close
examination and reappraisal of their treatment of the subject of
divine sovereignty and human responsibility reveals a stance much
less hard-line than that pursued by Luther and Calvin in the sixteenth
century, and that Tyndale's covenantal theme appears to echo the
moderation of the Wycliffe circle, and thus the Lollard foundations,
in some respects. Thus, we seem to be facing the possibility of an
extra-continental tradition opposed to the rigours of theological
determinism. In this light, perhaps even the much-maligned
Pelagius, whose works and thought have been subjected to reexami-
nation in recent decades, could be made to appear guilty more of
mistaken emphasis that outright heresy.[83]

What can be stated with greater certainty, however, is that
England's version of predestinarian thought remained, with few
exceptions, less extreme up to the beginning of the mid-Tudor era
than that generally favoured on the continent which, in the course of
things, provoked such intense objections from the likes of Desiderius

---

[80] *Ibid.*, p. 110.
[81] *Ibid.*, p. 111.
[82] *Ibid.*, p. 111.
[83] See John Ferguson, *Pelagius* (Cambridge: W. Heffer, 1956), especially p. 182. See
also the evaluation by Robert F. Evans in *Pelagius: Inquiries and Reappraisals* (New York,
N. Y.: The Seabury Press, 1968).

Erasmus and the evangelical Anabaptists.[84] Even the Edwardian phase of 'power and experimentation' failed to achieve anything approaching complete unanimity, as tensions were created by the struggle between 'Christian liberals' and 'Genevan Disciplinarians'. Then too, common enemies in the form of reviving Romanism and radical dissenters kept either party from relaxing too much. All in all, then, there were substantial numbers who ardently refused to worship at the 'shrine of Geneva',[85] and many of those who did appeared reluctant to endorse extreme predestinarianism in all of its details. Thus John Bradford, who figures prominently in the account about to be related, may well have been the first English Calvinist in a general sense, but lacked the intensity and zeal of the more strident Reformed element.[86] John Hooper saw the question of reprobation from a decidedly infralapsarian position,[87] and it was left to the Swiss-trained servant of Latimer, Augustine Bernhere, to display the more intolerant approach during the mid-Tudor predestinarian controversy.[88]

It is within this context, then, that the whole matter of official theology needs to be examined, with especial reference to such landmarks as the Forty-two Articles of 1553 and the Thirty-nine Articles of the early Elizabethan era. In particular, the relationship of these statements of the faith to popular religious movements such as Anabaptism, 'the fashionable menace of 1552'[89], and to the freewill radicalism of Edward's day, requires careful attention.[90]

Anabaptism in England: a case of mistaken identity?

We are assured by G. H. Williams that the radical movement in England in the sixteenth century featured the close interrelationship of Libertinism, anti-Trinitarianism, Anabaptism of the Melchiorite

---

[84] For a full discussion of Erasmus's possible influence in England, see below pp. 86 – 96, 100, 102; for the Anabaptist position, its relationship to Erasmus and its potential impact in England, see below pp. 96 – 102.

[85] Dickens, 'The Reformation in England', p. 451; 'Religious Toleration', p. 441.

[86] G. Rupp, 'John Bradford, Martyr, Ob. 1 July, 1555', *The London Quarterly and Holborn Review*, CLXXXVIII, 1 (1963), 52, as quoted by Hargrave, 'The Predestinarian Controversy', 138.

[87] Wallace, p. 18.

[88] Hargrave, 'The Predestinarian Controversy', 144. It is difficult to conjecture whether Bernhere developed his views on the continent or in England – or perhaps in both places. For more on his role, see below pp. 125 – 30 *passim*, and 159 – 63.

[89] Dickens, *English Reformation*, p. 252.

[90] See below pp. 207 – 13 for this discussion.

strain, and Spiritualism. Equally striking is the suggestion that the relationship between anti-Trinitarianism and Anabaptism may have been closer in England than anywhere else in Europe except Poland[91] – all the more remarkable a claim since virtually no proof is offered to substantiate it. The following assessment from Horst relating to the reign of Henry VIII is equally controversial:

> Anabaptism in England was in liaison with the movement in the Low Countries and Hesse. It was generally associated with sacramentarianism as a foreign heresy although it had continuity with traditional heresy in England. Its distinctive views were related to incipient anabaptism in the Netherlands and elsewhere in Europe, namely, to the doctrines promulgated by Melchior Hofmann and his followers . . .. The evidence suggests that the movement had some prominent supporters, especially merchants . . .. Despite the harassment throughout the period . . . anabaptism survived and entered the reign of Edward VI as a sizable and vigorous movement.[92]

Perhaps instead of inquiring at this juncture 'What has been said about Anabaptism in England?', it might be more appropriate to ask 'What hasn't been said about it?' As with the case of the freewill radicals of Edward's day, virtually everything has been stated at one time or another, yet with very little substantiation or certainty. We know from the publication of royal proclamations that the movement was deemed to have existed,[93] but we are justifiably sceptical about recent attempts to find an Anabaptist under every bed, in view of the absence of hard evidence pointing to the practice of rebaptism (surely the most convincing external sign of the movement) and the tendency of Tudor officials to sweep together all manner of objectionable opinions under a catch-all label. This is not to suggest that politicians and divines had no idea at all what they were speaking about, but merely highlights the official penchant for exaggeration, and consequently distortion.

In the special case of Tudor Anabaptism, one must be particularly careful not to attribute to Anabaptism that which could just as easily be attributed to 'late Lollardy'.[94] Herein lies the fault of both Williams and Horst, and it is best illustrated in connexion with one particular item of deviational thought which is supposedly in the

---

[91] Williams, pp. 778, 782.
[92] Horst, p. 95.
[93] See below pp. 29 – 32 regarding these royal proclamations.
[94] A. G. Dickens and John Tonkin, *The Reformation in Historical Thought* (Cambridge, Mass.: Harvard University Press, 1985), p. 227.

Melchiorite stream. This is, of course, the already-mentioned incarnational peculiarity commonly referred to as the celestial flesh doctrine. Understandably, Horst makes much of this aspect in his work, pointing to a report concerning the publication of a book on this very subject in the realm around 1538. Horst is thus easily convinced in his study that the celestial flesh notion 'has been coming to the fore as a leading tenet of English Anabaptism and thus a major mark of identification'.[95] Like Williams, he forgets, or seems unaware, that this same belief was displayed in England in the fifteenth century and in the early Henrician era, long before its heralding by Hoffmann and his devotees on the continent.[96] Thus, to see it purely in terms of a distinctive Anabaptist view seems overly simplistic, if not misleading. True, Joan Bocher was tainted with the same heresy and touted as an Anabaptist, while Hooper complained of Anabaptists who troubled him with their incarnational specula- tions.[97] Yet Joan could just as readily be claimed as a remnant of late medieval heterodoxy, and Hooper, far from being an expert on the radicalism of his day, seems to have completely misread (to the point of actually reversing) the Anabaptist position on determinism and freewill.[98]

Focussing on issues relating to the separation of church and state, a hallmark of continental Anabaptism, likewise supplies little help in clarifying the Tudor sectarian scene. Thus, with no substantiated cases of rebaptism upon which to draw as proof, and with a corresponding dearth of clear-cut evidence demonstrating the existence of organized alternative ecclesiastical structures, one would be inclined to agree with Loades that Anabaptism produced only a 'piecemeal and diffuse' effect in the Henrician era,[99] and would begin to look elsewhere for indications of continuity and interaction between the continental and the native English. During the course of this study, such an investigation will indeed be undertaken, primarily with reference to the Anabaptist (and perhaps Erasmian) position on the freedom of the human will in contradistinction to that of the emerging dominant consensus which looked to Saxony and Geneva for inspiration. It will be shown that, following a brief Dutch phase

---

[95] Horst, pp. 82 – 3.
[96] See above p. 8 and below pp. 38 – 41 regarding the celestial flesh doctrine and England.
[97] Davis, *Heresy*, pp. 104 – 5.
[98] For more on Joan see below pp. 32, 43, 101, 179 and 186; see Loades, p. 61, regarding Hooper, together with Hooper's letter to Bullinger in *Original Letters Relative to the English Reformation*, ed. Hastings Robinson, Parker Society, No. 52 (Cambridge: University Press, 1846), Part 2, 65 – 6.
[99] Loades, p. 59.

which may have been rather effectively controlled by the Henrician authorities, the survival or demise of Anabaptism in England as an appreciable influence can be best evaluated with reference to the presence of freewill ideas during the mid-Tudor years.

Freewill radicalism and the early English Reformation

At no point in the Henrician era is concern for Anabaptism in England clearly linked to the matter of freewill. One must recall, of course, that Catholic orthodoxy in England required the upholding of certain doctrines which even to a moderate man such as Tyndale could be construed as roughly akin to Pelagianism.[100] Accordingly, Henrican authorities looked carefully for signs of a denial of freewill in their monitoring of popular religion, not for indications of support.[101] For this reason, it is perhaps not too surprising that something which was regarded as a fundamental tenet of Anabaptism should receive little attention at this stage in England.

When the barriers to a more thoroughgoing doctrinal revolution were removed in Edward's day, however, the association of freewill ideas with Anabaptism became more pronounced. This requires close examination, particularly in the light of the controversy surrounding the nature of Anabaptism in England which has been briefly surveyed.[102] As intimated, the prime focus or test group will be the freewill radicals of Kent and Essex; their relationship to English Anabaptism, as well as their place within the broader context of the English Reformation, will be studied in considerable depth. We will hope to see how closely these radicals fit the pattern of left-wing movements on the continent, whose distinguishing marks have been listed by Bainton in terms of ethical concern, Christian primitivism (including New Testament literalism), a heightened eschatological fervor, anti-intellectualism and church-state separation.[103] It will be seen that the Edwardian freewillers meet some of, but not all, these criteria.

In addition, the Lollard contribution to the movement needs to be kept in view. Here we should wish to consider a plethora of possibilities: the tendency toward biblical rationalism and

---

[100] Wallace, p. 13.
[101] Davis, *Heresy*, p. 10.
[102] See above pp. 18 – 21.
[103] Roland H. Bainton, 'The Left Wing of the Reformation' in *Studies on the Reformation* (Boston: Beacon Press, 1963), p. 122.

fundamentalism; the 'puritanical streak' shown in some Lollard circles;[104] the 'practical spirit of Lollardy' which was expressed in its reliance upon the book of James;[105] and the lack of concrete connexion between Lollardy and social unrest.[106] We shall need to test the accuracy of Margaret Aston's assertion that 'mere coincidence of opinion' tells us little in these matters,[107] remembering to balance the necessity of guarding against overly facile and superficial judgements against that of making some deductions which will advance our understanding of Tudor religious radicalism. We shall have to assess the judgement of Claire Cross that the 'biblical fundamentalism' and interest in James evidenced by the freewillers gives more indication of Kentish Lollard origins than of direct continental links with Anabaptists.[108] And, if Lollardy and Lutheranism were combined in some way to produce the Christian Brethren of Henry's day we will want to ask whether it is plausible to suggest that Lollardy and Anabaptism were combined in some form to produce the freewillers of the Mid-Tudor years.

These are not the only questions to be asked. We will want to see if the Edwardian freewillers were legitimate heirs of a long standing dissenting tradition in the history of Christian thought in England which looked back to the medieval past and forward to the compromises of Elizabeth's reign (being reflected to some degree in the founding charter of the English church) and the Arminianism of the next. We will want to uncover the motivating dynamic of the south-eastern freewillers and consider their stance on the issue of freewill with reference to their entire world of thought. We will seek to discover why the subject of predestination came into such prominence when it did. What happened in the middle portion of Edward's reign to provoke such a determined outcry? Equally important, did the Edwardian divines overestimate the potential for disruption inherent in the freewillers' challenge and consequently over-react in their handling of the alleged crisis? Did the freewillers themselves merely react to what occurred around them – to what seemed likely to stifle and engulf – and take every step possible to separate themselves from it, or did they possess a positive programme which they hoped to see implemented on a broad scale? Are native influences sufficient to account for their origin and growth, or must continental input be included as well? And finally, how did

104 Davis, 'Lollardy', 221.
105 Dickens, 'Heresy', p. 375.
108 Thomson, p. 249.
107 Aston, p. 220.
108 Cross, p. 99.

developments in Marian times affect the course of the dispute, since both freewill radicals and orthodox Protestants found themselves on the defensive during the Catholic reaction? These then, are some, but not all, of the questions and issues which we will wish to keep before us as we proceed.

A closing word on terminology

We have by now had plenty of illustrations of what can occur when scholars become overly precise in attempts at definition on the one hand, and not precise enough on the other. J. F. Davis, for instance, in his preoccupation with terminology and movements, leaves the reader somewhat dazed (or perhaps running for cover) amidst a constant barrage of Erasmianism, Erastianism, Evangelism, and Sacramentarianism – in addition to the basic distinctions such as conservative, Lutheran, Lollard and Anabaptist. The situation is not really alleviated by the claim that a bifurcation occurs in the English reform tradition which saw Erastianism for a time set over against a combination of left-wing Evangelism and Lollardy which roughly equalled the sacramentarian party, nor by that which depicts a man such as Thomas Becon as 'an Erastian preacher who wrote for the Lollard presses of the Brethren in London and who subsequently developed in a more radical direction'.[109]

Along with this problem we have that of historians not sufficiently versed in theological definition (Professor Dickens's opening comments nothwithstanding) willing to cast their labels to and fro in a shower of half-truths and outright error. Thus Christopher Hill confidently refers to Arminianism, 'the doctrine that men may save themselves by their own efforts',[110] in terms which would be highly controversial if applied even to Pelagianism! In a discussion of sixteenth-century heresy which includes reference to Henry Harte, Hill states that numerous heretics of this era 'rejected predestination, attached greater value to works than to faith and emphasized human freedom and effort – a sort of pre-Arminianism, which can be found among Familists, as well as among continental Anabaptists, from whom it was taken over by the English General Baptists'.[111] Regrettably, such gems may be acceptable in approaches to history

---

[109] Davis, *Heresy*, pp. 33, 77.
[110] Hill, p. 58.
[111] *Ibid.*, pp. 58 – 9.

which care little for the inner workings of religion, but will never do in a serious treatment of Tudor radicalism which seeks to make a genuine contribution to our understanding of one particular phase in the history of Christian thought.

In the first place, it is necessary to state that men such as Henry Harte do not *a priori* oppose predestination. They oppose a particular interpretation of predestination. They accept the doctrine of justification by faith alone, but when faced with Wycliffe's dilemma, choose the path of least resistance. They do not believe that the sovereignty of God must preclude what they consider to be genuine human responsibility – the capacity to respond to or reject overtures of divine grace. They accept that salvific grace is available to all men equally, and that those who perish do so wilfully, not as a result of an inscrutable eternal decree.

Such an approach could now be referred to generally as Arminian, especially if the views of Arminius himself rather than those of his followers are kept uppermost. It would not be appropriate to label Henry Harte an Arminian, or even a pre-Arminian, however, particularly since the exact meaning of that term in all of its facets is still very much unclear when applied to the English scene. As intimated, the situation would be worsened by reviving the term Pelagian, since, for the most part, Harte's mature perspectives were not that far removed from that which might be referred to as one stream or branch of orthodox Protestantism in that day. Here we are referring to an emphasis upon the necessity of grace in all stages of the Christian life. Furthermore, there is little indication that Harte and his circle would altogether reject the concept of original sin, although it could be argued that there was a de-emphasis upon the said doctrine in their midst in an effort to preserve the capacity for response in man, which in turn is seen as an interpretation more glorifying to God than viewing humans as almost totally incapacitated. And, although Harte and his colleagues would affirm that true Christians must attain a significant measure of holiness in their lives, there is little to suggest that this was taken as being akin to absolute perfectionism – and accompanied by the pitfalls related to that position.

What remains for the present, then, is to refer to our protagonists in the simplest, least controversial terms. They are thus the freewill radicals of the mid-Tudor era. As intimated above,[112] it will not do, at least at this stage, to speak in terms of sectarianism or separatism either, since both of these imply a relationship to church and state

---

[112] See pp. 2, 20 above regarding sectarianism.

which is highly controversial with reference to the subjects of this inquiry. At no point is the record absolutely conclusive that they sought to cut themselves off permanently from contact with the established church.

Indeed, there is evidence suggesting that at least one wing of the freewillers was content with certain key aspects of the Edwardian church, and simply wished to correct the approach to the doctrines of sin and grace which were then carrying the day at the official levels. It is also possible to argue that in at least one phase of the freewill movement's existence the participants saw themselves, not in sectarian terms, but rather as divine instruments charged with the responsibility of challenging the entire nation to repent and adopt their radical brand of holiness. Thus, these traces of incipient nationalism suggest that some of the freewill leaders had fallen prey to the sixteenth-century version of the chosen people syndrome, and saw a special role for themselves in bringing the earth's most favoured people to their spiritual senses. This in turn would suggest a possible link with the research of James Stayer and Martin Haas into the early aspirations of the Swiss Anabaptists. Only when it became abundantly clear that the radicals program stood no chance of more widespread acceptance did the course of action shift to that of persecuted minority. Not all aspects of the English freewill movement fit this model precisely; yet its appearance to at least some degree necessitates a further look, since it is issues such as these which will ultimately provide clues in assessing the relationship between the freewill radicals and both separatism and sectarianism.[113]

In this light, the radicals may eventually appear more interested in reforming from within than in opting-out. At any rate, we should be safer for the moment in agreeing with Loades that a tendency towards nonconformity does not in any way prove the existence of separatism and sectarianism.[114] In fact, one might see considerable justification for adopting Christopher Hill's concept of occasional nonconformity until futher clarification is possible.[115] Other acceptable designations

---

[113] For instance, see Martin Haas, 'The Path of the Anabaptists into separation: The Interdependence of Theology and Social Behaviour' in *The Anabaptists and Thomas Muntzer*, eds. James M. Stayer and Werner O. Packull (Dubuque, Iowa: Kendall/Hunt Publishing Co., 1980), pp. 72–84. For more on the elect nation theme in the English context, see William Haller, *Foxe's Book of Martyrs and the Elect Nation* (London: Jonathan Cape, 1963). See also James M. Stayer, 'Reublin and Brotli: The Revolutionary Beginnings of Swiss Anabaptism' in *The Origins and Characterstics of Anabaptism*, ed. Marc Lienhard (The Hague: Martinus Nijhoff, 1977), pp. 83–102.
[114] Loades, p. 63.
[115] See Hill's essay, 'Occasional Conformity' in *Reformation Conformity and Dissent*, ed. R. Buick Knox (London: Epworth Press, 1977), pp. 119–220.

which could be applied to the freewill circle at this point would include 'fellowship', 'movement' and 'conventiclers'.

For reasons already enunciated, we must also resist all inclination at this point to refer to the freewillers as pure Anabaptists. One can only speak in terms of genuine Anabaptism in the presence of actual cases of rebaptism; that is, where the doctrine and practice of believers' (not 'adult') baptism is clearly in evidence in contrast to the prevailing notion of infant christening. In turn, the practice of infant baptism is inextricably bound to a peculiar understanding of the church as the community of the self-declared, self-committed faithful. There is no room for the wheat and the tares to grow together until the end of the age. Once again, it must be determined whether the freewill circle ever attempted to define itself in such uncompromising terms.

At the same time, it must be quickly stated that the possibility of Anabaptist influence cannot be ruled out. Indeed the probability of such influence appears at times to be rather high, especially with reference to the clear propounding of the relative freedom of the human will and in the attitude adopted towards the necessity of holy living — hallmarks which are indeed present in the native English milieu, but which are perhaps seen in much sharper relief in the continental examples. Thus, the association between Anabaptism and the English radicals' programme of freewill and ethical puritanism would seem too obvious not to have some basis or point of contact. The other possible source of these ideas in the early to mid-sixteenth century was Erasmus of Rotterdam, and it is not inconceivable that both the continental Anabaptists and English freewill radicals drew in some measure upon his theological and practical insights. Indeed, his disputation with Luther on the condition of the human will would be the primary model available to ideologists engaged in a similar controversy until the Arminian problem itself was examined at the Synod of Dort.[116] These possible channels of influence will be looked at before the full account of the mid-Tudor predestinarian battle is unravelled.[117]

Nor will the debt of English nonconformity to Lollardy be ignored, especially if it is agreed that its focus on the English Bible constituted the foremost element in its legacy, and if it can be maintained that the

---

[116] For more on the relationship between Erasmus and the continental Anabaptists, and on the radical emphasis upon holiness in the Anabaptists' scheme of things, see Kenneth R. Davis, 'Erasmus as a Progenitor of Anabaptist Theology and Piety', *MQR*, XLVII, (1973), 163 – 78, and his *Anabaptism and Asceticism* (Scottdale, Pa.: Herald Press, 1974).

[117] See below pp. 86 – 102 for a discussion of the possible influence of Erasmus and the continental Anabaptists upon the English freewillers.

freewill radicals were part of an ongoing native tradition of dissent somewhat distinct from established continental norms. At the same time, it is highly probable that Lollardy alone is insufficient to account for the entire freewillers' programme. Certainly there must be connexion between their origins and the Lollard tradition of dissent, and we can also be assured that the Lollard rejection of saintly intermediaries was very much implicit in the freewill stance. Yet the freewill radicals clearly moved beyond a merely negative posture. Denunciation of pilgrimages, images and even transubstantiation formed no appreciable part in their scheme of things, since they began to move beyond the rudiments of dissent and addressed themselves to genuine Reformational, not simply medieval, issues. Thus, although we sympathize with Thomson's warning regarding the fallaciousness of an overly rigid categorization of beliefs in the Reformation period,[118] we cannot allow this sceptism to stand in the way of identifying possible lines of transmission and influence; for even a cautious approach can convince us of the likelihood that we have as much of continental radicalism as native dissent in the case of the Kent-Essex conventiclers.

It is here that one last exercise in definition is required before proceeding to an examination of radicalism in the Henrician era itself. If the freewill nonconformists are to be viewed as the protagonists for purposes of this study, it is necessary to spend a few moments looking again at the antagonists — in this case the supporters of Saxon and then Genevan orthodoxy.

Here one can quickly enter a quagmire, especially having in mind Professor Elton's point that what might be appropriate terminology for continental models might not transpose itself intact to England.[119] We would thus hesitate to speak as glibly of Reformed or Calvinist orthodoxy here as we might in Switzerland or Strasbourg. We should perhaps do better with official theology and practice, or as suggested, with 'orthodox Protestants.' As for the maintainers of a Genevan-directed perspective in mid-century England, perhaps we can do no better than the predestinarians.[120] Certainly, it was the emphasis placed upon this particular aspect of the Genevan outlook which tended to dominate the minds of its opponents — even though for Calvin himself the subject of predestination was derived from a more encompassing vision which included 'the omnipotence of God' and 'the helplessness of man'.[121]

[118] Thomson, p. 250.
[119] Elton, 'England and the Continent', p. 12.
[120] See above p. 5 regarding the usage of this terminology.
[121] Charles D. Cremeans, *The Reception of Calvinistic Thought in England* (Urbana, Ill.: University of Illinois Press, 1949), p. 3.

Concentration upon the doctrine of predestination in the sixteenth century appears somewhat ironic in retrospect, since a more precise framework would have focussed on election rather than predestination.[122] The failure of contemporaries correctly to distinguish between the two terms (and the perpetuation of this error in some circles down to the present), is a genuine puzzle in the history of Christian thought. Somewhat greater precision in identifying different emphases within the 'predestinators' was beginning to maintain itself in England prior to the accession of Elizabeth, however, as the freewill party found itself able to distinguish between moderates and extremists. The former were hardliners in the Reformed world who affirmed that God's choice of the elect was made without reference to the fall of man. Indeed, the fall could be regarded by some as a virtual consequence of the electing activity of God and the decrees of God. The latter were the supporters of the infralapsarian branch of Reformed truth: God's eternal choice was made in full light of the consequences of fall. A remnant was graciously selected from the mass of fallen humanity. The fall in itself, although foreseen, was not willed by the divine majesty.

It seems clear that both these views had currency in pre-Elizabethan England, and that it was the unabashed perspectives of the more extreme element which drew the particular ire of the freewill exponents.[123] In the final analysis, however, neither view was terribly acceptable, since the freewill men were convinced that they were being called upon to defend biblical truth in what was first and foremost a 'moral dispute over the nature of God's love and goodness'.[124]

It is to the origins of this anti-predestinarian movement that we are now ready to turn.

<hr/>

[122] For further, contemporary theological discussion along these lines, readers may wish to consult the following: Wilber T. Dayton, 'A Wesleyan Note of Election' in *Perspectives on Evangelical Theology*, eds. Kenneth S. Kantzer and Stanley N. Gundry (Grand Rapids: Baker Book House, 1979), 95 – 103; Robert Shank, *Life in the Son*, 2nd ed. (Springfield, Miss.: Westcott Publishers, 1961); I. Howard Marshall, *Kept by the Power of God* (Minneapolis: Bethany Fellowship, Inc., 1969); Roger T. Forster and V. Paul Marston, *God's Strategy in Human History* (Wheaton: Tyndale House Publishers, Inc., 1974); Paul J. Jewett, *Election & Predestination* (Grand Rapids/Exeter: Erdmans/Paternoster Press, 1985); and *Grace Unlimited*, ed. Clark H. Pinnock (Minneapolis: Bethany Fellowship, Inc., 1975). My terminology and theological framework has been greatly influenced by the discussions contained in the above works, especially those found in Pinnock (e.g. Vernon C. Grounds, 'God's Universal Salvific Grace', pp. 21 – 30, and Jack W. Cottrell, 'Conditional Election', pp. 51 – 73).
[123] See below pp. 161 – 3, 180 – 1 and 199 – 201 for more on this theme.
[124] Jerry L. Wallis, 'The Free Will Defense, Calvinism, Wesley, and the Goodness of God', *Christian Scholar's Review*, XIII, 1 (1983), 33.

2

Anabaptists and Sectaries in the Reign of Henry VIII

Indications of Unrest

On 1 October 1538, a most intriguing directive went forth from Thomas Cromwell. As a result of mounting pressure and concern at the highest levels, the Archbishop of Canterbury was ordered to form a commission to extirpate the blight of Anabaptism in the realm. His commissioners were empowered to receive repentant heretics back into the church and to impose suitable penalties. The obdurate were to be handed over to the secular arm for punishment. Care was to be taken in searching for heretical books and papers, and all such were to be burned. The importance attached to the commission is clear from the sweeping powers with which it was entrusted, as the commissioners were declared exempt from any previous statutes which might interfere with the effective discharge of their duties.[1] Distinguished commissioners appointed to serve in this capacity included Dr Edward Crome, Nicholas Heath, and the sometimes controversial Robert Barnes.

This special commission, one of five issued during Cranmer's day,[2] represented the second stage of an official programme aimed at confounding the heretical dimensions which accompanied the Reformation stirrings. In March of 1535 — the year of the Münster reprisals — a royal proclamation had issued, ordering all Anabaptists to quit the realm within twelve days on pain of death.[3] In February, Cromwell had been advised of continental persecutions by William

---

[1] London, Lambeth Palace Library, The Registers of the Archbishop of Canterbury, Thomas Cranmer, 1532 – 55, fol. 67a.
[2] Davis, *Heresy*, p. 14.
[3] *Tudor Royal Proclamations: The Early Tudors*, eds. P. L. Hughes and J. F. Larkin (New Haven: Yale University Press, 1964), I, 155, 227 – 8.

Lok, who focussed on burnings in the Low Countries.[4] The vicegerent, together with the rest of the Council, must have been duly impressed with the perceived threat to the well-being of the realm, and indeed they might well have been concerned for there is an indication that followers of David Joris had visited England from the Netherlands in the middle of the previous year.[5] And Joris himself appears to have had plans to come across in 1535.

On 27 May 1535, Antony Wayte reported on some Flemings holding 'no less strange than damnable opinions' in a letter to Lady Lisle. These five opinions were:

> first, that Christ hath not the nature of God and man: secondly, that Christ born of the Virgin Mary took no part of the substance of her body: thirdly, that the bread consecrated by the priest is not the Incarnate body of Christ: fourthly, that baptism given in the state of innocency [that is, to children] doth not profit: fifthly, that if a man sin deadly after he be once baptised, that he shall never be forgiven.[6]

Barnes was evidently called upon to help with this examination too, although Wayte commented that 'they be so stiff that as yet there is small hope of their conversion'. Doubt was also expressed about the fate of those being questioned: 'the King's Grace' would have to choose between execution in England and returning the offenders to their native land. That choice may have been more complicated than it first appears, since Wayte mentioned both those who had come from Flanders of late and those who were 'dwellers' in the realm.

According to Wayte, there were twenty-three persons (including three women) in this initial group of heretics. Stow remarked that twenty-five persons (six of them women) from Holland were dealt with at St Paul's on 25 May. He also provided the judgement: fourteen condemnations, with the result that two persons were burnt at Smithfield and the rest were dispersed for suffering in various localities.[7] Foxe, who relied upon 'the registers of London' for his information, supplied the names of 'ten Dutchmen Anabaptists' who were executed in various parts of England in 1535, adding that ten others recanted and two were pardoned after the sentence had been delivered. Clemency such as this was seen as being 'contrary to the

---

[4] *The Lisle Letters*, ed. Muriel St Clare Byrne (Chicago & London: University of Chicago Press, 1981), II, 494. Cf. *L&P*, VII, 198, p. 76.

[5] Horst, p. 54.

[6] *Lisle Letters*, II, 193–4.

[7] *Ibid.*, II, 494–5. Cf. John Stow, *The annales of England* (London: G. Bishop & T. Adams, 1605 ed.) p. 963. RSTC 23337.

pope's law'.[8] Foxe cited the affair as the solitary example of religious persecution during the otherwise uneventful 'time' of Anne Boleyn.

A second royal proclamation touching upon the Anabaptist menace was forthcoming in November of 1538, some six weeks after the aforementioned commission was instituted. Anabaptists were advised to flee immediately.[9] Once again it is clear that the Council meant business. Within a week, three more Flemish Anabaptists were condemned after bearing faggots at St Paul's, while a fourth apparently abjured. According to Stow and Wriothesley, related burnings took place at Smithfield on 29 November.[10] John Husee, in correspondence to Lord Lisle during these days, must have spoken for many when he observed: 'It is thought more of that sect shall to the fire.'[11]

As if to confound the experts, these measures were followed by yet another proclamation of 26 February 1539, in which the King declared his desire to pardon all offenders not yet apprehended.[12] This gracious and highly surprising reversal was said to stem from the King's wish to win back his deluded subjects from the error of their ways, lest the fear of severe punishment transform 'their simplicity to obstinacy, whereby they might perish and be lost out of Christ's flock forever'. The clemency was not confined to 'Anabaptists', but was applied to 'Sacramentaries' as well.

The deeper motive for the pardon, if there was one at all, is rather difficult to discern. Perhaps the councillors were genuinely convinced that Cranmer's commission had matters so well in hand in such a short space of time that a relaxation was warranted. More probably, the situation reflected the high-level tug-of-war over the pace of reform being conducted at the time between Cranmer and Cromwell on the one hand, and the King himself on the other. As Professor Elton has convincingly demonstrated, the February reversal indicated that the former were enjoying a temporary victory in the ongoing campaign against previous conservative strictures.[13] At any rate, the problem did not altogether go away, although it is possible that the foreign input in Henrician sectarianism was being brought

---

[8] Foxe, V, 44.
[9] Hughes and Larkin, I, 186, 273.
[10] *Lisle Letters*, V, No. 1285, 307; cf. Stow, p. 971, and Charles Wriothesley, *A Chronicle of England During the Reigns of the Tudors*, ed. W. D. Hamilton, Camden Society Publications, New Series, Vol. XI (New York: Johnson Reprint Corp., 1965; orig. pub. 1875), I, 89 – 90.
[11] *Lisle Letters*, V, 307.
[12] Hughes and Larkin, I, 188, 278 – 80.
[13] G. R. Elton, *Policy and Police* (Cambridge: University Press, 1972), pp. 254 – 60, especially p. 258.

under control. It is reported, for example, that in the same year, thirty-one Anabaptists 'that had fled from England' were executed at Delft.[14] Clearly, the haven that had been sought in England had quickly vanished. Leadership must become a problem, especially since one of the victims of the previous November, Jan Matthijs, appears to have played a prominent role in keeping the lines of communication between the continental and English radicals intact.[15]

It is possible that three or four other persons who were executed during the spring and summer of 1540 suffered as Anabaptists,[16] though the accounts do not present a clear picture. Furthermore, it was reported in April of the same year that Robert Barnes and his colleagues had been placed in the Tower along with some local Londoners and up to twenty Anabaptists − many of them Flemish in origin.[17] All in all, Horst conjectures that some twenty persons suffered burning for Anabaptist opinions during Henry's reign, virtually all of whom were Dutch.[18] Although the King continued to receive reports concerning Anabaptist activity on the continent as late as 1544,[19] the early continental influence in England appears to have peaked and begun to wane. The next intensive examinations involving Anabaptism here did not occur until the reign of Edward VI, by which time the English movement had come to be closely identified with Kent and its most notorious radical, Joan Bocher.[20]

The place of freewill thought in the Henrician era

It is significant that there is no obvious connexion made between Anabaptism and freewill ideas in England before the reign of Edward VI. This is all the more striking given the furore created by the topic of freewill on the continent, when a major battle had occurred between Erasmus and Luther in the early stages of the Reformation

---

[14] Gerard Brandt, *The History of the Reformation and other Ecclesiastical Transactions in and about the Low-Countries* (London: Timothy Childe, 1720), I, 77.

[15] See Horst's largely speculative comments, pp. 80 and 88. Cf. *Chronicle of the Grey Friars of London*, ed. John G. Nichols, Camden Society Publications, No. 53, Old Series (London, 1842), p. 42.

[16] Horst, p. 93. Cf. Stow, p. 974; Wriothesley, I, 118−19; *L&P*, XV, 651, 310.

[17] Horst, p. 93. Cf. *L&P*, XV, 485, 205−6.

[18] Horst, p. 95.

[19] *Letters and Papers, Foreign and Domestic of the reign of Henry VIII*, eds. J. Gairdner and R. H. Brodie (London, 1862−1932), XIX, 2, 38, p. 17).

[20] See below pp. 43, 101, 179 and 186 regarding Joan of Kent.

and the radicals' position had become clearly identified before the Münster débâcle.

In accounting for the difference in emphasis, one must recall that predestinarian theology gained an early and wide acceptance on the continent, while in Henry's England, sympathy with the new doctrines had to be camouflaged somewhat by professions of adherence to conservative orthodoxy. Casting aspersions on the doctrine of freewill was enough to elicit condemnation at the highest levels in 1530,[21] and was being identified at the time with the writings of Tyndale. Affirming the role of freewill in the salvation process was part of Nicholas Shaxton's recantation proceedings later in the reign,[22] although Cranmer had the courage at one point to inquire of the King as to its actual existence.[23] And well he might, for by 1541 men such as Robert Wisdom were speaking out more openly on the subject. The first article at his trial in this year revolved around this very issue; by then, Wisdom had adopted the continental position regarding the necessity of regeneration prior to the coming of faith and the performance of good works in an individual.[24] The officials, however, were not favourably impressed with his stance, it being noted that he had 'preached against Free Will (and so derogated the grace of God and encouraged naughty men to flatter themselves in their unfruitful living)'.[25] Within a few years, the perspectives which Wisdom defended began to enjoy the royal favor, and those who opposed them became popularly associated with the excesses of the Anabaptists.

An early response to the emerging predestinarian theology

Just before the end of Henry's reign, Stephen Gardiner issued what might be taken as the definitive statement on freewill and predestinarian matters from the perspective of the declining conservative officialdom. Writing in response to criticisms levelled against him by George Joye, Gardiner's lengthy ' rebuttal was printed by John

[21] Davis, *Heresy*, p. 10; *Concilia Magnae Britanniae et Hiberniae*, ed. David Wilkins (London, 1737), III, 727 – 8.
[22] Davis, *Heresy*, p. 79.
[23] *Ibid.*, p. 69.
[24] *Ibid.*, p. 75.
[25] *L&P*, XVIII, 1, 538, p. 313.

Herford in 1546.[26] The career of Robert Barnes was obviously a
subject of mutual concern in this controversy, and Gardiner sought to
exonerate himself from charges of mishandling Barnes's case in the
early going.[27] Much of his later discussion revolved around the
subject of predestination, wherein he sought both to maintain
reverence for the ways of God and to disclaim the interpretation of the
Protestant mainstream which was then gaining ground. Gardiner
referred to his own day as one 'of vaine glory in knowledge'. Things
had proceeded so far in terms of the probing and defining of the
divine mind and plan that Gardiner could speak of it then being 'as
necessarie, to teache ignoraunce, for thexclusion of arrogancy &
presumption, & planting of humilite, as hath ben in tyme of extreme
darknes, expediente, to set forth knowledge to thincrease of gods
glory'.[28] He also caught sight of a scheme on the part of 'the
Captaines of the secte' which, by the use of semantics, was intended
'to decyve the simple, whom they wold seeme to desire, to teach
goddes truth, and under pretence thereof, do sowe abrode the devyls
falshed'. In this obvious reference to Lutherans and Calvinists who
held to a distinctly predestinarian position, Gardiner uncovered those
men who had:

> studied out a devise howe deceyvynge men, in the signification of
> fre wyll, as though it signified no choice at all but only a desirouse
> appetite, they have graunted that man hath fre wyl to his
> salvacion, whiche they call a wyll newe create of god, to be
> desyrouse of salvacion, and therewith defende styll their mere
> necessitie, and therwithall say this also, that a good man, doth
> necessarilye well, and also frely well, and an evyll man, doth
> necessarily evyll, and frely nought. They say also, that god doth
> compell no man, for compulsion (saye they) is contrary to free
> wyll, But not necessite, and for this they alledge the ethnyke
> philospher Aristotell, bicause he may helpe forwarde, who
> considering, the natural partes of the soule sayth that *violentum
> opponitur voluntati*, non necessitas. And yet Aristotell useth such a
> worde, in the steade of *voluntas*, as signifieth *Lubentiam* or *libidinem*,
> that is commen to man & beast and not *voluntatem* which is propre
> to man, and yet thus they shyft in the wordes, to deceyve the
> simple . . .. But Aristotell their author sayth, that absolute

---

[26] Stephen Gardiner, *A declaration of such true articles as George Joye hath gone about to confute
as false* (London: J. Herford, 1546). RSTC 11588.
[27] See for example *ibid.*, fol. xb.
[28] *Ibid.*, fol. lxxiia.

necessitie which is proprely necessitie, is contrary to fre choice, which man must have, or he is no man.[29]

In seeking to set the record straight, Gardiner maintained that 'the discussion of the scriptures' was not for everyone, since it 'requireth goddes further giftes of erudicion and lernynge'.[30] Perceiving that his opponents would accuse him of denying predestination outright, Gardiner made it clear that he would do no such thing. In fact, he declared 'god's predestination' to be a subject fit 'to be worshypped and reverenced'. He also expressed his regret at the way the topic, and the scriptures along with it, were being 'abused unsemely by noughty men, to suche ende and effecte, as the Greekes and infidels used the false opinion of destinie'. He then proceeded to lay down what he considered to be the proper principles of interpretation which must be utilized in approaching his grand subject. Scripture must be compared with scripture so that apparent contradictions may be overcome. It is not an open book as some maintain, but requires effort and diligence in the unlocking of its meaning or 'true sense', which 'hath ben by the spirite of god, preserved in the church, as certeine and inviolable, how so ever it hath been impugned in sundry ages.'[31]

Predestination was defined in Gardiner's work as 'the decree of god to helpe and directe men chosen, to thende of their glorification'. It is thus an aid and a comfort, as we are 'perswaded that god is with good men'.[32] Moreover, Gardiner stated with conviction that 'predestination doth not impugne the free choyse of man'.[33] He rejected the manner in which Augustine is utilized by some 'to conferme theyr opinion of necessitie', and proceeded to show that such interpretations are illogical.[34] He referred to Simon Magus as 'the fyrst auctour of the heresie of mere necessitie, which heresie hath ben in sundry ages renued, as it hath ben of late by luther& other, and not yet extinct'.[35] He also engaged in a lengthy argument designed to show the complexities of relating matters of eternity to the temporal realm. His design, of course, was to undermine the apparently presumptuous declarations of his opponents — those 'who when they perceyve not in dede the counsayle of hym that devysed fyrst any platte, they take upon them nevertheless, to set the frame

---

[29] *Ibid.*, fols. lxxiiib – lxxva.
[30] *Ibid.*, fol. ib.
[31] *Ibid.*, fols. xxib – xxiiia.
[32] *Ibid.*, fol. xxiiib.
[33] *Ibid.*, fol. xxviiia.
[34] *Ibid.*, fols. xxviiib – xxixa.
[35] *Ibid.*, fols. xxviia – b.

together, & marre some principal postes or cast them out as vaine, because they can not tell howe to joyne them with the rest, whom such men folow, who because they can not tell howe to frame gods choise, & mans choise togither, they mangle and denye mans choise, and cast it away as vayne, beinge a principall part to be beleved in our religion.'[36]

Gardiner's own position appeared to hinge on the conditional nature of God's election, coupled with a distinction between 'gods knowledge' and 'his election'.[37] He interpreted the Apostles Peter and Paul as teaching 'that goddes election is so done by hym, as it importeth no necessitie in man but requireth a confiormitie in us agreable for the same'.[38] Thus, 'the reconciliacion of god' does not imply any 'necessitie of continaunce'. Furthermore, 'goddes predestination as a superiour cause doth not violentlye work to the compulsion of the inferior cause'.[39] So, although 'god can not fayle in his promysse, so man maye fayle in the receyvinge and reteynynge of that is promised'.[40] Gardiner then came to the heart of his belief in the following passage:

> god choseth as he seeth in his divine providence those that shall receyve and use his gyftes accordynge to his wyl, and reproveth them that he seeth before wyl refuse them and worke their owne confusion, and so predestinateth such as he hath chosen, by which ordre goddes knowledge is the cause of his election, goddes election the cause of his predestination, predestinacion the cause of callyng &c.[41]

Gardiner, in this work, thus wanted nothing to do with the Protestant continental mainstream in his assertion that God's knowledge, though 'infallible, yet it is not the cause of all that is knowen, for in knowledge, god onely seeth moost perfitelye the workes of all natures, as they be, and mannes reason that wolde fynde faulte, can not considre goddes knowledge to be in priorite to goddes decre, to create man, wherebye that knowledge as it folowed, and was no cause of it, so it coulde be no cause whye to alter it'.[42] Similarly, although God created man, 'yet he is not author of their noughtiness,

---

[36] *Ibid.*, fol. xxxiiia.
[37] *Ibid.*, fols. xxxviiib, xlb.
[38] *Ibid.*, fol. xxxviiib.
[39] *Ibid.*, fols. xxxviiib – xxxixa.
[40] *Ibid.*, fol. xxxixb.
[41] *Ibid.*, fol. xlia.
[42] *Ibid.*, fol. xlib.

whiche is caused by their corruption engendred in them by their fall from god'. Then he argued:

> yf reason shulde contende with reason in discussion of goddes workes, necessite should be excluded, and not implyed in goddes provydence, election, or predestinacion.[43]

Although the question of election and predestination was not the only one to surface in Gardiner's response to Joye, it certainly raised issues near to his heart and gave him an opportunity to display his theological acumen. Like the freewill men of Edward's and Mary's days, he feared that all would be thrown into chaos if the doctrines of necessity should prevail. Thus he commented:

> This matter of free choice hath much troubled the church, by reason of such, as wolde presume, to have through knoweledge of all thynge after their discussion, and so entanglynge them selfe, with goddes high misteries, have ben authors of such opinions, of mere necessitie, as not onlye impugne the hole processe, of scripture, but also subverteth all staye of good direction, and endevour, either to godly exercise, or politique behavour. It is the extremite of all mischief, to saye that man can not chose whether he wyl use gods giftes or no, when they be offred him, whiche is the time of mans choice (as afore) for we must be persuaded that as god giveth to man his giftes frelye without necessitie or compulsion: so man receyvth them frelye without necessitie or compulsion to use them.[44]

In closing his treatise, Gardiner gave his readers the usual exhortation, urging them to return to the way of rectitude (which included their 'foueraine lordes obeysaunce').[45] His earnest appeal is significant in light of later developments, following which one would conclude that his words went largely unheeded:

> God graunt us to knowe him, truely and according to his will, so to worshyp and honour him, in bodye and soule togither, as all contencions, debates, malice and hatred, clearely extirpate & pulled out, we maye live here like christen men, with christen men, and englyshe men, with englyshe men, whiche of a good season, hath ben by dissention of opinions, somewhat letted and hyndred, whereof those have most cause to be sorye, to whom any

---

[43] *Ibid.*, fol. xliib.
[44] *Ibid.*, fol. lxxvib – lxxviia.
[45] *Ibid.*, fol. xcviia.

parte of the faulte maye be ascribed, And yet all must be sorye, for that is amysse, & eche man for his parte, begynne to amende, & with the prayer of the church, continually pray.[46]

No doubt Gardiner would have been surprised at the unreasonableness of Englishmen over the next decade with respect to these issues, and doubly so were he to learn that the prime defenders of his freewill cause proved to be radicals tarred with a Pelagian brush in a protracted struggle with mainstream Reformed thought; for, although the divines embroiled in the predestinarian controversy would undoubtedly claim to see a place in their doctrinal schema for 'free choice', their talk would not be 'worth a greane chease'[47] as far as Gardiner and the radicals would be concerned.

Incarnational deviations

Although there is little if any evidence of a connexion between freewill ideas and Anabaptism in the early English Reformation, there is a considerable amount linking English heterodoxy to incarnational peculiarities.[48] As already indicated, however, even this case is far from being clear-cut, since examples of heretical thought along these lines were detected before the emergence of Anabaptism on the continent. Thus, one can just as easily ascribe the existence of celestial flesh ideas in the Henrician era to Lollard survival as to Anabaptist infiltration.

An outstanding illustration of this point comes out of Archbishop Warham's vigorous efforts to curb heresy within his own diocese in 1511. The Kentish weald proved to be a particularly fertile field for nonconformity, with evidence of Lollard views revealed in places such as Tenterden and Ashford.[49] Off to the east in the parish of Waldershare, one Simon Piers confessed to having held that Jesus Christ 'was god and man Incarnate at the begynnyng of the worlde and before he was conceyved and borne of his said blessed moder and virgyn mary'.[50] Piers was now ready to own that Christ had taken 'fflesshe and bloode of the moost pure and glorious virgyn our lady

---

[46] *Ibid.*, fol. xcviib.
[47] *Ibid.*, fol. lxxiiia.
[48] See above p. 8.
[49] Thomson, pp. 188 − 9.
[50] Davis, *Heresy*, pp. 4, 38; London, Lambeth Palace Library, The Registers of the Archbishops of Canterbury, William Warham, I, fol. 175r − v.

seynt mary'. In the 1530s, the view was still current in east Kent, this time being promoted by a clergyman. The curate of Hothfield created quite a stir through his distinctive preaching, insisting among other things that the virgin Mary was similar to a saffron bag in her role as the bearer of the Christ-child.[51] The bailiff of Folkstone suffered especial affront at such talk, and succeeded in having the curate removed from the pulpit at the hands of the vicar. Evidently the damage was already done, however, as it was lamented that one hundred persons had been won over to the curate's views.

By this point, it is likely that Melchiorite forces had begun to share the spotlight with native dissent in the area of Christology. In September of 1538, the Duke of Saxony sent Henry VIII a copy of materials obtained from an Anabaptist 'in which mention was made of England, showing that the errors of that sect daily spread abroad'.[52] About the same time, the continental radical, Peter Tasch, referred to 'a printed book "De incarnatione Christi" ', which had been put out by the 'brethren' in England. Tasch expressed his approval for the sentiments contained in the volume, and commented: 'In England the truth silently but widely is propagated and powerfully increases; God knows for how long!'[53] It is probable that these two episodes are connected: that is, incarnational speculations were at the heart of the perceived spread of Anabaptism, and a blending of continental and English heterodoxy was indeed under way.

The Archbishop's troubles in Kent

Another protracted episode from the closing stages of Henry's reign indicates that opinions such as the celestial flesh of Christ continued to find fertile ground for development in Kent for some time to come. The occasion for the disclosure proved to be the discontent against Cranmer stirred up by his not inconsiderable opposition in that region. Complaints about his competence were presented to the Council in the form of articles, and a commission was appointed to investigate the charges in 1542. Unfortunately for the protesters, Cranmer headed the commission himself, so that the parties which had formally raised the issue were ultimately forced to comply with

---

[51] Davis, *Heresy*, p. 83.
[52] *L&P*, XIII, 163 (427).
[53] *Ibid.*, 105 (265).

his policies or risk a prison term. As a further step toward uniformity, another commission, to be empowered with 'certeyne speciall articles', was recommended by the Council in 1543 and ordered to examine 'all abuses and enormites off religion' in Kent more critically.[54]

During the course of these investigations, some truly amazing depositions were gathered. At the eye of the storm was one Robert Serles, vicar of Lenham. Serles, who appears to have been a Fellow of Merton College,[55] had been in trouble as early as September of 1541 when the Council ordered him 'to repair to the abp. of Canterbury by 10 Oct. next and deliver a letter which he has received from the Council, without opening it, and abide the Abp.'s judgement in the matter touching his preaching, which he says is depending in the Abp.'s consistory'.[56] Evidence collected in 1543 indicates that Serles was ultimately imprisoned as a result of Cranmer's 'complaint made for his preachings'.[57]

Cranmer, for his part, apparently relied upon accusations which were said to have originated with men who 'did unjustly', and fresh evidence was now being received to the effect that Searles's 'preachings were godly'. Further testimony indicates that considerable feeling had been stirred up in Kent between conservative clergy and supporters of the new learning. Cranmer was accused of listening to complaints against men such as Serles, 'for whose preaching Catholic most men that have heard him will witness with him', and letting the likes of Launcelot Ridley and John Scory go unmolested.[58] Those who had come to testify on Serles's behalf 'could not be heard'.

As for the specific nature of Serle's offences, we know that his position on images brought personal censure from Cranmer at some point. Edmund Shether, another cleric who was under suspicion along with Serles, answered that he had heard Cranmer 'rebuke Mr. Serles for that he preached so much of images'. Cranmer had

---

[54] *VCH*, ed. William Page (London: The St Catherine Press, 1932), II, 76 – 7; *APC*, I, 126. M. E. Simkins, who wrote the *VCH* work in this portion of its 'Ecclesiastical History', gives numerous citations from the *L&P* material discussed below, pp. 40 – 4 (i.e. from vol. XVIII).

[55] C. W. Field, *The Province of Canterbury and the Elizabethan Settlement of Religion* (n.p., n.d.), p. 41. Simkins, writing in the *VCH*, comments that 'Serles and Dr. Willoughby, vicar of Chilham, seem to have been actually responsible for the conveyance of articles . . . to the council' regarding Cranmer. He also remarks that 'a record of the investigations survives and shows them to have been clearly one-sided, and against maintainers of the old learning'. See *VCH*, II, 77 for Simkins's description of these rather complex events.

[56] *L&P*, XVI, 1189, p. 553.

[57] *L&P*, XVIII, ii, 546, p. 348.

[58] *Ibid.*, 365.

challenged 'that "imago" and "idolum" was one' at this point.[59] Other testimony concerning Serles in the 1543 depositions revealed his conservatism to be of a curious sort. In a sermon at Lenham, he displayed a definite inclination towards incarnational speculations, insisting that Mary 'nourished her son with milk, not material milk but milk that came from heaven; for no woman can nourish her child with material milk but she that is conceived by knowledge of man'.[60] More predictable was his attitude towards Bible reading, as he was quoted as remarking in the parish church of Ashford: ' "You fellows of the new trickery that go up and down with your Testaments in your hands, I pray you what profit take you by them?" ' Thus, ' "meddling with the Scriptures of Christ" ' would lead only to misfortune. Cranmer himself recorded the charge that Serles ' "preacheth no sermon but one part of it is an invective against the other preachers of Christ's church'." Undoubtedly, these were only some of the reasons Serles was not numbered among his favourites within his diocese.

It is clear that Serles's opinions were shared by others in the region, though not always in identical conjunction. A cleric referred to as Sandwich (apparently an alias for William Gardiner of Christchurch, Canterbury),[61] also held forth against 'preachers that were lately come hither', and stated 'that they should never be rid of them till they purged them with smoke and fire'[62] — an eerie enough prediction of things to come. He had chosen the Easter season as an occasion for 'beating into the people's heads that some had called Our Lady a saffron bag, and that they would Our Lady to have no honour'. While Serles seems to have supported these celestial flesh notions, Gardiner appears to have been more consistently conservative. Perhaps he even had Serles in mind at this juncture, or, more likely, he was thinking back to 1539 when the curate of Lenham, Thomas Dawby ('now parson of Wycheling'), had denigrated the status of Mary and asserted that 'she was but a sack to put Christ in'.[63]

It was also through these depositions that some initial tensions were revealed regarding the subject of the freedom of the will. The conflict was apparent amongst the clergy at Christchurch, as Gardiner's conservative colleague, the aforementioned Edmund Shether, was accused of making 'invections against the other preachers of this

---

[59] *Ibid.*, 356.
[60] *Ibid.*, 304.
[61] *Ibid.*, 292.
[62] *Ibid.*, 294.
[63] *Ibid.*, 315.

Cathedral Church, making the people believe that the preachers of the Church preach nothing but a carnal liberty, new fangle errors and heresies against the blessed Sacrament of the Altar, against free will, auricular confession, prayer, fasting and all good works'.[64] Shether's own stance was quite clear, as he had preached at Sandwich 'that every man since the Passion of Christ has as much free will as Adam had in Paradise'.[65] Likewise, the chantry priest at Tenterden, in addition to possessing 'a book of prophecies' and holding that the Bible contained 'heresies', said 'that every Christian man being baptized and holpen by the grace of God, is in as full state of free will as Adam was before his fall'.[66]

One can appreciate Cranmer's dilemma in the midst of such turmoil, particularly when caught between the poles of maintaining official orthodoxy on the one hand and keeping the Reformation fires burning on the other. The situation was particularly delicate where the work of reformist preachers (who may have enjoyed Cranmer's covert blessing) was beginning to produce division among the clergy in Kent. Scory, in particular, had managed to create quite a stir by means of his uncompromising approach. During the Lenten season in 1541, he had provoked the conservative faction at Christchurch through his sermon on justification by faith alone, asserting boldly: 'he that doth deny that only faith doth justify would deny, if he durst be so bold, that Christ doth justify'.[67] His presence at nearby Faversham during the following year is also noteworthy,[68] since the clergy there were definitely divided in their opinion of the new learning. Here the vicar, Clement Norton, appears to have been somewhat in league with Serles and Shether against reformational principles,[69] although he also came in for censure for his negligence at ceremonies and for suspicion of incontinence. It was further declared that he had urged a parishioner 'to use his paternoster in English no more, for he knew not how soon the world would change';[70] he had disobeyed the royal injunctions in removing the Bible from the parish church; and he 'bade one Young wife take holy water and other sorcery for the piles'.[71] The depositions regarding Norton proved that it was sometimes difficult to distinguish between incompetence and conservatism in the Kentish clergy.

[64] *Ibid.*, 305–6.
[65] *Ibid.*, 305.
[66] *Ibid.*, 294.
[67] *Ibid.*, 304.
[68] *Ibid.*, 305.
[69] *Ibid.*, 377.
[70] *Ibid.*, 293–4.
[71] *Ibid.*, 308.

At the same time, more controversial strains were being introduced at Faversham through the sermonizing of John Bland, vicar of Adisham. In language reminiscent of Zwingli, Bland had maintained that 'the mass was no satisfaction for sin but only a remembrance of Christ's passion'. Other favourite targets for denunciation included images, saintly intercession, auricular confession, and the appointment of ignorant clergy by avaricious bishops.[72] Bland sprinkled his wisdom throughout much of the region, alleging at Staple that men were then suffering the breaking of their heads 'for speaking of the truth'. In Northgate parish, Canterbury, he suggested that the current ceremonies of the church contained elements which were both heretical and treasonous. This was also the site of his declaration 'that in the christening of children priests be murderers'. Perhaps even more serious were his remarks on the Trinity, said to have been made in his own church: 'that the image of the Trinity is not to be suffered and he cannot find "Trinitas" throughout Scripture, but that Athanasius put it in his "Symbolum" '.[73]

Bland was reported to have been entertained at the home of one John Toftes of Canterbury, together with other questionable types – including Joan Bocher 'after she was accused'.[74] Thus, Bland was undoubtedly connected to the underground network then operating in East Kent. Toftes, for his part, was active in defending Joan before the consistory court at Canterbury 'when she was detected as a sacramentary'. It was during this interval that Joan 'did bring forth the King's pardon which was given to the Anabaptists for their deliverance, repenting themselves'.[75] Other members of the Toftes family also seem to have figured prominently in the unrest of those days, one lamenting that 'It is the more pity that God's Word shall so little be set by that it may not be read openly.'[76] Such sentiments as these were evidently becoming more common in the area. Thomas Dawby, already mentioned in connection with the Kentish interest in the celestial flesh doctrines,[77] was of the opinion 'that it was lawful for all manner of men to read the Bible at all times and that no one ought to discourage them'.[78]

The battle lines were obviously being drawn in Kent towards the end of Henry's reign. Conservatism, along with moderate dissent (some of which was very possibly receiving Cramner's sympathy),

---

[72] *Ibid.*, 311.
[73] *Ibid.*, 312.
[74] *Ibid.*
[75] *Ibid.*, 314.
[76] *Ibid.*, 307.
[77] See above p. 41 regarding Dawby.
[78] *L&P*, XVIII, ii, 546, p. 315.

was joined by definite heretical tendencies. These lines, to be sure, were extremely fluid and tentative at the best of times; yet the air was full of contention and unsettledness. The Kentish depositions closed with the optimistic yet rather pathetic directive: 'These towns following are specially to be remembered that in them be placed learned men, with sufficient stipends: Sandwich, Dovor, Folkeston, Ashforde, Tenterden, Crambroke, Faversham, Hearne, Whitstable, Marden, Maidstone, Wye, Wingham.'[79]

Henry Harte and the origins of Kentish freewill radicalism

Thus, a partisan spirit was beginning to manifest itself in Kent, especially between those who became committed to some measure of reforming doctrine and practice and those who staunchly resisted all such attempts to make inroads on the Kentish scene. Thus, the rector of Pluckley, William Lancaster, exhibited a sense of exclusivism which must have been gaining currency at the time. Lancaster (it was noted in the same depositions) failed to use holy water 'in the church porch' and was reluctant to distribute holy bread to his parishioners. He appears to have abandoned the invocation of the saints. More significant, however, was his reaction when informed that an acquaintance continued to bless himself regularly and repeat the traditional prayers and creed. Lancaster affirmed 'that if he knew it of truth that the said Stevyn used the same form of prayer, he would not accompany him, nor once drink with him'.[80]

This information is critical to an examination of the south-eastern freewill movement for two reasons. In the first place, Lancaster represents a link in a tradition of exclusivism which was clearly seen among the Kentish freewillers in Edward's day.[81] And secondly, the village of Pluckley figures somewhat prominently in the story of the freewillers' development in itself, since it appears to have been the home of the best-known freewill radical of the mid-Tudor years, Henry Harte.

Our first definite impression of Harte is gleaned from a letter sent by Cranmer to Thomas Cromwell in April 1538 — a mere five months before the institution of the royal commission to deal with

[79] *Ibid.*, 378.
[80] *Ibid.*, 209 and 306 – 7.
[81] See below pp. 54, 66 – 7.

Anabaptist radicalism.[82] From the contents of the dispatch it is clear that several men from Pluckley and nearby Smarden, including Henry Harte, had been recently indicted at the Canterbury Court of Quarter Sessions for 'unlawful assemblies'.[83] Cranmer seems to have been personally involved with the case, and perhaps even supervised the inquiry when the incident was first reported to him. He learned that their crime was nothing more than favouring 'God's word' and being reckoned as supporters of 'the new doctrine, as they call it'. Unfortunately, Cranmer did not enlarge upon his terminology, so that we do not know for certain if the reference was to the beliefs of Luther and his followers or to a more radical variety of opinion such as Anabaptism itself. Cranmer's own handling of the case, however, would seem to suggest that he meant the former.

The Archbishop was clearly concerned about the matter and, in this instance, took the side of the defendants. He advised Cromwell that 'much sedition' would likely be stirred up within the realm if such unjust vexations were to continue 'at sessions', and requested of Cromwell 'that some remedy may in time be devised for the redress of such indictments'. It is worth noting that Cranmer had expressed similar irritation in 1536 when corresponding with a justice in Kent who was reportedly intimidating the populace through his pronouncements against the reading of the scriptures. Ironically, this was the very year in which Cromwell had instructed that all parish churches should be issued with Bibles.[84] The cantankerous official in Kent had replied that he would eagerly proceed to indict some of Cranmer's own personnel for heresy were it not for the regard in which he held the Archbishop. Then, during his visitation of 1540, Cranmer was presented with information regarding one Vincent Ingeam, justice of the peace, who had 'commanded on Easter-Monday, 38° of the king, that no man should read, or hear the bible read, upon pain of imprisonment, and cast two into prison, the one for speaking against him therein, and the other for shewing him the king's injunctions concerning the same'.[85] Although it cannot be said that these developments are definitely linked, they do suggest something of a likely sequence of events for Harte and his compatriots. And once again the complexity of Cranmer's task is brought clearly to the fore.

---

[82] Thomas Cranmer, *Works*, ed. John Cox (Cambridge: University Press, 1846), II, 367.
[83] I have been unable to find a record of this episode in the Quarter Sessions Records for the diocese of Canterbury which are located in the archives of Christchurch Cathedral.
[84] *VCH*, II, 73.
[85] Cranmer, II, 367.

It seems that Cranmer became fully acquainted with Harte's activities during these years, and that he was in the best position to assess Harte in the days to follow.[86] At this stage, Harte does not appear to display a hardened sectarian bias; he is evidently distressed because his right to examine the Bible in English has been restricted, contrary to his understanding of the official directives. He is the only one of this particular band to reappear in any identifiable way in the Edwardian freewill proceedings, the other five men remaining obscure. Four of the six were reported to be from Smarden, a village located to the south-west of Pluckley en route to Biddenden and Cranbrook. Only Harte and one John Stanstrete hailed from Pluckley.

The local setting

The village of Pluckley was situated to the south-west of Canterbury roughly between the North Downs and the Weald of Kent. Along with Smarden and numerous other villages in the region, Pluckley was influenced by the growth of the cloth industry from the fourteenth century onwards.[87] It also seems to have been dominated by the Dering family for some time. For example, Richard Dering the elder had provided approximately £50 for the erection of the chapel of the Virgin Mary in 1480, and was buried there in the following year.[88] Earlier in the same century, discontented weavers and clothmakers from both Pluckley and Smarden had participated in Jack Cade's revolt,[89] furnishing clear evidence of the resolute nature of the Wealden mentality. In addition, unlawful assemblies, perhaps similar to those involving Harte and his colleagues, were noted at nearby Lenham in 1534.[90]

The parish of Pluckley lay under the jurisdiction of the deanery of Charing. The church was dedicated to St Nicholas. Robert Collens

---

[86] This was clearly the opinion of Nicholas Ridley. See his remarks on the subject in John Bradford, *The Writings of John Bradford*, ed. Aubrey Townsend (Cambridge: University Press, 1848 – 53), II, 169 – 73.

[87] Frank Jessup, *A History of Kent* (n.p.: Kent Archaeological Society, 1974), p. 86.

[88] W. K. Jordan, *Social Institutions in Kent, 1480 – 1660: A Study of the Changing Pattern of Social Relationships* (Ashford: Kent Archaeological Society, 1961), p. 115; Edward Hasted, *The History and Topographical Survey of the County of Kent* (Canterbury: E P Publishing Ltd., 1972, in collaboration with Kent County Library; orig. pub. 1798), VI, 467.

[89] D. W. Cooper, 'John Cade's Followers in Kent', *AC*, XXII (1868), 238.

[90] *VCH*, III, 299.

had been appointed rector in 1534 and held this post for five years.[91] During his term there, he was assisted by a curate, Nicholas Ealner, while John Dering served as one of two churchwardens.[92] Collens was succeeded briefly by Henry Markeham before the above-mentioned William Lancaster took over in July 1541. Lancaster remained until 1554, at which time he was deprived.[93] His Protestant sympathies, already noted, can also be seen in his sale of the old Latin service books before he received official notification to remove them.[94] Thus, when the Kentish inventory of church goods took place in 1552, the only outstanding items revealed were a pair of organs, a silver chalice weighing over ten ounces, and 'a greate emptie cheste'.[95]

The search for Harte's family tree in the Pluckley area is predictably challenging. The name was extremely common. Several Harte brothers — John, Nicholas and Thomas — seem to have possessed extensive landholdings in the area at the end of the fifteenth century.[96] Much of this land lay in nearby Little Charte. Both Nicholas and Thomas Harte had sons named Harry, while John's only son, another Thomas, may have fathered yet another Harry who is perhaps the most likely choice of the lot. This Harry (Herte) was destined to receive significant properties lying in the parish of Pluckley upon his father's death.[97] As suggested elsewhere, it is possible that Henry Harte, the freewill radical, may well have been 'a person of considerable means'[98] — possibly through involvement in the cloth industry or even property ownership and management.

Indeed, Horst has speculated that Harte may have been wealthy enough to sponsor an English delegation to the Anabaptist conference held in Bocholt, Westphalia, in August of 1536.[99] An extremely diverse assortment of radicals were represented at Bocholt, and the

---

[91] Francis Haslewood, 'The Rectors of Pluckley, Kent, For Upwards of Six Hundred Years', *AC*, XXII (1897), 85, 87.

[92] Canterbury, Christchurch Cathedral Library, Archdeaconry Visitation Act Book, Z 3/5, 1538–1541, fol. 42.

[93] Haslewood, 'The Rectors of Pluckley', 87.

[94] C. E. Woodruff, 'Extracts from Original Documents Illustrating the Progress of the Reformation in Kent', *AC*, XXXI (1915), 105.

[95] Mackenzie Walcott and Scott Robertson, eds., 'Inventories of Parish Church Goods in Kent, A. D. 1552', *AC*, X (1876), 289.

[96] Maidstone, Kent County Record Office, Archdeaconry Register, PRC 17/6/248, PRC 17/7/110. Dur to the plethora of possibilities regarding Harte's family tree, these findings are necessarily somewhat tentative. See also PRC 17/12/550 and PRC 17/7/82.

[97] The surnames Hart, Harte, and Herte seem highly interchangeable in the various sources, as do the given names Henry and Harry.

[98] Horst, p. 122; see below regarding Harte's possible residence in London during the 1540s.

[99] Horst, p. 122.

English delegates were reported to have been unsympathetic toward the surviving Münsterite faction. Nonetheless, an Englishman named Henry had been an enthusiastic supporter of the conference itself,[100] and had paid the expenses of the English party led by Jan Matthijs of Middelburg.[101] Although it has been suggested that this Henry from England may have been the continental mystic, Hendrik Niclaes, this is quite untenable.[102] It has also been postulated that the English were in fact the organizers of the entire conference and that they were 'in the forefront of leadership in the anabaptist movement' at this juncture[103] – surely an imaginative if not demonstrable piece of conjecture. These speculations are at least suggestive of the degree of success which emerging radicals such as Harte may have begun to enjoy during the closing stages of Henry's reign. Although we can (and will) conjecture further regarding his whereabouts during this time,[104] it is not until the Edwardian era that he emerges again in a recognizable way. By that time, the freewill movement was in full swing.

---

[100] *Ibid.*, pp. 79, 122; Friedrich Nippold, 'David Joris von Delft' in *Zeitschrift fur die Historische Theologie*, ed. Christian W. Riedner (Gotha, 1863), p. 53.
[101] Robert Barclay, *The Inner Life of the Religious Societies of the Commonwealth* (London: Hodder and Stoughton, 1876), p. 77. See above p. 32 regarding Jan Matthijs.
[102] *Ibid.*, p. 77.
[103] Horst, p. 80.
[104] See below pp. 77 – 8 regarding Harte's possible movements in the 1540s.

3

The Emergence of the Conventiclers

The Bocking incident

As the realm entered the second half of Edward's reign, renewed concern over the threat of the Anabaptist presence in the south-east was clearly demonstrated. For example, the visitation articles of 1550 for the diocese of London, where Nicholas Ridley was now bishop, gave much attention to the detection of Anabaptism. Undoubtedly, Ridley's earlier encounters with Anabaptism in Kent had served to permanently alert him to the dangers inherent in the movement. According to Strype, Ridley, then Bishop of Rochester, and Stephen Gardiner, Bishop of Winchester, had been called upon to deal with two men in Kent who were reported to be anabaptists. Strype relates his impression that many of this sect had fled to England from Germany at this time, and had proceeded to 'infect the realm with odd and heretical opinions'. In this instance, the Anabaptists were reputed to have spoken of the sacrament with contempt – hardly sufficient evidence to distinguish them as true Anabaptists. Ridley had also used this opportunity to urge Gardiner to come to terms with the doctrine of justification, and requested that he be faithful in refuting Anabaptism in his own diocese. He further assured Gardiner that he would be resolute in upholding the mystical holiness of the sacrament against the same group in his own sphere.[1]

Although there is no further evidence on this incident, the account serves to indicate that Ridley had been initiated into the world of proceedings against Anabaptism. He was then translated to London in early 1550.[2] In his twelfth visitation article of that same year under the section dealing with preaching, he instructed that inquiry be made to see if any did 'preach and defend, that private persons may make insurrections, sturre sedition, or compel men to geve theim

[1] Strype, *EM*, II, 1, 107.
[2] *VCH*, II, 79.

their goodes'.[3] The question of surrendering goods appears to have been raised with Anabaptist communalism in mind, even though the sect was not specifically mentioned. The next three articles left no doubt at all about the bishop's intentions, however, as he dealt with such items as the holding of all things in common, the denial of the office of the magistrate and the refusal to swear oaths when lawfully required of Christians, and the avoidance of the court system when clearly wronged.

Perhaps the most telling of this series of articles, though, was that which enquired 'whether any teacheth and sayth, that Christ tooke no fleshe and blood of the blessed virgine Mary'.[4] This was yet another reference to the doctrine of the celestial flesh of Christ, which was propogated on the continent by Melchior Hoffmann in the 1520s and incorporated into the thought of Menno Simons. Bishop Hooper had linked this tenet directly to English Anabaptism in 1549, when he complained to Bullinger that the radicals attended his services in droves and gave him much difficulty regarding the Incarnation of Christ.[5] As we have already observed, the concept was also very much a part of the native English heretical tradition long before the days of Hoffmann and the continental Anabaptists.

Although Ridley did not mention the Anabaptists by name in this article, he did instruct that search should be made for them in article forty-four. He required that it be determined whether any of this or another sect was congregating privately and engaging in doctrinal discussion and sacramental observance apart from the parish churches. A subsequent article dealt with the denial of infant baptism,[6] while item fifty-two concerned repentance for wilfully committed post-baptismal sins. This would indicate that the authorities were linking Anabaptism with some form of sinless perfectionism. Such an identification appears to have been quite common on the continent as well as during the early Reformation, when the magisterial reformers reacted caustically to Anabaptist teaching regarding relative perfection.[7]

Thus we have Ridley's preoccupation with the Anabaptist menace in his diocese in 1550. Further attention was given to these matters in January 1551, when a royal commission of thirty-one worthies was formed to 'correct and punish all Anabaptists, and such as did not

---

[3] Church of England, *Visitation Articles: Articles and Injunctions*, Diocese of London (London: R. Wolfe, 1550), pt. 1, sig. a. ii. RSTC 10247.

[4] *Ibid.*, sig. a. ii.

[5] *Original Letters*, ed. Robinson, Part 2, p. 65.

[6] Church of England, *Articles*, sig. a. vii, 48.

[7] For example, see the list of charges brought against Felix Mantz as described in Williams, p. 144.

duly administer the sacraments according to the Book of Common Prayer'.[8] Cranmer and Ridley were included in the assignment, along with such dignitaries as William Cecil, John Cheke, Hugh Latimer, Miles Coverdale, Matthew Parker, Nicholas Wotton and Rowland Taylor. As Strype noted, there were many in England, other than papists, who could not accept the changes in religion then being administered. These various elements, which included those holding Arian and Pelagian views as well as the fundamentals of baptist beliefs, were commonly lumped together as Anabaptists.[9] It was these factions, then, along with those which found fault with the Prayer Book, that became the object of this latest initiative in counteracting heresy within the realm.

Perhaps as an immediate return on the royal investment, a significant pocket of conventiclers was uncovered and apprehended in Essex later in that same month. Evidence was conveyed to the Privy Council concerning a meeting held at Bocking during the Christmas season just past. As a consequence, on or about 26 January 1551, the Lord Chancellor was instructed to send one 'Upcharde' of Bocking for examination. The Chancellor had apparently been dealing with the accused personally prior to this date. When presented to the Council, Upcharde owned that some Kentishmen had come to Bocking to stay with 'goode man Cooke', later identified as the Bocking clothier, Robert Cooke.[10] When the men from Kent arrived at Cooke's home, they found his wife alone. They were then directed to Upcharde's dwelling where Cooke was 'at dinner'. Since Cooke's wife was pregnant, he asked that his visitors remain at Upcharde's for the night. This being agreed upon, the home of Upcharde served as a meeting-place on the next day around noon. This meant a Sunday gathering, and numerous inhabitants of the town joined with the Kentish guests in discussing the 'thinges of the Scripture, speciallie wheather it were necessarie to stand or kneele, barehedde, or covered at prayer'. The assembly eventually concluded that it was the attitude of the heart which mattered before God, and not external appearances at ceremonies. Since the group consisted of at least sixty persons, the Council decided to detain 'the said upcharde and one Sympson of the same sorte' in the Marshalsea until further examinations could be held. Accordingly, despatches were sent to the authorities of Essex and Kent on 27 January for the arrest of those

---

[8] Strype, *EM*, II, 1, 383.
[9] John Strype, *The Life and Acts of Matthew Parker* (Oxford: Clarendon Press, 1821), I, 54.
[10] J. R. Dasent, ed. *Acts of the Privy Council of England*, New Series (London, 1890 – 2), III, 206.

deemed the 'chief of that practise'. Sir George Norton, the sheriff of Essex, was given a list of nine men from the Bocking area and was instructed to see to it that none of the apprehended should have recourse to discussion amongst themselves. The objects of his search included two clothiers, one being the aforementioned Robert Cooke and the other John Eglins, also of Bocking. Others identified as offenders from Bocking were John Barrett, a 'Cowehered' from nearby Shawforde, along with Richard Bagge, Thomas Piggerell, John King and Thomas Myxer. In addition, Robert Wolmere and one Boughtell of no determined address were to be confined when found.[11]

Similarly, a letter was sent to Sir Thomas Wyatt and Sir Edward Wotton in Kent regarding the troublemakers there who were apparently based at Faversham.[12] The outstanding culprit on the Kentish list was 'Cole of Maydestone', whose occupation was listed as 'Scholemaster'. The remaining five suspects hailed from the Wealden area. William Sibley and Thomas Yonge were from Lenham. John Ledley and one Chidderton were stated to be from Ashford, while Nicholas Sheterden came from Pluckley.

Obviously, not all sixty of the conventiclers were included on the original lists, although several others appear to have been gathered in during the process of arresting the few. On 3 February 1551, five of the Kentishmen and seven men from Essex came before the Council and told about the nature of their scriptural discussions. Included in their confession was the admission that they had not received communion for over two years.[13] Their reasons for avoiding the sacrament were declared to be extremely 'superstitiouse and erronyose', and were accompanied by various other opinions considered to be worthy of severe punishment. Accordingly, Sheterden, Sibley, Cole, Boughtell and Barrett seem to have been further detained, or were perhaps committed to the trust of local officers for a time. Eglins, Myxer, Bagge, Piggerell and King were all released, each on bail of £40 and upon condition that they appear when called for and 'resorte to their ordinarie for resolucion of their oppynyons in case thei have any doubte in religion'. Recognizances were also taken from Thomas Sharpe of Pluckley and Nicholas Yonge of Lenham.

Further investigations in connection with these disclosures were evidently being carried out on the local level in Kent. An undated series of depositions touching upon the Kent-Essex connexion

---

[11] *APC*, III, 206 – 7.
[12] *Ibid.*, III, 207; Strype, *EM*, II, 1, 369.
[13] *APC*, III, 215.

suggests that many of the Kentish sectarian leaders were not apprehended at Bocking.[14] A significant proportion presumably escaped from the pursuing authorities. Perhaps several Kentishmen were among this number, or else they were already being detained in Kent as a result of previous allegations. At any rate, the principle figure in the Kentish depositions was clearly Henry Harte, a character not mentioned at all in the previous hearings. In addition, these declarations by local informants prove that the key issue within the Kentish side of the movement was the doctrine of predestination and not conduct and apparel at worship. The presiding officials, who were probably conducting their examinations under the auspices of the 1551 royal commission, questioned several men according to a prescribed series of articles.

The first informant, John Grey, reported that one Cole of Faversham, 'upon Lammas daye paste', had declared that the doctrine of predestination was more suitable for 'divilles' than for Christians.[15] Likewise, Henry Harte, 'aboute bartholomew tide laste', had stated in a gathering that 'ther was no man so chosen but that he might dampne hime self'. The Apostle Paul himself might have fallen away if he had so desired. Conversely, there was no such thing as a man 'soo reprobate' that he might not keep the commandments of God. Finally, Grey reported that Harte had an aversion to 'Learned men', deeming them to be 'the cause of grete errors'. Laurence Ramsay concurred with Grey's statement, as did William Forstal. Forstal added that Harte had said that his faith did not depend upon learned persons, since these were responsible for the introduction of 'all errors'.[16]

Three other examinees, namely Richard Dinestake, clerk, Thomas Broke and Roger Linsey, testified that another radical, George Brodebridge, had made the claim one year earlier that divine predestination was conditional and not fixed or 'certeyne'.[17] They also confirmed that the Kentish 'congregation' had been travelling up to Essex, and that Cole of Maidstone had flatly denied that children were conceived in original sin. William Greneland, who was obviously in sympathy with the conventiclers' outlook, stated that playing 'annye game for money' was sinful and fleshly. He also informed his inquisitors that the local assembly was wont to hold its

---

[14] London, British Museum, Harleian MSS, 421, fols. 133a – 134b; also printed in Champlin Burrage, ed., *The Early English Dissenters in the Light of Recent Research* (Cambridge: University Press, 1912), II, 1 – 6.
[15] Harl. Mss, 421, fol. 133a.
[16] *Ibid.*, fol. 133b.
[17] *Ibid.*, fol. 134a.

meetings in various spots, and that they had indeed gone over to Essex. His final declaration was a confession that he had 'contrybuted' to the group, undoubtedly referring to financial or material support of some kind.

The last witness listed was John Plume of Lenham. Plume admitted to being a conventicler, and reported hearing many times within the fellowship that its members should not salute or recognize a sinful man or a stranger. It was also affirmed that it was not sinful to lust for something evil if the act itself was not committed. Plume further identified Humphrey Middleton as a visitor at Cole's house in Faversham upon the previous occasion. Middleton had reasoned that all men 'were predestynate to be salvid', since Adam had been elected unto salvation and all men were contained in his 'Loynes'.[18] Thus, there were simply 'no reprobates' whatsoever. The recorded depositions closed with Plume's assertion that Nicholas Yonge had inveighed against communicating with sinners. Another witness listed in the record, Edmund Morres, does not appear to have given a separate testimony at this time.

Thus one is presented with a rather meagre portrait of the Bocking-Faversham radicals as far as the official records go. As already seen, the original discovery of the Kentishmen in Bocking occurred near the end of 1550 or the beginning of 1551. The principle meeting definitely took place during the Christmas season, but it is not clear whether some of them were arrested at the actual site or if the arrests all occurred sometime later in various locations. Upcharde was the first to be brought before the Council and the Lord Chancellor, Richard Rich, and his testimony led to the arrest of several of his comrades from the Bocking area as well as some Kentishmen from the Weald and nearby communities. Following their appearance before the Council, most of these were probably released. Meanwhile, further proceedings were launched in Kent by the delegated authorities, and the Faversham basis of the Kentish segment was thereby established. In addition, Henry Harte and Cole of Maidstone emerged as principal figures within their ranks, and the critical issues which were collectively discussed included predestination and election, separation from ungodliness, and higher learning. At some stage the Kentish society, comprising some kind of formal organization, had travelled well into Essex in order to propogate their views or meet men of similar interests.

It is unclear whether these Kentish delegates were invited or not, and the references to argumentation in the account by Upcharde

---

[18] *Ibid.*, 421, fol. 133b.

suggests that not all were of the same mind. It is quite likely that the majority of the conventiclers escaped detection altogether, and that the authorities did not get wind of the gathering until it had been over for some days. Despite the arrests and hearings which followed, the officials seem to have been rather lenient toward the offenders once the nature of the meeting was known. Little could anyone have realized at that point that the very same issues and individuals involved in this incident would continue to plague the ruling powers well into the reign of Queen Mary. Before relating these later aspects of the story, however, it will be necessary to examine the careers of the Bocking-Faversham conventiclers more closely in order to lay the foundation for the Marian episode. As an integral part of this examination, a brief survey of Bocking's history is offered so that the framework surrounding the early apprehensions in Essex is made more meaningful. This will be followed by a similar introduction to Faversham as well as the Kentish Wealden region which figured so prominently in Kentish dissent and radicalism.

The town and parish of Bocking

It is exceedingly ironic that the Kentish sectarians should have been discovered in the parish of Bocking in Essex, since this area was one of several 'peculiars' which came under the direct jurisdiction of the Archbishop of Canterbury. Peculiars were always outside the geographical scope of Canterbury diocese, but were not subject to the diocese in which they were situated as would normally have been the case. Hence, Bocking parish, exempt from the Bishop of London's care, was entrusted to a Dean. Jurisdiction over peculiars was never clearly stated in law, as most simply developed around holdings belonging to the Archbishop of Canterbury. Some of these manorial lands had at one time been in the possession of the Prior and Convent of Christ Church, Canterbury, but these seem to have been exchanged for other sites with the Archbishop along with the advowsons of six benefices in the deanery of the Arches.[19]

By the thirteenth century, the diverse holdings were grouped into eight deaneries, each left in the hands of an officer commissioned by the Archbishop. For instance, the peculiar of Croyden and Shoreham, which was the most important of the lot, was generally

---

[19] This information is found in the index to the Vicar-General Records, Lambeth Palace Library, under the heading, 'Archbishop's Peculiars'.

supervised by the Dean of the Arches in the sixteenth century. The other deaneries came under separate administration. Most of the properties, however, were given to the Crown between 1536 and 1547, with the Archbishop retaining only the rights to ecclesiastical supervision and presentations.[20]

Generally speaking, Bocking appears to have achieved some notoriety by the end of the thirteenth century, in that the Archbishop of Canterbury chose the parish as a site for ordination on various occasions.[21] Early in the next century, emigré cloth-workers from Bruges were said to have moved into Essex and Norfolk, some of them settling in Shalford and Bocking and setting up their trade.[22] This seems to have happened even before Edward III's famous measures on the cloth industry in the 1330s. From here the craft spread to other localities such as neighbouring Braintree and Coggeshall. By the middle of the fifteenth century, officials at Braintree were boasting that the art of cloth-weaving was proving to be the most productive trade ever practised in that region.[23] Formal authorization to weave cloth in Bocking and Coggeshall was forthcoming at the beginning of Elizabeth's reign, and these towns, along with Colchester, Braintree, Dedham and Halstead became the mainstays of the cloth industry in Essex. The industry was apparently threatened in Bocking during the Marian years by a statute which restricted cloth-making to market towns, cities, boroughs and corporate towns.[24] Since Bocking and several other communities fell under none of these categories, a special exemption was necessary in 1558 in order to relax the tenor of the previous bill and permit the continuation of the craft.

The church at Bocking, St Mary's, may have existed as far back as the thirteenth century. In the middle of the fifteenth century, the Dorewood family founded a house for poor men in Bocking known as 'Maison Dieu'. It was to have housed seven men initially, and seems to have survived as an almshouse for centuries after the Reformation era.[25]

---

[20] This form of jurisdiction by peculiars prevailed until the early nineteenth century, at which time it was abolished.

[21] Irene Churchill, *Canterbury Administration* (London: Church Historical Society, 1933), pp. 96 – 9.

[22] William Page and H. A. Doubleday, eds. *The Victoria History of the County of Essex* (Oxford: University Press for the London Institute of Historical Research, 1907), II, 381.

[23] *Ibid.*, II, 330.

[24] *Ibid.*, II, 385 – 6.

[25] *Ibid.*, II, 183. In the nineteenth century, it was being supervised by the Dean of Bocking and the parish officials.

Faversham and the Weald

Faversham appears to have ranked as the Kentish focus for purposes of the original investigation, and thus the counterpart there to Bocking in Essex. Located at the head of a navigable creek running into the Swale, Faversham was reckoned to be a significant port by the sixteenth century. Situated to the north-west of Canterbury approximately half-way to Rochester, its prominence among Kentish towns was seen as early as the ninth century when a 'royal residence' was established there, and in time it came to be regarded as a subsidiary of Dover.[26] King Stephen founded an abbey in Faversham, and much of the subsequent economic life of the community in the medieval period revolved around that establishment. Perhaps the most noted enterprise in the town, however, was the oyster fishery. Hasted referred to it as the 'only staple commodity of this town'.[27] Another activity which may have been providing handsome returns by the early sixteenth century was the export of wheat to the Netherlands.[28] In 1539 several townsmen were exporting large quantities of corn, wheat, barley and malt to Zeeland, utilizing two hoyes from Flushing. One of the individuals engaged in the wheat trade was Robert Cole, described as the bailiff of Faversham at the time,[29] while another seems to have been the local abbot.[30] Cloth products were also being shipped by enterprising Faversham businessmen, including kersies destined for Flushing as well.[31] In addition, tons of beer and oysters, bags of saffron, and 'flytches of baconne' appear in the trade records.[32]

Thus, trade flowed freely between Faversham and the continent, as well as towards London. There is some indication that trading activity with the continent served to link Faversham with other south-eastern centres too, including Colchester in Essex. Vessels from Colchester were often found at Middelburg and other ports alongside

---

[26] Roger Higham, *Kent* (London: B. T. Batsford Ltd., 1974), p. 35.

[27] Hasted, VI, 351 – 2.

[28] London also depended upon the shipment of cereals from Kentish ports such as Faversham and Sandwich. See Peter Ramsey, *Tudor Economic Problems* (London: Victor Gollancz Ltd., 1968), p. 22.

[29] *Bronnen Tot De Geschiedenis Van Den Handel Met Engeland, Schotland en Ierland*, ed. H. J. Smit, Rijks Geschiedkundige Publicatien, Tweede Deel, 1485 – 1585; Erste Stuke, 1485 – 1558 ('S-Gravenhage: Martinus Nijhoff, 1942), 634. This may have been the same man who shared a common outlook with Henry Harte until the Marian years. For more on his early career, see below pp. 74 – 5 and 110 – 12.

[30] *Ibid.*, nos. 530 – 1.

[31] *Ibid.*, no. 528.

[32] *Ibid.*, nos. 528, 592, 548.

their counterparts from various Kentish communities, including numerous vessels from Faversham.[33] Shipping was evidently one of several points of contact which developed over the decades between the two counties, while others were cloth manufacturing, fishing and agriculture. One could wish to add intellectual stimulation to the list, since these economic activities would also serve as potential avenues for the dissemination of novel ideas.

Although Lambarde later wrote that Faversham was 'well peopled' and flourishing 'in wealth',[34] it bears mentioning that the dissolution movement caught up with the community in 1538. The number of monks had fallen off in the years prior to the end, and those still there at the time were given pensions. The lands pertaining to the grammar school reverted to the crown until the reign of Elizabeth, when the town petitioned the Queen for a new one in keeping with the instructions of the original benefactor, Dr John Cole.[35]

At some point, the church at Faversham had been dedicated to St Mary of Charity, or, as it was otherwise known, to the Assumption of our Lady of Faversham.[36] The vicar of Faversham during the turbulent years under Edward and Mary was Clement Norton, a controversial figure whom we have already met, while Richard Maupas held neighbouring Preston-by-Faversham.[37] At least two cases were heard against Norton before the Commissary-General, Robert Collens. In one instance, it was alleged that the vicar had never been known to encourage anyone to read the Scripture, 'but contrariwise he had been heard to rebuke some for reading it'.[38] Moreover, it was said in October of 1550 that the cleric had grossly overindulged in the sacramental wine, and had told the wife of the deponent that she could not expect salvation if she did not believe in the pyx which held the consecrated bread.[39]

Evidently Norton's religious conservatism had been a cause for much concern among the town's Protestant faction for some time, and Thomas Arden, son-in-law to Sir Edward North, chancellor of

[33] *Ibid.*, nos. 628, 646, 818.

[34] William Lambarde, *A Preambulation of Kent* (London: Chatham, Baldwin Cradock, and Joy, 1826; orig. pub. 1576), p. 281.

[35] John Lewis, *The History and Antiquities of the Abbey and Church of Faversham in Kent* (n.p., 1727), p. 70; Edward Jacob, *History of Faversham* (n.p.: The Faversham Society, 1974), p. 53.

[36] G. A. Cooke, *Topographical and Statistical Description of the County of Kent* (London: Sherwood, Neely, and Jones, N.D.), p. 147.

[37] Scott Robertson, 'Rectors and Vicars of Preston-by-Faversham', *AC* XXI (1895), 146 – 7. See p. 42 above regarding Norton and other Kentish depositions.

[38] Woodruff, 'Extracts from Original Documents', 102.

[39] *Ibid.*, 98.

the Court of Augmentations, was most instrumental in Norton's censure in that same year.[40] Arden, who had become one of the principal landholders in the vicinity of Faversham, was regarded as a firm supporter of Edwardian policy in the region. It would appear that progressive sentiment in Faversham was not confined to spiritual issues either, since radicals within the community seem to have used the occasion of the new incorporation of the town in 1546 to try and wrest control of local politics as well.[41] Such fervor was clearly not uncommon in the region, as one could also mention the destructive treatment meted out to the Faversham abbey in the years following its dissolution.[42] It is not surprising, therefore, that religious sentiments and emotions continued to run at a fever pitch throughout the county and elsewhere during the Marian reaction.[43]

During the later Middle Ages, Faversham's prominence had been reinforced by regular sittings of the Archdeacon's Court. Faversham and nearby Ospringe were visited on an alternating basis so that matters pertaining to the deanery of Ospringe, within which jurisdiction Faversham lay, could be handled conveniently. These were but two stops on a fifty-mile circuit which also included Cranbrook, Ashford and Milton on occasion.[44] In 1416, a statute of Convocation had stipulated that all archdeacons and suffragans of Canterbury province should inquire at least biannually into the state of each rural deanery. They were also required to examine all parishes and deaneries wherein heretics were rumoured to reside with equal frequency, and to receive sworn testimonies regarding conventicling activities, heretical ideas and forbidden books.[45] When any names were confirmed, the offenders were to be sent to the diocesans for formal proceedings. In some cases, the accused might be handed over to the secular authorities. Otherwise, they were to be incarcerated until the next session of Convocation at Canterbury or perhaps even later. In order to facilitate proceedings against Kentish heretics, the Archbishop began utilizing the Bishop of Rochester in such investigations during the early part of the fourteenth century.[46]

---

[40] Peter Clark, *English Provincial Society from the Reformation to the Revolution* (Sussex: The Harvester Press, 1977), p. 74.

[41] *Ibid.*, pp. 82, 68, 62.

[42] Peter Clark and Paul Slack, eds., *Crisis and Order in English Towns, 1500 – 1700* (London: Routledge & Kegan Paul, 1972), p. 26.

[43] Frank V. Barchard, Jr, 'Reginald, Cardinal Pole, 1553 – 1558' (unpublished Ph.D. thesis, Tulane University, 1971), p. 198.

[44] Brian Woodcock, *Medieval Ecclesiastical Courts in the Diocese of Canterbury* (London: Oxford University Press, 1952), pp. 35 – 6.

[45] Thomson, pp. 222 – 3.

[46] *VCH*, II, 56.

And plenty of heretics there were, many of whom undoubtedly managed to escape the detection of Archbishop Chichele following the execution of Oldcastle in 1418.[47] Despite persecution, Lollardy survived in Kent and the south-west, so that, as Dr Thomson noted, 'there are numerous indications that unorthodox doctrines were flourishing in Kent' by the last decade of the fifteenth century.[48] Potential trouble spots included Maidstone, Tonbridge, Canterbury and Bridge. As a result of Warham's relentless pursuit of heretics early in the sixteenth century, it is indeed possible to find support for the notion that Lollardy had made significant inroads into the life of the county. As indicated, the year 1511 brought a thorough visitation of Canterbury diocese, and there was also the appointment of a commission to try heretics there.[49] One of Warham's judges was Dean Colet, while Cuthbert Tunstall served as his commissary. The Weald proved to be a particularly fertile field for nonconformist ideas, especially the town of Tenterden near Cranbrook. William Carder of Tenterden was the most notorious victim, espousing many traditional Lollard views regarding images and pilgrimages, prayers to the saints, and the sacramental system. His trial in the spring of 1511 launched a year-long investigation in which persons from Tenterden, Maidstone and Ashford clearly stood out above the rest.[50] For example, it was discovered that Edward Walker of Maidstone had been hosting Lollard gatherings in his home, probably due to his possession of a copy of Matthew's Gospel in the vernacular. Thus, there were obvious precedents for the conventicling movement of the Edwardian era prior to the Reformation years; and although the issues for discussion underwent some change by that time, the patterns for radicalism and independence of spirit were firmly in place beforehand.

Before moving on, it is perhaps important to reiterate that religion was not the only matter deemed to be worth fighting over in Kent. Going back to the fourteenth century, for example, one is immediately struck by the high proportion of leadership and general support for the Peasants' Revolt which came from Canterbury and the Weald. Disenchantment with royal policy on the French war was an important factor in Kent's anxiety level at that time, as the county seems to have been made to bear the brunt of the hardships which

---

[47] J. F. Davis, 'Lollard Survival and the Textile Industry in the South-east of England' in *Studies in Church History*, ed. G. J. Cuming (Leiden: E. J. Brill, 1966), III, p. 194; *VCH*, II, 58.

[48] Thomson, p. 184.

[49] *VCH*, II, 63.

[50] Thomson, pp. 188–9.

accompanied the hostilities. Add to this the imposition of an aggravating poll tax and the situation became highly volatile in this first of a series of uprisings in which Kent and her populace played a key role.[51] During the next century, trouble once again erupted, as artisans, husbandmen and labourers from every conceivable trade participated in Jack Cade's revolt. Most significantly, weavers and workers from Smarden and Pluckley were found among Cade's followers.[52]

In the sixteenth century, discontent associated with enclosure led to trouble in 1548. Near Canterbury five hundred persons overran an enclosure made by the Lord Warden of the Cinque Ports, and officials had to request artillery in order to subdue the rebels who were threatening to lay siege to the city. Once order was restored, a commission sent to examine the grievances of the malcontents complied with their wishes in bringing about the destruction of the offending object. The situation in Kent was still being monitored closely for signs of potential trouble as late as 1550.[53]

That trouble, although of a different sort, was of course forthcoming early in 1554, as Sir Thomas Wyatt organized an armed display at Maidstone on 25 January.[54] Although this demonstration took place when the proceedings under investigation in the present study were in full swing, and none of the religious disputants encountered here were noticeably involved, it is nonetheless noteworthy that both Maidstone and the Wealden villages, which supplied much of the impetus for the Kentish freewill movement, contributed heavily to Wyatt's Kentish support base. Indeed, D. M. Loades's research indicated that Maidstone parish provided more men than any other single area in the country, while a group of villages which included Smarden and Pluckley ranked second in numbers.[55] While Loades noted that none of the identifiable Kentish rebels were included in Foxe's table of Kentish martyrs,[56] it is possible that one of the dissidents, John Spice, hailed from Pluckley parish – the apparent home base of Henry Harte[57] – while another

---

[51] *VCH*, III, 348 – 9.

[52] W. D. Cooper, 'John Cade's Followers in Kent', *AC*, VII (1868), 238 – 9.

[53] W. E. Tate, 'A Handlist of English Enclosure Acts and Awards. Part 17. Open Fields, Commons and Enclosures in Kent', *AC*, LVI (1943), 58.

[54] *VCH*, III, 300.

[55] Loades, *Two Tudor Conspiracies* (Cambridge: University Press, 1965), pp. 76 – 7.

[56] *Ibid.*, p. 87.

[57] John Spice is listed as a parishioner at Pluckley in the visitation return for 1538. See Canterbury, Christchurch Cathedral Library, Archdeaconry Visitation Act Book, Z 3/5, fol. 45. Evidently Spice was still attending there in 1557. See *Archdeacon Harpsfield's Visitation, 1557*, ed. L. E. Whatmore (London: Catholic Record Society, 1951) XLV, 118. Cf. Loades, *Conspiracies*, p. 255.

rebel, William Symming, may have been a good friend of Harte.[58] At any rate, it is obvious that the Weald and vicinity could embrace a fairly wide variety of radical, and even dangerous, opinions and causes without a great deal of outside encouragement.

The identity of the conventiclers

Having briefly surveyed the regional and historical context out of which the original conventicling movement emerged, it remains now to examine the identity of the first participants as far as the record allows. Of the thirty-three persons identifiable from the sources who were officially implicated in the proceedings of 1550 – 1, at least eight appear to be still active later on in Marian England in connexion with the King's Bench prison dispute – one of the prime foci of this work. Here, as we shall see, the Bocking controversy was carried on with renewed zeal and vehemence.[59] Another eight persons have left behind mere traces of information through various channels, while the rest appear to evaporate as far as the records are concerned.

One of the less difficult men to identify is 'Upcharde' of Bocking, the individual first singled out by the Council as one of the key participants. He was almost certainly Thomas Upshire, or Upcher, a man who later spent some time in prison under Mary before being released and fleeing to Frankfurt.[60] He appears to have been a weaver, quite possibly coming to Bocking from nearby Kelvedon.[61] Kelvedon had a long tradition of both cloth-making and Lollardy, as two local weavers from here joined the ranks of Oldcastle's followers in 1414.[62] Kelvedon became a secondary producer of woollens behind such places as Colchester, Bocking, Braintree, and Coggeshall following the arrival of numerous Dutchmen in Essex after the middle

---

[58] A William Symming or Dymning was listed in Harte's administration. Apparently he also hailed from Pluckley. See Maidstone, Kent County Record Office, Archdeaconry Act Book, PRC 3/15/22. Cf. Loades, *Conspiracies*, p. 255.

[59] James Oxley, *The Reformation in Essex to the Death of Mary* (Manchester: University Press, 1965), p. 192.

[60] Christina Garrett, *The Marian Exiles* (London: Cambridge University Press, 1966), p. 316. See Doris Witard, *Bibles in Barrels: A History of Essex Baptists* (n.p.: Essex Baptist Assoc., n.d.), p. 21, for reference to a Richard Upchard who may have been part of the same circle.

[61] Chelmsford, Essex Record Office, Archdeaconry of Colchester, D/ACR 3, fols. 109 – 110.

[62] E. J. B. Reid, 'Lollards at Colchester in 1414', *English Historical Review*, XXIX (1914), 103.

of the sixteenth century.[63] A Thomas Upcher was resident here during the 1540s, and he was evidently a man of considerable possessions and wealth. He employed five servants and had one son named John. These facts agree reasonably well with Garrett's findings, as she suggested that Upcher was 'a man of some substance' by 1557, and that he then had two sons, John and George.

Upcher's involvement in the Bocking episode is not immediately clear, and his selection as the first witness in the case was probably due to his function as host to the gathering. It must be remembered that the original target for the Kentish representatives was the home of Robert Cooke, not that of Upcher. Cooke, being a clothier, may also have been moderately wealthy by this time, and was perhaps connected to the Lollard tradition associated with Essex cloth-workers. Although not terribly likely, it is somewhat feasible that this man was the same Robert Cooke who had been causing such a stir in the royal court since the days of Queen Catherine Parr. Strype cast this fellow as an Anabaptist who 'crept into the Court' and displayed considerable knowledge and skill at music.[64] He became the keeper of the royal wine-cellar, and used his position to debate with some of the most noted churchmen of that age on various points of doctrine. He was known to oppose infant baptism and he held odd views relating to the Lord's Supper at various stages in his career.

In his most famous polemical encounter Cooke clashed with Dr William Turner, ordained Dean of Wells by Ridley in December of 1552.[65] The subject of the argument was the doctrine of original sin, as Cooke vehemently denied its existence. Then Cooke virtually disappeared from public view for several decades, save for the appearance of a manuscript work against a Calvinist understanding of election which he may have written during the Marian period.[66] He emerged again in the Elizabethan era as a gentleman attached to the Queen's chapel, having apparently abandoned his radical views.[67] His activities between 1547 and 1573 are something of a mystery, however, and the time span would certainly permit a period of proselytizing and controversy in connection with the emergence of the Kent-Essex sectarians. The fact that an Essex clothier implicated in the Bocking incident bore the same name as a mysterious eccentric who may have contributed to the King's Bench contention does not prove that they are one and the same. Yet the possibility is too

[63] Page and Doubleday, II, 386.
[64] Strype, *EM*, II, 1, 111.
[65] *Ibid.*, 2, 62.
[66] See chapter 7.
[67] Strype, *EM*, II, 1, 111–12.

intriguing to be entirely overlooked.[68] Certainly the mobility of the cloth trade would allow for the dissemination of Cooke's ideas, and his occupation may have been an extension of his courtly activities or even a front for radical involvement.

It will be remembered that one 'Sympson' was detained by the Council in 1551 along with Upcher. The identity of this man presents some problems, although he may well have been one Cutbert Symson, who was known to be a tailor at one time.[69] Although Symson may have been living in Essex when first apprehended, it is probable that his family came from Elham parish in Kent.[70] During the Marian years, a Cutbert Symson served as a deacon in the underground church in London which was pastored by several men during this period, including John Rough.[71] Since Symson was to die a martyr's death in sympathy with the Reformed faith, it was likely that he was in the formative stage of his spiritual outlook in 1551, and that he, along with others, later switched allegiances under the influence of mainstream Protestant orthodoxy in London.

Predestination hotly defended: Elham Parish

The possibility of participation from the parish of Elham seems all the stronger when it is remembered that the local minister, John Lamberd, had set forth his opinions 'Of predestinacion & election' only a short time beforehand in 1550. Drawing upon Augustine and Bonaventure for support,[72] his tract is extremely significant since it indicates, or rather confirms, the kind of topics being discussed so energetically in East Kent during those days. In examining the tract, one first observes Lamberd's adoption of a relatively strident form of predestinarian teaching. One is also struck by the emphasis upon separation from wickedness and especially, from the wicked — just

---

[68] Cooke's career is fully explored below in chapter 7. See also Witard, p. 21.

[69] Foxe, VIII, 446. See also appendix 2 below for the problem of identification in connexion with Symson.

[70] Maidstone, Kent County Record Office, Archdeaconry Register, PRC 17/18/123. See appendix 2 below.

[71] Foxe, VIII, 454 – 9; see also his section on John Rough, 443 – 9; see B. R. White, *The English Separatist Tradition* (Oxford: University Press, 1971), pp. 10 – 11 regarding the leadership of the underground congregation during Mary's reign; for further details of Symson's career see below pp. 144, 153 – 4 and 172 – 3, and appendix 2.

[72] John Lamberd, *Of predestinacion & election made by John Lambard minister of the church of Elham* (Canterbury: J. Mychell, 1550). RSTC 15181. For an example of his reliance on these scholars, see fol. Bia.

the sort of topics being heatedly debated by the Kent-Essex conventiclers and thus reported to the authorities.

It is further clear that Lamberd was on the defensive to some extent. Thus, when he declared his 'councell' to be 'that no man dyspute with God why he hath ordeyned the vesselles of wrath to dampnacion,' one can be almost certain that plenty of his parishioners (possibly including Cutbert Symson) had been asking that very thing. Lamberd expressed the hope that when his 'reader' had finished with his 'lytle treatyse', he might then be in a position to 'consulte or counsell with his owne conscience and so examyne the same, whether he do lyve lyke a reprobate or one that is electe of God to salvacion'.[73] His uncompromising rigidity is most evident in his description of the reprobate, whom Lamberd refers to as 'mynysters unto the salvacyon of the electe, which are Goddes workmanshyp'.[74]

Though professing humility, 'good wyll', and a willingness 'to knowe the truthe',[75] Lamberd, like so many others who were to be drawn into the swirl of the predestinarian controversy, had obviously staked out his own position and intended to occupy it staunchly until the very end. In predictable fashion, he asserted his belief in key doctrines related to the attributes of God. Thus, we have His eternality and also His omnipotence − 'he maye do what he wyll and none but he' − along with His omniscience − 'all thynges good and bad were ever presently in the syghte of God or ever they were' − which included his foreknowledge of men's conduct and destinies − 'he dyd know by his prescience who shulde goo the brode way that leadeth to perdicion.'[76] Only those belonging to Christ's flock would come to faith; those who were not his 'shepe' would never 'beleve'.[77] Further, 'the passion of Christe can not save a reprobate, that is he that refuseth the trueth and always doeth stryve agaynste the holy Ghoste, whose dampnacion is just & true. For such are dampnable creatures knowne of God before the worlde was layde and are called the vessels of wrathe to declare Goddes glory on the vessels of mercy'. On the other side of the ledger: 'The electe also was predestinate of God to be saved.'[78] Proof of one's election lay in the presence of 'lyvely fayth'.[79] Moreover, as if to counter the likes of Harte and his fellows, 'it is impossible that the elect should be dampned'.[80]

[73] *Ibid.*, fol. Aiia.
[74] *Ibid.*, fols. Aiia − b.
[75] *Ibid.*, Ciib.
[76] *Ibid.*, fol. Aiiia.
[77] *Ibid.*, fol. Aiva.
[78] *Ibid.*, fols. Aivb-Bia.
[79] *Ibid.*, fol. Cib.
[80] *Ibid.*, fol. Cib.

Lamberd also defended the concept and reality of both original and actual sin in the following passage:

> Therfore yf Adam and Eve had not transgressed Christe should not have dyed, nowe seinge they did offende they and all their posteryte were infected with that contagyouse poysin of sinne . . . . Adams disobedience dampned us all, yet we our selves wrought evyll. Therfore seynge we were the causers of Christes death god myght have dampned us Justly, although he elected us before the worlde was made . . . . God fyrst predestinate us & elected us in him before the worlde was made that we shulde be sayntes, for Christe was predestinate to be the Sonne of God. And then beynge lost through synne, yet god knowynge by his prescience suche thinges would come to passe.[81]

Continuing with his apologetic tone, Lamberd affirmed that the elect had been chosen 'accordynge to the pleasure of hys will'. In a telling section, he reasoned that those who were so chosen 'should not blame God because he hath predestinate some to be the chyldren of perdicion, onlesse they would be sory for their owne salvacion, he ordeined some to be punyshed accordynge to their dedes'.[82]

Again, it would seem all too obvious in light of what later transpired that some of the saints in Elham parish (and in other localities) were very much perturbed about the very issues raised by men such as Lamberd. Thus, although the predestinarian message seemed to be gaining ground steadily throughout the Edwardian years, pockets of resistance surfaced from time to time at the popular level, as Englishmen began to wrestle with the picture of divinity which emerged from such pronouncements. At the root lay the question of the goodness of God. If one's theology did not allow for this basic proposition in terms understandable via the approach of common sense rationalism, of what practical use could it possibly be? Either God was fair and just according to one's inner standards, or He was not. Although Lamberd himself was convinced that He was not at all deficient in 'charytie . . . for he is very love it selfe',[83] others in East Kent were evidently not so sure.

As indicated, a secondary issue was revealed in the course of Lamberd's discourse. This concerned the need to identify the reprobate and steer clear of them. To facilitate the problem of knowing 'the reprobate now frome the electe',[84] Lamberd published

---

[81] *Ibid.*, fols. Bib – [B]iib. The tract incorrectly reverts to A at this point.

[82] *Ibid.*, fol. Biib.

[83] *Ibid.*, fol. Cib.

[84] *Ibid.*, fol. Biiib.

his authoritative list of identifying marks which included the sin of 'presumynge to much on goddes mercy'. Following his review of these 'very tokens of a reprobate', Lambard warned that 'with such we should not company nor eate, so longe as they persever in that wycked estate'.[85] The notion of exclusivity was reinforced by his admonition to the elect that they 'be servauntes to al men that be our brothers in Christ, and minyster unto theim the fruytes of faythe in all their nede'.[86] As will be seen during the proceedings of the King's Bench prison dispute,[87] there were many who later lived up to the spirit of Lamberd's directives most faithfully. Whether Lamberd's treatise, which was printed at Canterbury by J. Mychell,[88] became a widespread source of inspiration or not, it is unquestionable that he touched on matters of extreme importance to religious men in an age when religious issues pressed for attention. Thus, despite his caution to 'never clymbe any hygher or serche any further, why God hathe predestinate some, to be the chyldren of perdicion',[89] numerous men from the south-east could not resist the temptation. Symson was evidently one of them.

More identities revealed

The second clothier mentioned in the royal schedules at the time of the exposé was John Eglins of Bocking, possibly the father of two children.[90] Although Eglins was found in the conventiclers' circle in 1551, he may have conformed to the Elizabethan church and was probably buried in St Mary's churchyard in September 1562.[91] A similar pattern appears likely in the case of John King of Bocking, a weaver whose will may have been drawn up in the same year as the investigation.[92] According to this document, he possessed significant quantities of cloth, much of which lay in 'Blakwellhall' in London. A John King was interred in St Mary's churchyard in February 1592.[93]

[85] *Ibid.*, fol. Bivb.
[86] *Ibid.*, fol. Cia.
[87] See chapters 4 to 7.
[88] *Ibid.*, fol. Ciiia.
[89] *Ibid.*, fol. Cib.
[90] Chelmsford, Essex Record Office, Archdeaconry of Colchester, D/ABW 13/23.
[91] James Goodwin, ed. *The First Register of St. Mary's Church, Bocking, Essex, England* (n.p., 1903), p. 61. A 'Johnes Egling' was buried here on 25 September of that year.
[92] Chelmsford, Essex Record Office, Archdeaconry of Colchester, D/ABW 22/48.
[93] Goodwin, p. 95.

Thomas Cole and his 'flowers'

The remainder of the native Essex conventiclers must remain obscure,[94] so that attention may now be focussed on the Kentish delegation which precipitated the entire affair by their journey into Essex. One of the spokesmen for this group was the aforementioned schoolmaster from Maidstone, Thomas Cole. Situated strategically on the road from London and Sevenoaks, Maidstone completed something of a nonconformist triangle in Kent, with Faversham and the Wealden towns around Ashford and Pluckley being the other points. Maidstone's population was tabulated at 2,041 in 1550.[95] Fuller's earth was obtainable in the vicinity of nearby Boxley, and the Flemings introduced the production of linen-thread here toward the end of the sixteenth century.[96]

Cole's interests, however, were primarily intellectual and not economic. Originally a native of Lincolnshire, Cole attended King's College, Cambridge, receiving his B.A. in 1546 and his M.A. in 1550.[97] During this time, he was appointed headmaster of the grammar school in Maidstone in 1546,[98] an institution which came into being as a result of the suppression of the College of All Saints. Between 1507 and 1519, education in the College had been under the guiding hand of William Grocyn, the humanist scholar known as the first instructor to teach Greek at Oxford.[99] Although Thomas Cole did not quite attain the heights of his predecessor, he did manage to make a name for himself.

Around 1550, Cole began to preach in All Saints' Church against the doctrine of original sin as it was then being espoused at Geneva.[100] The corporation of Maidstone was sufficiently alarmed to appoint a committee to deal with Cole and make him aware of his errors. It was believed that others in the district agreed with him, but the

[94] One possible exception to this statement is John Barrett, also designated as 'Barrey'. A John Barry from Essex was later closely involved in the King's Bench proceedings, but he does not appear to have been a farmer. His story is chronicled below, pp. 159 – 63.
[95] Walter Gilbert, ed. *The Accounts of the Corpus Christi Fraternity, and papers relating to the Antiquities of Maidstone* (Maidstone, 1865), p. 136.
[96] Jessup, p. 88.
[97] *DNB*, IV, 729.
[98] Gilbert, p. 161.
[99] Frank Streatfield, *Account of the Grammar School . . . of Maidstone* (Oxford: Rogers & Browne, 1915), p. 14.
[100] J. M. Russell, *The History of Maidstone* (Maidstone: William S. Vivish, 1881), p. 173.

schoolmaster received most of the attention.[101] It seems as though nothing much became of the inquiry, and little further is known of Cole until his dealings with the Privy Council in February 1551.[102] He must have deeply impressed the authorities on that occasion, since he found himself preaching before the Archbishop himself in All Saints' Church during the Lenten season of 1552.[103] The sermon was a most intriguing item, since it contained information concerning the kind of discussions held by the Kentish conventiclers and gave insights into their views. Apparently it was also delivered in the presence of 'two simple men' who were guilty of maintaining the errors Cole was now refuting, but the identity of these men was nowhere revealed by Cole. They were presumably from the Maidstone area, although the presence of Cranmer leaves open the possibility that they may have been transported some distance in order to attend.

In the sermon, Cole subtly declared that he had 'never held or taught any of these or such like errors' personally,[104] and that, save for two men present, he did not even know of any who did. His purpose in addressing his audience was to forewarn them of the subtle activity of Satan, who sought to deceive and beguile as many victims as possible. In keeping with his goal, Cole enumerated 'a great heap of noisome flowers' which the Devil utilized to entice men away from the truth.[105] These flowers were obviously the opinions held by some of the radicals. The first dealt with the universalist aspect of salvation. According to this flower, all men were destined for salvation and 'none at length' were to be damned. Cole felt this to be a deadly doctrine since it bred 'a false security' within a man and elevated the mercy of God at the expense of his justice.[106] Although God is merciful towards all men in Christ, only those who are true believers in Him will be saved for His sake. Those who die in unbelief will be justly condemned.[107]

If this flower is not enticing enough, Satan introduces a second which denies the existence of any divine predestination. Therefore, 'none shall be saved' in the end according to this argument since, for

---

[101] Streatfield, p. 14.
[102] It is possible that the furore created by Cole on this occasion may have led to the Kentish inquisitions referred to above. If so, this would seem to place the Kentish depositions prior to, and not subsequent to, the Bocking arrests. It is also possible that Cole was simply examined by the local town fathers at the outset. Cf. Russell, p. 173.
[103] *Ibid.*
[104] T. Cole, *A godly sermon, made at Maydstone the fyrste sonday in Lent* (London: R. Wolfe, 1553), sig. D. iiib. RSTC 5539.
[105] *Ibid., sig. B. iiia.*
[106] *Ibid.*, sig. B. iiia.
[107] *Ibid.*, sig. b. va.

Cole, justification is an effect of predestination.[108] If the latter is denied, then the former is soon renounced as well, as men conclude that Christ died in vain — if, indeed, there is a Christ. This means that faith itself would be destroyed; and, if faith is destroyed, then none can be saved. Such reasoning is entirely beside the point for Cole, however, since God's predestination is certain in Christ, even though it may be uncertain in men.[109] Thus, men should not attempt to 'rashly judge' in the matter of divine predestination, but should humbly submit their judgements to God's Word and be free of idle curiosity.[110]

Moving on in his discourse, Cole developed his understanding of predestination even further, this time addressing himself to the question of evil and its relationship to divine activity. He declared it to be a 'flower of hell' to 'hold that by predestination God is the author of sin'. To maintain this opinion, as evidently the Kentish dissenters did, was to exceed the limits of Scripture. God never moves anyone to sin and is therefore not the author or it; for 'He is the author of nothing but of that which He alloweth.' He warns men to flee from sin and wills that all men should keep clear of it. Satan is the one ultimately responsible for the presence of sin, and sin is the sole reason why the divine wrath is poured out upon men. Those who do not respond to God are condemned, while those who believe receive 'undeserved mercy' and are saved.[111]

The fourth flower on Cole's list was something of an oddity, since it does not appear to have been an issue during the later contention. It was stated that 'Christ died for his own sins as well as for the sins of the people'.[112] Cole obviously abhorred the very suggestion, which may have arisen in connexion with speculation about the humanity of Christ amongst extremely radical circles. The next error may also be construed as being related to radicalism, especially the type which surfaced at Münster in 1535. It was alleged that a true Christian could 'have his neighbour's wife in common'. Cole considered the idea to be so blasphemous that it scarcely needed a reply. The sixth error also gave evidence of some continental influences, as it held that 'the inward man sinneth not, when the outer man sinneth'.[113] Cole rejected this on the ground that it was the soul which the Devil assailed in order 'to make it obedient to the lusts of the flesh'. When the soul consents to the suggestion, it gradually becomes a slave to the

[108] *Ibid.*, sig. B. via.
[109] *Ibid.*, sig. B. vib — viia.
[110] *Ibid.*, sig. B. viia.
[111] *Ibid.*, sig. B. viib — viia.
[112] *Ibid.*, sig. C. ib.
[113] *Ibid.*, sig. C. iiia.

flesh. Thus, evil actually proceeds from the soul or the inner man, when it responds to Satan.[114]

This particular question was somewhat reminiscent of the discussions among the continental Anabaptists, even though the perspective as stated in Cole's flower would not find much sympathy in their midst. Yet Hubmaier's conviction that the spirit of man was not involved in the Adamic fall was sufficiently similar to this concept to suggest some point of contact.[115] At least the same questions were being asked, even if the answers differed from place to place.

The remainder of Cole's flowers also gave evidence of possible Anabaptist links, including the two which followed on the subject of free will. These dealt with the old Pelagian question involving man's capacity to please God and attain salvation with or without the aid of divine grace.[116] Cole could conceive of no greater 'blasphemy'; he argued that faith was a gift from God which depended upon His grace alone. He also affirmed that no man could please God without reference to Christ Himself. Cole did not argue that the human will was inoperative in these matters, but merely asserted the uselessness of the will apart from grace.[117]

In the next portion of his sermon, Cole began to attack the exclusivist and isolationist stance of his former associates from Kent. He declared it to be unlawful to 'invent orders in religion' when the common or public order was considered to be defective in the sight of an individual. Those who opt for 'ceremonies and doctrines of their own inventions, are authors of sects'. Those who avoid having fellowship with their fellow believers and who piously keep clear of them 'as from wicked and damned men' would do well to remember the example of Christ, Who came to save the lost and not to condemn them.[118] True believers, therefore, ought to seek to recover the wanderers from their wayward paths rather than separating themselves 'uncharitably' from their company. It is clear that Cole believed such behaviour to be presumptuous, particularly since humans cannot always judge which men are in sin and which are not. Even if a congregation failed to perform its duties in disciplining 'notorious' members, separation was not justified. One should instead remain within the local church fellowship and entrust the issue to God, realizing that only personal purity is required. Cole

---

[114] *Ibid.*, sig. C. iiib – iiiia.
[115] Balthasar Hubmaier, 'On Free Will' in *SAW*, eds. G. H. Williams and Angel Mergal, *LCC*, No. 25 (Philadelphia: Westminster Press, 1957), p. 118.
[116] Cole, sig. C. iiiia&b.
[117] *Ibid.*, sig. C. va.
[118] *Ibid.*, sig. C. vb – via.

asserted that he was not aware of any who did practise 'such separation'.[119]

Next on the list of flowers came a many-headed hydra which rejected both 'original sin' and the 'baptism of infants', and also seemed to broach the subject of the unpardonable sin in very confusing terms. According to Cole, the errors in these beliefs were all confuted by the Word of God, although he confessed that he did not have time to elaborate upon them. Accordingly, he moved on to yet another flower, namely that 'it is lawful to be a public preacher in a Christian commonwealth, without the authority of the Christian magistrates'.[120] Once again the allusion to the Anabaptist tradition is unmistakable, and Cole saw this tenet as another 'enemy to Christian order'. Likewise, the thirteenth article dealt with the flower of sinless perfection, yet another principle commonly associated with the continental Anabaptists. Cole denied the possibility of living sinlessly in the absolute sense, choosing instead to concentrate upon the believer's ultimate perfection in Christ.[121] Moreover, God desires unity 'which is the bond of perfection'.

The final flower analyzed by Cole appeared to be related to the extreme asceticism or puritanism of the Kentish conventiclers. This puritanism came out very strongly in the ecclesiastical depositions and Privy Council hearings, and it resurfaced again during Mary's day to play a prominent role in the King's Bench controversy itself.[122] In Cole's sermon, the subject turned to gambling or playing at games for money, which was a 'deadly sin' according to this evil flower of Satan. Cole was suspicious of such an attitude, since to him it seemed 'to thrust into man's heart such a preciseness, that at length a good man might judge everything, although it were but indifferent, to be damnable sin'. He argued that the mere playing of a game in itself was not sinful, but the 'abusing' of oneself in the playing was indeed 'damnable sin'. Such abuse would include the swearing of evil oaths or the neglect of one's family through an addiction to dice and other games.[123] Thus, Cole appears to have been aware of some social ills pertaining to the times in which he lived, and he was not afraid to voice an opinion on them publicly.

As for the overall tenor of the sermon, it could be described as moderately Calvinist at most points. Undoubtedly the presence of Cranmer went a long way in determining Cole's perspectives. It was also clear that Cole was directing his clever remarks at a specific

---

[119] *Ibid.*, sig. C. vib – viiia.
[120] *Ibid.*, sig. C. viiia.
[121] *Ibid.*, sig. C. viiib – D. ia.
[122] See below, p. 153.
[123] Cole, sig. D. iia – b.

group of men – men who were 'good livers',[124] and who were attempting to be 'sober' in their conduct. Nevertheless they were in danger of receiving the grace of God in vain since they were espousing 'ill doctrine' under the facade of 'good living'.[125] Cole had apparently rejected the vices of his former way of life and was now seeking to correct his old comrades and bring them into the pathway of truth.[126]

Cole was rewarded for his efforts late in 1552 when he was appointed Dean of Salisbury,[127] but he was forced to flee the scene soon afterwards with other Protestant divines and wound up in Frankfurt. Here he came to know John Knox and was included in the leadership of the church as early as September of 1554 when it was decided that Knox should be called to the pastorate.[128] Following the outbreak of strife at Frankfurt amongst the exiles, Cole became a supporter of Whittingham's flock, although he remained behind for a time following the departure of the others for Geneva. Presumably, he was to serve as an informant to the departed faction.[129] His whereabouts during the later Marian years remain something of a mystery, although he appears on Bale's calendar of exiles made in 1557.[130] Following the death of Mary he returned to his native land and was named rector of High Ongar in Essex as of 1559.[131] In 1560 he became Archdeacon of Essex and was also given the prebend of Rugmere in St Paul's Cathedral. A subscriber to the original articles of religion of the English Church, Cole received an honourary D.D. in 1564 and was appointed rector of Stanford Rivers, Essex. He also preached before the Queen at Windsor during this year, and was asked to preach the Spital Sermon by the Lord Mayor of London in 1566. He was, however, prevented from conducting this service by Archbishop Parker who was apparently still concerned with Cole's tendency toward heterodoxy.[132] This fact suggests that Cole may never have completely abandoned some of the perspectives of the early Kentish radicals. At any rate, he died in 1571 after a rich and

---

[124] *Ibid.*, sig. B. iiib.

[125] *Ibid.*, sig. D. iiib.

[126] It is most significant that Cole affirmed their admirable life-styles, since this was precisely the factor which later concerned Bradford and his fellows when debating with the freewillers in prison. Also, the theme of reclaiming the lost radicals was a constant one during the prison debate. For example, see below, chapter 4.

[127] Streatfield, p. 15; *DNB*, IV, 729.

[128] William Whittingham, *A Brief Discourse of the Troubles at Frankfort, 1554 – 1558 A.D.* (London: Elliot Stock, 1908; orig. pub. 1575), p. 36.

[129] Garrett, p. 122.

[130] Joanne Baleo, *Scriptorum Illustrium maioris Brytannie, quam nunc Angliam & Scotiam vocant* (Basileae, 1557, 1559), p. 742.

[131] *DNB*, IV, 729.

[132] Streatfield, p. 16

varied career which took him far beyond the original conventiclers' circle, and he stands as something of an enigma in the episode under examination.

Of the remaining identifiable members of the Kentish faction, all but one seem to have come from the vicinity of the Weald. This exception is another Cole – Cole of Faversham, not Maidstone. Robert Cole, perhaps originally from Bedfordshire, may also have been a graduate of King's College, Cambridge.[133] He is most clearly identified with the town of Faversham in Kent, however, and may have served as town bailiff in 1539. This bailiff, who bore the same name, engaged in the shipping of English wheat to Zeeland, using hoyes owned by two men from Flushing. It has already been established that townspeople from Faversham and other south-eastern centres were heavily involved in this kind of activity with the continent during the late Henrician period.[134] Not only would this enterprise supplement Cole's income, it would also serve as a direct link with continental religious ideologies and trends, perhaps including Anabaptism. It should also be remembered that 1539 would be only four years after the ill-fated scene at Münster, and numerous Hollanders were undoubtedly still desperate to flee their homeland.

Shipping links with the south-east of England, then, could serve as immigration channels to the north of the Strait of Dover. One might also realistically expect to find in these circles the type of religious and heretical literature which the royal proclamations inveighed against during those years. The transportation of prohibited literature was undoubtedly a significant factor in the persistence of late Lollardy,[135] and it would be most plausible to expect that similar activities might develop in the dissemination of continental concepts as well. Thus, Robert Cole, bailiff, may have absorbed some tenets of continental radicalism while dealing with the Netherlands, and then gone on to propagate these views amongst his Kentish associates. It is unlikely that his involvement in shipping Kentish produce to the continent was merely part of his function as bailiff, even though it may well have been an extension of it; for the barons and bailiffs of the port of Faversham had been receiving royal instructions regarding maritime matters since the thirteenth century.[136] At that time, the bailiff was either elected or appointed by the Crown and was responsible for

---

[133] Garrett, p. 121. Garrett claims that Robert Cole graduated M.A. from King's College in 1550 and was named a fellow of the College in 1545.

[134] See above, pp. 57 – 8.

[135] Davis, *Heresy*, p. 195.

[136] F. F. Giraud, 'The Service of Shipping of the Barons of Faversham', *AC*, XXI (1895), 274.

acting as the king's local administrative assistant in putting royal directives into force. In some instances, a complementary function of the bailiff was to serve as the principal executive officer for the English boroughs on behalf of the burgesses, thus acting as a go-between for the Crown and the boroughs.[137]

Cole's position would have been an extremely responsible one, therefore, and if he and others of like influence were attracted to nonconformist ideas while active in capacities such as this we may have a partial explanation for the relative leniency of Cranmer and his subordinates in dealing with Kentish heresy. In this light, it is significant that another of the Faversham entrepreneurs, William Castlocke, was quite possibly Mayor of Faversham during this period, or at least for part of it.[138] Furthermore, these factors would help to account for the conventiclers' associations with Essex, since the Colchester area participated in a similar trade.

Robert Cole's opposition to continental predestinarianism was well known to the Kentish informants by the Edwardian years, suggesting the probability of continental ties or even an indigenous heretical substratum. The latter is perhaps less likely than the former, given the basically Augustinian approach of John Wycliffe, although perhaps a combination of the two is most likely. Cole's eventual role in the King's Bench drama, which will be examined later, and his subsequent incorporation into the Church of England as a clergyman, are yet other fascinating aspects of this case.[139] His development ran somewhat parallel to that of John Ledley of Ashford who was discovered to have been at Bocking, and who remained a close confidant of Robert Cole during the Marian upheaval.[140] Nothing is known of Ledley's career prior to the Bocking affair.

The same might be said of at least nine other Kentish sectarians. Of the remainder, two of the recorded informants, Edmund Morres and William Forstal, were still acting in this capacity during the Marian inquisition.[141] At that time they offered written testimony concerning the behaviour of the eventual martyr John Bland, parson of Adisham in Kent. Thus, their involvement in the radical episode was basically from the outside only. Another original witness to the activities of the Kentishmen, the clerk Richard Dinestake or perhaps Dunslake, may have been rewarded for his reporting with the

---

[137] C. R. Young, *The English Borough and Royal Administration, 1130 – 1307* (Durham, N.C.: Duke University Press, 1961), p. 30.

[138] F. F. Giraud, 'Expenses of the Corporation of Faversham, Temp. Hen. VIII', *AC*, x (1876), 241.

[139] For example, see below, pp. 110 – 12; 122 – 3; 140 – 3, *passim*; 182; 193.

[140] See pp. 110 – 12, 122 and 143 below for Ledley's subsequent activity.

[141] Foxe, VII, 290.

vicarage of Rolvenden in 1555;[142] and if so, he continued in this capacity under Elizabeth. Dunslake may have been parish clerk in Faversham or another of the affected centres at the time of the hearings.[143] One of the original offenders, William Sibley of Lenham, does not appear to have survived the reign of Edward. He probably died intestate in the spring of 1552.[144] The disposal of this man's goods was left in the hands of John Castlocke of Faversham and Edward Partridge of Lenham, perhaps two more of the group's number. Another defendant before the Council with Sibley on 3 February 1551, had been Thomas Sharpe of Pluckley. Sharpe may have been involved in the cloth trade, as one of the men entrusted with his possessions at his decease in January of 1563 was a clothier from nearby Egerton.[145] Nicholas Sheterden also hailed from Pluckley, and the family seems to have been associated with that part of the Weald for quite some time.[146] Although his profession is unknown, his end was most carefully chronicled by Foxe, as Sheterden went through a long series of investigations for heresy in 1555 before being condemned in July of that year along with John Bland and another conventicler, Humphrey Middleton of Ashford near Pluckley.[147] Middleton, it will be remembered, had been present at Robert Cole's home in Faversham and, according to John Plume of Lenham, had come close to espousing some form of universalism.[148] Yet another conventicler and Marian martyr was George Brodebridge of Broomfield, located just north of Canterbury. Brodebridge suffered at Canterbury in September of 1555 after denouncing auricular confession, the real presence in the sacrament of the altar and the Roman mass.[149] In June of 1557 his widow was apparently burnt as well. According to the Kentish ecclesiastical depositions, Brodebridge set forth the most advanced theological proposition of the entire group, arguing for the conditional election of all men to salvation.[150]

---

[142] Peter Clark, 'The Prophesying Movement During the 1570's', *AC*, XCIII (1977), 89.

[143] In 1548, it had been determined that the number of parish clerks in Faversham should be reduced from two to one. F. F. Giraud, 'On the Parish Clerks and Sexton of Faversham, A.D. 1506 – 1593', *AC*, xx (1893), 209.

[144] Maidstone, Kent County Record Office, Archdeaconry Act Book, PRC 3/12/89.

[145] *Ibid.*, PRC 3/17/23.

[146] A Walter Sheterenden who resided at Great Charte in the early sixteenth century may have been related to Nicholas, as the latter wrote to his brother named Walter during his imprisonment in 1555. Foxe, VII, 314 – 16. See also Maidstone, Kent County Record Office, Archdeaconry Register, VII, fol. 340.

[147] Foxe, VII, 306 – 18.

[148] *Ibid.*, 383.

[149] *Ibid.*, VIII, 326.

[150] Harl. MSS, 421, 134a.

The introduction and survey of the Bocking-Faversham conventiclers who participated to some extent in the prison proceedings
of the Marian reign is now complete, save for a further examination
of the figure who evidently played one of the most prominent roles in
mid-Tudor radicalism in the south-east. This, of course, is Henry
Harte of Kent. Harte had made extremely heretical claims concerning the subject of predestination and the accompanying doctrine of
the perseverance of the elect, and had also expressed an intense
aversion to higher learning. As pointed out, Harte's original place of
residence was probably Pluckley in the Weald, the home of other
activists such as Sheterden and Sharpe.[151] Harte's movements
between his initial indictment for unlawful assembling and his
association with the Faversham radicals are not easily chronicled.
The presence of a John Harte serving as a sacrist at the abbey in
Faversham in 1534 suggests that the name was not unknown in that
vicinity.[152] The most probable centre of Harte's activity prior to the
Bocking episode, however, is not Faversham but London. Near the
beginning of Edward's reign, two tracts produced by Harte appeared
in print, and it is not unreasonable to suspect that he may have spent
these years in writing and seeking out publishers in London. Robert
Staughton of London printed the first of Harte's tracts in October of
1548, while a second edition under an altered title appeared on 1
January 1549 under the sponsorship of John Day.[153] Later in the
same month, John Oswen of Worcester set forth Harte's other extant
work, indicating that Harte may have spent a considerable amount of
time preparing his tracts before finding his publishers.

The 'Returns of Aliens' residing in London for these years lend
substantial support to this hypothesis, as a Henry Harte is
consistently listed in the records between 1541 and 1549 − the silent
years as far as Harte's links with Kent are concerned. From 1541 to
1544 he was residing in St Andrew's Parish in Holborn, while in 1545
he was listed twice simply under 'Holborn' and 'High Holborn'.[154]
Finally, from 1547 to 1549 he was listed as dwelling on the 'Streate'
or 'the streate side'.[155] His possessions were variously evaluated
during this period, from £20 in the early years to £14 in 1545.

---

[151] Martin, 'English Protestant Separatism', 58. See above, pp. 44 − 8 regarding
Harte's early activities.
[152] *VCH*, II, 140.
[153] Martin, 'English Protestant Separatism', 60.
[154] 'Returns of Aliens in London' in *Hugenot Society of London Publications*, eds. R. E. G.
Kirk and E. F. Kirk (Aberdeen, 1900 − 7; rep. 1969, Kraus Reprint), X, pt. 1, 58, 96,
108; pt. 3, 317. Apparently Percival Harte, 'knight', had a son named Henry as well.
See *Calendar of the Patent Rolls, Edward VI*, (London, 1924), I, 207.
[155] 'Returns of Aliens,' X, 1, 132, 183.

Sometimes he was classified as an 'alien' while on other occasions he is listed as a 'stranger'. In one instance the term 'denyson' appears along with 'straunger', posing something of a problem of interpretation. If this is indeed a reference to the Kentish conventicler of the same name, it would seem as though he was being classified officially as both a resident and a foreigner.

Although one can only speculate at this point, it is possible that Harte may have encouraged the authorities to regard him as an alien in order to conceal his true identity. It is also possible that classification as a foreigner was related to his having recently come to London. At any rate, Henry Harte, radical leader from Pluckley and loyal citizen of the realm, may well have retained possessions and properties in Kent during the years in which London served as his base of operations, if indeed he did live there prior to the Bocking escapade. He could also have chosen to keep his family at home in Kent, away from the hubbub of the city.

As for the themes and contents of Harte's tracts, we can see at least one of the radical tenets he displayed in Kent coming through clearly and immediately, namely his wariness of excessive learning and natural reason. In his first work, Harte began with a reference to Nicodemus who, being a Pharisee and 'a man lerned', could not fathom the teachings of Christ until aided by divine grace.[156] He went on to explain that 'knowledge is a gyfte of the spryte, and in the hand of god and he measureth hys gyfts to hys creatures at hys owne pleasure and wyll'. Therefore, men should be content with the level of understanding granted to them, and should not attempt presumptuously to go beyond their individual capacities. Harte warned that knowledge was actually a dangerous commodity when it is not accompanied by obedience and love; 'for it tyckelyth the mynde of foles, and lefteth them up wyth vanyty'.[157] Thus Harte concluded that many claim a true knowledge of God, 'but wyth their dedes they shamfollye deny hym, in that they refuse to lyve accordyng to his commaundements'.[158]

Harte tied this undesirable situation to the fall of the human race 'in adam', so that man cannot obtain 'the trewe knowledge, peace and love of god' through the strength available by his 'first byrthe'. Thus, although man had originally possessed a 'Reasonable soule', reason became blinded and 'nature corrupte'. Now, all men are naturally conceived in 'orygynall Synne, that reygneth in all fleshe',

---

[156] Henry Harte, *A godly newe short treatyse instructyng every parson, howe they shulde trade theyr lyves* (London: Robert Stoughton, 1548), sig. A. iia – b. RSTC 12887.
[157] *Ibid.*, sig. A ixa.
[158] *Ibid.*, sig. B. ib.

and are accordingly 'chyldern of wrath'. Thus, men are 'not obedyente . . . to that goodnes that naturall reasone teacheth them'. Although it is true that all men were dead in Adam, there is still hope for mankind, since 'in Chryste we are al made alyve, as manye as beleve in hys name'.[159] Quoting from the prophet Ezekiel, Harte stressed that God has no pleasure whatsoever in the death of a sinner, but wills that men should repent and live.[160] This involves consenting to the truth of God with the whole heart,[161] and must be accompanied by 'amendement of lyfe', which is the essence of repentance.[162]

Other themes related to the Christian life which Harte chose to emphasize included the necessity of suffering and growth in personal holiness as one is conformed to the likeness of Christ — the purpose of God's calling.[163] Harte stated that 'we are called . . . to suffer wyth Chryst, that we myght be made partakers wyth hym in glory'. Just as Christ suffered 'for us', even so He left an example for His disciples to follow. If men would be glorified with Him, they must first take up the cross and share in His sufferings,[164] thus fulfilling God's call to holiness and sharing in the divine nature through the power of the Spirit of God.[165] This theme was closely related to that of obedience, which dominated Harte's thoughts as much as anything throughout his tract: thus, the 'lacke of obedyence' predisposes men to 'fall into wyllfull synne';[166] 'the holy Relygyon of Chryste' is said 'to stand . . . in obeyng to the wyl of the Lorde GOD to do the same';[167] 'true fayth' flourishes 'Through perfecte obedyence to the wyll of god'.[168]

A thread of warning ran throughout Harte's tract, and in this instance he exhorted his readers, who were 'made the temple of God', to 'defile not . . . this holy place least the lord be angry, and so ye perysh from the ryght way'.[169] In sounding this grave warning, Harte came close to propounding another theme which characterized the conventiclers' discussion. This topic concerned the possibility of falling from grace and was held to be contrary to the major themes of the magisterial reformers. It also became a storm centre during the King's Bench controversy.

[159] *Ibid.*, sig. A. iib-ivb.
[160] *Ibid.*, sig. B. iia.
[161] *Ibid.*, sig. A viib.
[162] *Ibid.*, sig. B. via.
[163] *Ibid.*, sig. A. viia.
[164] *Ibid.*, sig. B. iiib — va.
[165] *Ibid.*, sig. B. viiib.
[166] *Ibid.*, sig. A. va.
[167] *Ibid.*, sig. A. vib — viia.
[168] *Ibid.*, sig. B. via.
[169] *Ibid.*, sig. B. viiib.

Although Harte was generally restrained and moderate in his printed works, he came closest to espousing the typical freewill position when handling this question of perseverance. On several occasions he seemed to concede that a believer could actually fall from a state of grace and be ultimately lost. He remembered the solemn words of Peter regarding those who had 'escaped from the fylthines of the woorlde' through the true knowledge of Christ the Redeemer and yet had become 'entangled agayne' and eventually 'overcome'.[170]

His clearest pronouncement on the subject came in his benediction when he prayed for the grace of perseverance for his readers, lest they 'also be plucked away in the erourre of the wycked, and fall from . . . stedfastnes'.[171] He had previously cautioned against departing from the straight pathway of the Word of God, lest a similar tragedy occur,[172] and constantly exhorted them to refrain from hardening their hearts.[173] Instead, they should look inside themselves with a critical eye,[174] and keep themselves free of worldly evils so that they might 'be saved'.[175] He reminded them that God is not a 'respecter of persons', and that He will justly recompense all men according to their deeds in this life.[176]

Thus, we have in Harte a clear emphasis upon the responsibility of man to persevere and work out his own salvation before God in order to make his calling sure through proper conduct.[177] Yet, at the same time, Harte was careful to base the achievements of man upon the unmerited favour of God. Indeed, there is no trace of the hasty radicalism in this work which was attributed to him shortly thereafter by his accusers in Kent. Rather, there is a common-sense Biblical rationalism devoid of excessive theological systematization, stemming perhaps from Harte's firsthand encounter with the Scriptures in his own tongue.[178] Indeed, much of Harte's work consisted of Biblical quotations interwoven with a brief commentary. Yet it would be erroneous to view the piece as the construction of a backwoods simpleton, for at some points Harte gives evidence of what can only be considered advanced evangelical thought for this stage in sixteenth-century England. He clearly understands the nature of the Protestant faith, and his Christocentric focus is anything but

170 *Ibid.*, sig. A. vib.
171 *Ibid.*, sig. B. ixb.
172 *Ibid.*, sig. A. viiib.
173 *Ibid.*, sig. A. viib.
174 *Ibid.*, sig. B. iib.
175 *Ibid.*, sig. B. ixa.
176 *Ibid.*, sig. A. vib.
177 *Ibid.*, sig. B. vib.
178 For a similar conclusion, see Martin, 'English Protestant Separatism', 56.

underdeveloped. He fully comprehended the principle of identification with Christ in His suffering and death, together with its significance for the future. Thus he comments: 'Truly we are called as ye know to suffer wyth Chryst, that we myght be made partakers wyth hym in glory for yf we were grafted lyke him in death Then shall we be lyke hym also in the resurrectyon.'[179] Further, he gives no indication of entertaining unorthodox views relating to the person of Christ — no celestial flesh, to be precise — as he refers to 'the sonne of God takying oure nature upon hym' in a manner which would be acceptable to the most godly divine then in England. He also displays what might be considered an Erasmian emphasis in his understanding of the relationship between divine sovereignty and human responsibility; thus, 'yf ye put to a wyllyng mynde ye shall fynd the lorde readye wyth hys grace at youre hande'.[180]

A similar pattern is discernible in Harte's other original tract which was published a year later in 1549. This second work, *A Consultorie for all Christians*, was several times longer than the previous item and contained an even more urgent prophetic call to repentance from spiritual pride, hypocrisy and deceitfulness. Harte included a strong appeal to England, a nation in desperate need of true conversion, and gave evidence of a freer style and a more personal approach.

Acknowledging that his own spiritual eyes had been enlightened by the grace of God, and that the Creator had brought about a 'perfect repentaunce' and amendment of life in him personally, Harte stated his desire to see others of his 'brethren and natural countrymen . . . of England', as well as other nations and professing Christians, being provoked in order that they might produce fruit of eternal worth and reward.[181] He thus adopts the tone and approach of both the evangelist and the prophet, displaying a particular concern for the spiritual welfare of his nation and his fellow countrymen. His purpose in writing was twofold: firstly, 'to declare unto you the daungerouse harmes that synne bryngeth to suche as delyte and continew therein'; and secondly, likewise to make known 'the unspeakable reward of the righteouse whiche god hath prepared for those that withe their hole hartes tourne from theyr synnes and walke wyth theyr god in the way of rightuousenesse'.[182]

True to form, he warned against a fleshy foundation built upon 'naturall reason' and recommended the pursuit and acceptance of the

---

[179] Harte, sig. B. iiib – iva.
[180] *Ibid.*, sig. b. viia.
[181] H(enry), H(art), *A consultorie for all christians* (Worcester: J. Oswen, 1549), sig. A. vb & viia. RSTC 12564.
[182] *Ibid.*, sig. A. via.

divine 'doctrine of wisedome'.[183] He was disturbed by the non-chalance and worldliness of the people of God and believed the remedy lay in placing the standards of the Kingdom of God in a position of preeminence. This involved a daily striving against inner lusts, a mortification of one's affections, and a rigid subjection of the flesh to the authority of Christ.[184]

Harte also displayed a keen historical consciousness in this work by developing an analogy between the nation of Israel in the Old Testament period and the 'Israel of god' — God's true people in the sixteenth century.[185] Perhaps alluding to the gradual ascendancy of Romanism in the professing church, he called on Christian nations to remember their long captivity and spiritual blindness which had by then exceeded in length of time the experiences of the Jews. Harte seemed to view the Protestant Reformation as a divine deliverance: God had heard the groans of His people and had 'come downe to delyver Jacob his chosen wyth a myghtie hand'. Referring either to worldly human wisdom or perhaps its manifestation in the papacy, Harte recalled Daniel's prophecy concerning 'the man of synne' who would exalt himself in the place of God.[186] Harte pronounced woes upon hypocritical 'bishops, pastours and lawiers' who had no concern for the condition of their own souls but sought holiness through external signs and sacraments only.[187] Such are but corrupt mediators. Thus, as far as the current state of affairs was concerned, it was not enough to merely 'have gods word and his holye Sacramentes'.[188]

Time and again Harte bemoaned the state of Christendom at large and England in particular, especially since God had favoured and loved it 'above many other'. He believed that England was perishing through its own wilful folly, and that the only solution lay in confession of sin.[189] As things then stood, he could see no difference at all between Christendom and 'other Hethen nacions', save for superficialities. Even further, if an infidel should be truly converted in his heart and do that which is just and right, he would receive the benefits of salvation 'although he never receive christen name nor outward sacrament'. Since it is the circumcision of the heart that is crucial before God, receiving the sacraments and Christian baptism avail nothing if the required change in conduct does not ensue; for

---

183 *Ibid.*, sig. A. viiib; B. iib.
184 *Ibid.*, sig. B. vb & viib.
185 *Ibid.*, sig. H. iiia.
186 *Ibid.*, sig. B. viiia & C. iib.
187 *Ibid.*, sig. C. viib.
188 *Ibid.*, sig. E. iia.
189 *Ibid.*, sig. D. iiia & D. iiiib.

baptism, which signifies 'repentaunce, the new regeneracion and amendment of lyfe', has become 'an open witnesse' against those who are false Christians and pretenders.[190] To Harte, therefore, Christendom's plight was all the more lamentable, since it had fallen from such lofty heights and had been held captive for so long.[191]

It is this repeated concern for the fate of Christendom and his own country which is worthy of special note at this juncture, especially bearing in mind the question of Harte's alleged separatism and sectarian bent. It is clear that at this point he has not seriously considered giving up on his call to national repentance; his appeal is really directed at the English church and its membership – in fact, toward all true Englishmen. He is attempting to provoke his fellows into adopting what he considers to be the genuine evangelical perspective: to bring the reality of life in Christ into close approximation with the ideal. As far as he is concerned, there are far too many professing Christians in England, and not enough real ones. Perhaps at some later point he will grow weary in his appeal and adopt a more radical strategy. For the present, he is a loyal son of the nation and of the church, hoping earnestly that his brethren will come to their senses in what must obviously be the last days. Perhaps he almost expects that his warnings will go unheeded as in the days of old; yet he is not thereby relieved of his responsibility faithfully to proclaim his message, especially since the prophets of the church were then guilty of teaching 'falsely'.[192] Thus he must remind the 'Englysshe nation' that 'god hath loved the[e] above many other and hath sent hys worde, the sonne of god . . . unto the[e] too call the[e] frome thyne own waies that thou mightest be made his owne people'.[193] God's truth had been proclaimed by 'his beloved messengers as wel within this rea[l]me of England as in all other regions on the earth'.[194]

Throughout the treatise Harte repeated several of his earlier themes. He wrote again of God's impartiality, as He is not a 'respecter of person, nacion, lande, tyme nor place'. Rather, He accepts those who do what is right in any locality, so that He might fulfil His promise to 'chose out his elect' from every nation on earth.[195] Harte also made reference to the divine will regarding

[190] *Ibid.*, sig. E. iiiia & b. Here, as elsewhere, Harte was in close agreement with both Erasmus and the Anabaptists.
[191] *Ibid.*, sig. D. vib.
[192] *Ibid.*, sig. G. viiia – H. ia.
[193] *Ibid.*, sig. D. iiia.
[194] *Ibid.*, sig. A. viib.
[195] *Ibid.*, sig. E. iib & iiia.

universal repentance so that sinners might live and not die.[196] He continued his tirade against human wisdom and reason, along with that counterfeit holiness and false teaching which serve to deceive 'the symple ignoraunte synners'.[197] He reminded his readers of God's promise to destroy worldly wisdom and understanding,[198]and how the Almighty had chosen the weak and foolish of the world to be His own. He urged that men cast aside 'hygh reasons, and let gods word although it seme simple and rude, lede' the way. He also continued the theme of self-renunication as the means to share in God's glory and everlasting kingdom.[199]

It is worthy of note that Harte gave no definite clues as to his attitudes or relationship to Anabaptism, even though the views expressed in his works would be well received by members of that sect and also by the followers of Erasmus. And, although he was most emphatic in his stress upon human responsibility in matters of salvation and sanctification, he was anything but a Pelagian. To Harte, the grace of God was far too crucial for him to be placed in that category. As noted, he referred to being personally enlightened through an act of grace, and to the perfect work being performed within him by the Word and the Spirit.[200] He besought the Lord to remove the sinfulness of His people and turn their hearts unto Himself, so that they all might seek to do His will and praise His name.[201] He spoke of the 'everlasting atonement' and of God's 'everlasting love' in strains which would warm the heart of the staunchest Augustinian. Indeed, the ultimate answer behind the question of the atonement rests with the will of God alone.[202]

Thus, Harte's discourses gave evidence of a certain balance in his perspective at this point in his career, closely resembling the typical Lollard pattern in some respects, which, as observed, has been summarized by Thomson as tending towards both 'a scriptural fundamentalism' and 'a commonsense rationalism'.[203] Here is no frenzied heretic uttering irrational statements guaranteed to alarm all and sundry, but a serious lay believer who, along with his fellows, appears to be the product of a first-hand encounter with the English Bible only recently made generally available.[204] Harte's tendency to

---

196 *Ibid.*, isg. G. va.
197 *Ibid.*, sig. C. ib & iia.
198 *Ibid.*, sig. C. iiiib.
199 *Ibid.*, sig. E viiib – F. ib; F. iib.
200 *Ibid.*, sig. A. vb.
201 *Ibid.*, sig. D. iib.
202 *Ibid.*, sig. F. va.
203 Thomson, p. 244.
204 See Martin, 'English Protestant Separatism', 56, 72.

incorporate numerous biblical quotations from both the Old and New Testaments indicates a relatively high degree of familiarity with the contents of the Scriptures, although there are signs that this knowledge was perhaps hastily acquired and as yet to some extent unsystematized. The hostility displayed by the parish priest at Faversham towards the private reading of the Scriptures may be indicative of a clerical response to an extremely speculative mood amongst his flock, or, by the same token, his previous obstinacy and discouragements may have helped to stir the curiosity in the first place. Harte's strong statement against false bishops and pastors who mislead the simple may be significant within this context. He is angry with those who would prevent God's truth from being made known. He will have the Scriptures in his own tongue, and will interpret them himself aided only by higher wisdom.

Moreover, the Faversham priest's proneness to superstitious observances in connexion with the Eucharist may also have served to disturb a budding nucleus of increasingly articulate laymen who had come to believe that salvation was a matter of individual concern based on the objective truth of the Scriptures as the revealed Word of God and therefore something which was independent of hierarchical pontification. In other words, the apparent adherence of the local clergy to the tenets of the passing Romanist regime may have served as a stimulus to Harte's group which favoured many of the perspectives of continental Protestantism – especially those which were at numerous key points closely in step with the Lollard residuum of the mid-Tudor years. The most prominent point of divergence between Harte's circle and the Protestant mainstream, of course, came to be the subject of predestination and the capacity of the human will to respond to grace in the salvation process. It would seem that Harte came ultimately to identify those who maintained the rigid predestinarian outlook with the worldly, unacceptable type of wisdom and learning which he always vehemently denounced. Here, the possibility of some external stimulus – something other than the various native influences explored previously[205] – warrants consideration, and would appear to lead us quite naturally to a consideration of the potential for intellectual influence vested in Erasmianism and continental Anabaptism.

[205] See above in chapter 1, pp. 6 – 18.

The place of Erasmus

To the discussion regarding potential avenues of influence and intellectual transmission may be added the royal decision to make available the first volume of Erasmus's *Paraphrases* in every parish church in the realm. The specific significance of this measure lies in Erasmus's open adherence to theological views on the relationship between divine grace and human response in the salvation process which were often at variance with the Calvinist doctrines coming into vogue in official circles under Edward VI. Erasmus's position on the subject had been well known since his celebrated battle with Luther over the role of grace and the human will in salvation.[206] It should also be remembered that Erasmus could be intensely sceptical about the capacity of worldly wisdom unaided by divine grace as his work, *The Praise of Folly*, clearly shows.

In 1548, the first tome of Erasmus's *Paraphrases upon the Newe Testament* was published in English, thanks to the initial labours of Katherine Parr, the Queen Dowager, in support and encouragement. Although she persuaded the Lady Mary to spend some time working on the translation of the paraphrase of John's Gospel, she relied most heavily upon the services of Nicolas Udal. Udal translated the portion on Luke's Gospel and edited most of the rest.[207] The first volume included only the paraphrases of the four Gospels and Acts, while the second tome, which contained the remainder of the New Testament, was not forthcoming until 1549.[208] As a result of the royal injunctions of 1547, each parish church was to possess one copy of the Great Bible in English as well as Erasmus's *Paraphrases*. From the surviving records of the church inventories of the period, it would seem that most churches in Kent had met these requirements by the end of the Edwardian era.[209] Thus, one can speak with some certainty about the possibility of Erasmian influence on the faithful community, either indirectly through the local clergy who were reading the amplified

---

[206] It must be remembered that Erasmus's work on this subject had not yet been translated into English.

[207] E. J. Devereux, 'The Publication of the English *Paraphrases* of Erasmus', *Bulletin of the John Rylands Library*, LI (1969), 357; Strype, *EM*, II, 1, 45, 48. Strype says that the first volume was published 'about' the year 1547, and the second 'about' the year 1549.

[208] Strype, *EM*, II, 1, 48. Devereux points out that the second volume 'was not specifically ordered by the *Injunctions*, and no doubt many churches refused to buy it'. See p. 359 of his article. Also, see his *A Checklist of English Translations of Erasmus to 1700*, Oxford Bibliographical Society, Bodleian Library, Occasional Publications, No. 3 (Oxford, 1968), pp. 23–5.

[209] *VCH*, II, 78.

translations, or even directly in the case of those who may have managed to obtain personal access to the parish books. In time, we shall find it profitable to explore the *Paraphrases* in an attempt to discover whether Erasmus's perspectives in the areas critical to the present inquiry come through as clearly as in his debate with Luther. Before proceeding to that point, however, his argument during that controversy will be briefly reviewed.

Erasmus and Luther on the freedom of the will

As is well known, Erasmus's most direct encounter with Luther involved a heated exchange of polemics on the freedom of the human will at the very time when evangelical Anabaptism was experiencing its birthpangs in Switzerland. Reacting against what he considered to be Luther's excessively forensic and deterministic approach to redemption, Erasmus charged the great reformer with espousing a system devoid of moral responsibility and incentive. Luther's stress on divine sovereignty seemed to be nothing less than morbid fatalism to Erasmus, so that no motivation toward realistic growth in holiness and relative perfection was possible. Luther's understanding of *vim liberi arbitrii* conveyed to Erasmus the notion of meaninglessness and absurdity, since Luther had described this phenomenon as being the completely passive entity 'qua homa aptus est rapi spiritu et imbui gratia Dei, ut qui sit creatus ad vitam vel mortem aeternam'.[210] Erasmus objected to this notion of passivity, and yet at the same time was careful to establish that all human merit and man's ultimate salvation itself depended upon divine grace. By looking at the Scriptural injunctions to holy living and active obedience, he concluded that these would not make sense 'Si nihil operatur homo'.[211] Other passages seemed to place the responsibility for meaningful progress squarely upon the divine initiative, however, so

---

[210] Martin Luther, 'De servo arbitrio' in *D. Martin Luthers Werke, Kritische Gesamtausgabe* (Weimarer Ausgabe), (orig. Weimar, 1883; 1908; 1964), 18 Band, 636; for English translation see Luther, 'The Bondage of the Will', in *The Works*, gen. eds. Jaroslav Pelikan and H. T. Lehmann, trans. and ed. P. S. Watson (Philadelphia: Fortress Press, 1972), XXXIII, 67.

[211] Erasmus, 'De libero arbitrio Diatribe seu collatio' in *Opera Omnia* (repub. London: The Gregg Press, 1962), Tomus Nonus, p. 1234; 'The Free Will' in *Erasmus – Luther: Discourse on Free Will*, trans. and ed. E. F. Winter (New York, N.Y.: Frederick Ungar Publishing Co., (1961), p. 59.

that man's contribution appeared to be microscopic. Realizing that the Spirit of God could not contradict Himself, Erasmus sought to convey his personal assessment of the situation: 'Sed interpretatio quaerenda quae nodum explicet'.

Erasmus's solution then, was to develop a theory based upon synergism in which the human will was free to respond to the divine initiative at various stages in the redemptive process. He established a scholarly progression involving different levels of grace: *gratia naturalis*, with which all men are endowed without exception; *gratia peculiaris*, or *operantem*, whereby God 'stimulat ad resipiscentiam'; *cooperantem*, which is necessary for the performance of good works; and finally, 'est gratia, quae perducit usque ad finem'.[212] In the crucial stage involving cooperation, grace is primary but not exclusive, as a power or capacity to choose is given to the human will. Thus, there is no coercion involved, but only the excitement of the spiritual dimension in man by the Spirit of God. Grace still predominates, but is not automatically infused once the *natura* stage is passed. Human responsibility is thereby maintained, and the basis of rewards is established: 'Et tamen Deus hoc ipsum nobis imputat pro meritis, quod non avertimus animum nostrum ab ipsius gratia, quod naturae vires ad simplicem obedientiam appellimus.'[213]

When we submit to God's will at this point, we embark on a life-long journey, 'ut per gradus virtutum perveniamus ad perfectionem'.[214] To Erasmus, this seemed much more meaningful than Luther's concept of Christian obedience wherein man, in all his doings, was portrayed as a mere 'instrumentum Deo, quale securis est fabro'. Ever the humanist, Erasmus considered that Luther grossly exaggerated original sin and the fallen nature of man, so that man is able only to hate and ignore God rather than actively obey him; 'ac ne per fidei quidem gratiam justificatus ullum opus possit efficere, quod non sit peccatum.'[215] Instead of exalting divine grace, Erasmus believed this to be an unforgiveable deprecation of the same.

Thus, the perspectives of Erasmus were clearly presented during the formative years of the Reformation. Given the high degree of interest in Christian humanism in England at this time, especially as seen in Thomas More, it is not difficult to envisage a keen familiarity with Erasmus's position in learned circles in the period following the debate with Luther. Erasmus had visited England in the past, of course, and had found a patron in the Bishop of Rochester, John

---

212 Erasmus, *Opera Omnia*, pp. 1223 – 4; 'The Free Will', pp. 29 – 30.
213 Erasmus, *Opera Omnia*, p. 1241; 'The Free Will', p. 77.
214 Erasmus, *Opera Omnia*, p. 1229; 'The Free Will', p. 44.
215 Erasmus, *Opera Omnia*, p. 1246; 'The Free Will', p. 90.

Fisher.[216] While he was staying at Fisher's residence in Rochester during August 1516, More had visited him — this after an interval earlier in the same month when Erasmus had lodged at More's Bucklersbury residence.[217] Erasmus seems to have remained something of a favourite in high circles for several decades in England, until the Marian reaction brought a condemnation of his works.[218] Of course, even before this point he was not regarded with universal fondness, as Robert Cooke evidently learned when he tried to cite him as an authority on the subject of infant baptism and was pounced upon by his adversary, William Turner.[219] Nevertheless, the fact that he enjoyed an immense reputation as a man of letters without equal would seem to warrant granting him special consideration in this study.

Erasmus and the *Paraphrases* Reconsidered

As already stated, the Edwardian endorsement of Erasmus's *Paraphrases* provided Englishmen of varying social and spiritual ranks with an opportunity to study the reformer's thought on a first-hand basis, as the first volume or 'tome' was available in English translation as early as 1548. Since his discourse against Luther was not translated into English at the time, the *Paraphrases* became highly significant as a potential channel for transmitting Erasmus's views to the English populace. The original Latin works had been produced gradually between 1517 and 1524 when Erasmus was also engaged in his revision of the Greek and Latin New Testaments. This era, according to one scholar, represents 'the most intense period of Biblical scholarship in Erasmus's career', and his works during these years indicate an attempt to enjoin Christian scholarship to 'the active practice of the imitation of Christ'.[220]

---

[216] W. B. Rye, 'The Ancient Episcopal Palace at Rochester, and Bishop Fisher', *AC*, XVII (1887), 68.

[217] Richard Marius, *Thomas More: A Biography* (New York: Alfred A. Knopf, 1984), pp. 238 – 9. Marius speculates that 'More's galloping visit to the departing Erasmus probably had something to do with *Utopia*'. Cf. Rye, pp. 69 – 70.

[218] Strype, *EM*, III, 1, 417 – 18.

[219] William Turner, *A preservative, or triacle, agaynst the poyson of Pelagius, lately renued, & styrred up agayn, by the furious secte of the Anabaptistes.* The English Experience (New York: Da Capo Press, 1971; orig. pub. 1551 [by R. Jugge] for A. Hester), fols. C 8a – D. 2a. RSTC 24368.

[220] Erasmus, *The First Tome or Volume of the Paraphrases of Erasmus upon the Newe Testament*, ed. John Wall (Delmar, N.Y.: Scholars' Facsimiles & Reprints, 1975; orig. pub. 1548), p. 4.

In evaluating the *Paraphrases* and their possible effect on English radical thought and action under the mid-Tudors, it is necessary to determine firstly whether the views expressed in the brief elucidations are in agreement with Erasmus's perspectives in his debate with Luther, and secondly, whether these views can be considered sufficiently extreme to influence the thoughts of Englishmen in an era when the learned divines of the realm were generally looking toward Geneva for inspiration. At first glance, the answer might seem to be negative on both counts, since the tone of the *Paraphrases* is not in keeping with the reported incendiary pronouncements of the Faversham conventiclers.[221] Yet there can be little doubt that they both share the same basic outlook on the subject of free will and a common desire to remain free of excessive systematization in key areas of doctrine. In his paraphrase of Matthew's Gospel, for example, Erasmus discusses Christ's grief over Jerusalem's obstinacy in terms which leave little room for questioning where his sympathies lie. He paraphrases:

> Nothing is let pass on my behalf, whereby thou mightest be saved, but contrary wise thou hast done what thou canst to bring destruction to thee, and to exclude salvation from thee. But to whom free will is once given, he can not be saved against his will . . . .. Ye shall be left to your blindness, until that being taught with so great miseries, ye fall to repentance.[222]

Furthermore, Erasmus's stress on human responsibility in the light of God's universal provision in matters pertaining to salvation, which was a constant theme of the English radicals, came through clearly in the paraphrase of John's Gospel. Here he presented Christ as the Light of the World Who shines upon all men impartially, so that 'none might pretend any excuse, when willingly and wittingly he perisheth through his own fault'.[223] Thus, Christ has omitted nothing whereby He may 'draw all folk to eternal salvation'.[224] Everlasting life is available to 'what man so ever would believe in Him' regardless of race or condition. When someone perishes, the situation is analogous to a sick man who endeavours to hide his disease from his physician and thereby 'resisteth that thing, whereby he might have recovered health'.[225] The only solution to spiritual sickness, then, lies in full confession of sin and faith toward God. Over and over again

[221] See above, pp. 52 – 4 regarding the Faversham depositions.
[222] *First Tome*, Matthew, Cap. xxiii, fol. xciiia.
[223] *Ibid.*, John, Cap. i, fol. iiiib.
[224] *Ibid.*, Cap. xiii, fol. lxxviiiib.
[225] *Ibid.*, Cap. ii, fols. xviiiib – xxa.

Erasmus affirms that this divine cure is intended for 'the whole world', since it is the will of the Father 'that all men should be saved by faith'.[226] Indeed, the theme of Christ as the Saviour of the world occurs frequently throughout the first tome,[227] as does Erasmus's conviction that God is impartial in dealing with mankind.[228] It seems clear, therefore, that Erasmus's perspectives as presented in the first volume of the *Paraphrases* are compatible enough with his remarks upon the freedom of the will and the universality of grace in the debate with Luther. It is also abundantly clear from local diocesan injunctions and parish records that the first tome should have been generally available to Englishmen in the south-east by the mid-Edwardian era. Ridley's visitation articles for London diocese in 1550 instructed that each church should display the English Bible and 'the Paraphrases of Erasmus upon the gospels likewise in english' in a 'convenient place'.[229] The inspectors were also required to determine whether the ministers were discouraging 'any to look and read theruppon'. Ridley's visitation injunctions of the same year required that similar notice be taken.[230] In the Kentish parish records, moreover, there is further evidence that the English Bible and Erasmus's *Paraphrases* were generally available to interested persons. In the 1552 inventory of church goods, copies of the latter were listed at various locations including Eynsford, Farnborough, Hartley, Orpington, Stone-next-Dartford and Sutton-at-Hone.[231] According to the Churchwardens' accounts of Smarden church, five shillings had been expended for the *Paraphrases* in 1548, the year of initial publication.[232]

Furthermore, as another scholar has pointed out, 'it is unsafe to assume that because a church has no record of an expenditure for the book it did not buy it'.[233] It is highly probable, therefore, that most, if not all, churches possessed a copy of Erasmus's work long before the accession of Mary, at which time the government appears to have taken some measures to limit its influence.[234] Moreover, the presence of one copy in Smarden church prior to the uncovering of the Kentish

---

[226] *Ibid.*, Cap. vi, fol. xxxviiiia. It should be mentioned that 'all' to Erasmus sometimes appears to mean 'all nations' rather than 'all individuals'.
[227] *Ibid.*, Cap. i, fol. viiiib; Cap. vi, fol. xxxxb.
[228] *Ibid.*, Acts, Cap. x, fol. xla.
[229] Church of England, *Articles*, sig. a. v, 29.
[230] *Ibid.*, pt. 2, sig. A. iii & iv, 16.
[231] Mackenzie Walcott and Scott Robertson, eds., 'Inventories of Parish Church Goods in Kent, A.D. 1552', *AC*, VIII (1872), 152 – 3; IX (1874), 267; X (1867), 287; XIV (1882), 290, 293.
[232] *Ibid.*, IX, 227.
[233] Devereux, 362.
[234] *Ibid.*, 365.

conventiclers suggests interesting possibilities regarding transmission, especially since the radicals dated their alleged separation from the established church from the same general period.

Perhaps a stronger case for a connexion between Kentish radicalism and Erasmus's works could be made if a direct link were to be established between the affected areas and the publication of the second volume or 'tome' which contained the paraphrases of many theologically rich books of Scripture such as Romans and Ephesians. Admittedly, no such links can be found as yet, although this does not preclude a certain degree of indirect influence, since Erasmus's approach to predestination and redemption is often unsystematic and non-Calvinist. Such an interpretation would seem all the more striking during the late Edwardian era when official religious policy began to assume a more rigorously Calvinist approach.[235] To be sure, Erasmus espoused a firm belief in human depravity, yet his pronouncements fell far short of the Genevan perspective in most instances. The subject of original sin, for example, was handled somewhat ambiguously, as Erasmus stated that sin had come into the world through Adam's disobedience and death through sin. Yet he appeared to vacillate on the key issue of transmission, and the concept of Adam as the federal head of the human race was not always clear.[236] He appeared to stop short of attributing the full guilt of Adam's sin to all of his posterity, even though man was now conceived in sin and the effects of sin were passed on to all because all men sinned.

At the same time, Erasmus preferred to stress the surpassing power of Christ's redemptive work as the world's Saviour rather than human corruption. In this, he was in agreement with the Kentish radicals once more. Through the death of Christ, 'the sins of all the world . . . are at once . . . wiped away', so that Adam's sin is 'turned to our weal and advantage'. Erasmus was no universalist, however, since he made it clear that the full benefits of redemption could only be applied to those who trusted and obeyed God.[237]

Moving on to the controversial subjects of election and predestination, it is clear that Erasmus was determined to let the Scriptures

[235] It is certainly a tribute to Erasmus's catholicity that he should have such widespread appeal in such seemingly diverse circles.
[236] *The Second Tome or volume of the Paraphrases of Erasmus upon the Newe Testament* (n.p., 2 June, 1552), Romans, Cap. V, fol. xiia – b. Erasmus maintained that sin spread gradually to all of Adam's posterity as men 'followed the example of their first parent'. Thus, 'the sin of one man' infected all his descendents, and all became subject to death. This was necessary, since all who 'had offended, as Adam did', must be brought under 'the same yoke'.
[237] *Ibid.*, Cap. v, fol. xiiia.

speak for themselves, even if it meant that his interpretations might appear unsystematic. He maintained that God had chosen some from the human race 'before all time', and that these were called unto godliness and salvation to demonstrate the mercy of God.[238] At the same time, some are passed over or forsaken in their sinfulness in order to set forth divine justice.[239] He does not ascribe the plight of the wicked to secret, unconditional divine decrees, but states simply that only 'such as through malice and stubbornness refuse to believe' are rejected. Correspondingly, faith is the sole requisite which makes a man 'worthy to be taken among the chosen children of God'.[240] Moreover, the cause of unbelief is not a divine decree, but man's persistence in evil and refusal 'to believe'.[241] God can never be charged with being the author of sin, therefore, even though he permits men to engage in sin for a time so that they might clearly perceive their wickedness and come to accept His mercy.[242] Nevertheless, there is still a mysterious element in all this, since men are not informed 'why he calleth some one lately, and some other more timely, nor why he draweth one which hath not so deserved, and forsaketh another, which hath deserved better'.[243] Thus, in paraphrasing Ephesians, Erasmus added that 'all things are ordered and disposed of by his unsearchable counsel . . . according to his own will'.[244]

Although one might wish that Erasmus had expressed his opinions more clearly, it seems certain that his desire to keep above excessive systematization compelled him to state the apparent paradoxes of Scripture without seeking to unravel them. Accordingly, his emphasis upon divine sovereignty in the process of redemption appears side by side with his stress upon man's role in cooperating with divine grace

---

[238] *Ibid.*, Cap. viii, fol. xxxib.

[239] *Ibid.*, Cap. viiii, fol. xxiiiib.

[240] *Ibid.*, Cap. viiii, fol. xxiiiia. In keeping with this approach, Erasmus says that God inflicted punishment upon Pharaoh in order to provoke him to repentance. Similarly, there is no injustice with God in His dealings with Jacob and Esau, since the purpose of this Old Testament story is to illustrate the connexion between chosenness and faith. Romans, Cap. viiii, fol. xxiiiia – b.

[241] *Ibid.*, Cap. X, fol. xxviiib; Cap. xi, fol. xxxa. Unbelief is also viewed repeatedly as the key to Israel's sad demise and rejection.

[242] *Ibid.*, Cap. xi, fol xxxia.

[243] *Ibid.*, Cap. viiii, fol. xxiiiib.

[244] *Ibid.*, Ephesians, Cap. i, fol. cxxxb. Erasmus also touched upon the subject of predestination here, speaking of an eternal divine decree. He seemed to be referring not so much to individual election to salvation as to that process whereby the faithful are chosen in Christ to become 'holy and faultless' children of God. A little later, however, he implied a more unconditional aspect with regard to individual salvation, as he made the choosing of believers dependent upon the divine initiative in predestinating men to eternal life through the ancient decree. Ephesians, Cap. i, fols. cxxviiiib – cxxxa.

and the universal dimensions of Christ's atonement.[245] Since Christ came to be the Saviour of Jew and Gentile alike, it is necessary for believers to strive so that 'his death may be indifferently available unto all'. Men should even pray for the salvation of the 'Ethnics' in this light, just 'in case he died' for these as well.[246] Thus, the essence of Christianity lies in showing kindness to all men, so that 'even the very wild beasts are overcome and made tame'.[247] Indeed, it is the very 'imitation' of Christ which makes one a true member of His body, and not the mere 'profession' of Him.[248]

In the paraphrase of I Peter, Erasmus linked the growth in 'Christlikeness' to the Second Coming of Christ and the eternal order, stating that only those who 'fortaste' immortality in the present life will experience it in its fullness in the future; for 'the father will not acknowledge any to be his sons, but those that be like mannered unto him'.[249] Believers should always remember that Christ is coming again in judgement and should not be lulled into a false sense of security and consequent slothfulness. Instead, they ought to be diligent in pursuing holiness, and recognize that the 'sufferance of the Lord' is intended to give 'all man space to repent'.[250] Although no one knows the exact hour of Christ's return and it is unwise to speculate on the matter, believers should live 'as though he would come this day', as the Apostle Paul was wont to stress this point so that men might be pricked 'forward to the study of godliness'.

Thus we have Erasmus's interpretations in the second tome in which he upholds universal accessibility to salvific grace and a corresponding need for practical godliness to be manifested in those who claim to be children of God. These are perspectives with which the English freewillers readily agreed, although it must be granted that they occasionally went to far more radical extremes in their formulations than did Erasmus. He, for example, maintained a mystery dimension to the subject of election – something which the later extremists professed to observe verbally but appear to have lost sight of in practical terms.

One further tenet which formed an integral part of the Kentish freewill programme, but which has not yet been specifically considered with reference to Erasmus, concerns the need for believers

[245] As for the latter, he states that God has 'freely redeemed all from the bondage of sin'. *Second Tome*, Ephesians, Cap. i, fol. cxxxb.
[246] *Ibid.*, I Timothy, Cap. ii, fol. clxxviib.
[247] *Ibid.*, Titus, Cap. iii. fol. ccib.
[248] *Ibid.*, I John, Cap. ii, fol. cclxxiiib.
[249] *Ibid.*, I Peter, Cap. i, fol. ccxxxiiiia.
[250] *Ibid.*, Cap. iii, fol. cclia.

to be constantly watchful lest they should fall from grace.[251] The Kentish radicals seemed to accept the possibility of falling away without question, whereas Erasmus appeared to have reservations about the matter and stopped short of stating in unequivocal terms that a believer could fall and be ultimately lost. In his paraphrase of the Epistle to the Hebrews, he spoke of the need to increase in godliness daily and attain a 'higher perfection' rather than relapsing into former evil habits. To turn back is unthinkable for Erasmus, since the process of spiritual enlightenment and the forgiveness of sins which takes place through baptism cannot 'be repeated and ministered again'.[252] This is necessarily so because a man can become a 'new creature' only once. Those who require a further renewal through repentance do nothing else than crucify Christ 'a fresh' and make a mockery of Him through their conduct, while those who seek to walk according to the significance of their baptism are diligent to ensure that the 'seeds of virtue and goodness' which He has implanted in them 'grow and come to good'.

Thus, Erasmus simply reaffirms the biblical perspective that men cannot be 'renewed again through repentance' once they have responded to truth, and fails to draw any rigid or binding conclusions. At the same time, he does not attempt to soften the impact of the biblical warnings, nor seek to explain them as being merely hypothetical. His approach, which might be described as a biblical fundamentalism, was also clearly seen in the early works of Henry Harte.[253]

In addition, Erasmus's views on the freedom of the will and the consequent necessity for purified lifestyles among Christians were remarkably similar to the perspectives of the continental Anabaptists. Indeed, it was once reported that Stephen Gardiner had been arrested for opposing the public introduction of the *Paraphrases* 'on the ground that Erasmus was an anabaptist'.[254] Since Erasmus's relationship to the Anabaptists has been the object of several recent studies,[255] a

[251] The historic Calvinist response to this issue is contained in the doctrine of the perseverance of the elect.
[252] *Second Tome*, Hebrews, Cap. vi, fols. ccxiib – ccxiiia.
[253] See above, pp. 84 – 5.
[254] *Calendar of State Papers – Spanish*, eds. M. A. A. Hume and R. Tyler (London: His Majesty's Stationery Office, 1912), IX, 187. Bainton has even referred to Erasmus as the sole legitimate claimant to the title Anabaptist in the sixteenth century, since he had at one time expressed the opinion that youths should be rebaptized when approaching puberty in order to impress the significance of the sacrament upon their hearts and minds. R. H. Bainton, 'The Paraphrases of Erasmus', *Archiv fur Reformationsgeschichte*, LVII (1966), 73.
[255] For example, see Kenneth R. Davis, 'Erasmus as a Progenitor of Anabaptist Theology and Piety', *MQR*, XLVII (1973), 163 – 78, and Thor Hall, 'Possibilities of

detailed examination is unnecessary here; but a brief overview of several critical points will serve as a basis for further discussion regarding the Anabaptists' possible role in the transmitting of freewill ethical puritanism to the English radicals.

Reconsidering the Anabaptist link

The Anabaptist stress upon the universal availability of divine grace and the corresponding unlimited potential for growth in Christian holiness needs particular attention. Hans Denck, for instance, believed that a man could actually imitate God in his conduct and even assume 'the traits of the divine generation, as one who is the son of God and coheir with Christ'.[256] It was clear to Denck that God had granted man the capacity to either accept or reject His will for human life, since He only desires spontaneous praise from His creatures. Thus, He 'could never with full praise have been praised' had he given man the capacity of a stone and forced him to please Him, for this would have defeated the very purpose of creation.[257] Moreover, since God is not a respecter of persons, He gives to all 'the chance, grace and strength to be converted' through the presence of the 'invisible Word of God' Who shines upon everyone.[258]

Thus, Denck agrees with Erasmus that freewill had not been withdrawn from man at any point. He also stressed that man could not succeed in the spiritual dimension without the assistance of grace, since man cannot even 'accept grace without grace'. He cannot come to God 'undrawn' of his own accord, since no one may rightfully presume 'to give God something which he has not received from him'.[259] Like Erasmus, he warned against laxity in the Christian life, although he went considerably further in stating that God is able and even willing 'to reject again' one whom He has 'received in faith' but who 'does not remain in faith'.[260]

Touching upon the difficult question of how God hardens the hearts of men, Denck again came close to Erasmus, maintaining that

---

Erasmian Influence on Denck and Hubmaier in their Views on the Freedom of the Will', *MQR*, xxxv (1961), 149−70.

[256] Hans Denck, 'Whether God is the Cause of Evil' in *SAW*, p. 99.

[257] *Ibid.*, p. 90.

[258] Hans Denck, 'Divine Order' in *Selected Writings of Hans Denck*, eds. F. L. Battles et al. (Pittsburgh: Pickwick Press, 1976), p. 78.

[259] Denck, 'Evil', p. 107.

[260] *Ibid.*, p. 105.

men were only hardened in this manner in order to provoke repentance. This is in keeping with His will that sinners should not die but rather be converted and live.[261] Denck was also concerned about the relationship between divine foreknowledge and foreordination: he cited the case of Jacob and Esau in order to prove that God had foreseen the wickedness of the latter and the righteousness of the former prior to their conception. As a result of his sin, Esau was punished, since 'God punishes no one undeservedly'.[262]

It is evident from this brief survey that the views and attitudes of Erasmus and Denck were very close in several important areas relating to the role and capacity of man in the salvation process. Indeed, Hall has suggested that Denck may have been aware of Erasmus's quarrel with Luther on the subject and even utilized some of Erasmus's arguments for support in his own writings.[263] This conjecture is all the more probable given the fact that Denck had met Erasmus in Basel when studying there in 1523.[264] Furthermore, the personal contact between Erasmus and Balthasar Hubmaier, the Anabaptist leader who had many ideas in common with both Erasmus and Denck, has been shown to have been more intimate still. Hubmaier had placed a high value upon Erasmus's paraphrases of the Pauline Epistles as early as 1521,[265] and had gone to Basel to consult Erasmus personally in the following year.[266] Since one of the topics discussed on this occasion had been the significance of the human will in the process of regeneration,[267] it is beyond question that Erasmus's influence weighed heavily with Hubmaier during these critical years when his theological perspective was in its formative stages.

A clear indication of Erasmian influence upon Hubmaier is seen in the latter's view of the fall of man and original sin. Although Hubmaier's estimation of the extent of these developments was not as extreme or severe as Luther's, it still gave evidence of Erasmus's determination to let the Scriptures speak for themselves. Thus, the fall was indeed a calamity, although not an irremediable one, since the spirit escaped the horrors of the Edenic catastrophe.[268] There is

---

[261] *Ibid.*, pp. 108 – 9.
[262] Denck, 'Divine Order', pp. 79 – 80.
[263] Hall, 'Erasmian Influence', 155.
[264] *Ibid.*, 154.
[265] Torsten Bergston, *Balthasar Hubmaier: Anabaptist Theologian and Martyr*, ed. W. R. Estep, trans. I. J. Barnes and W. R. Estep (Valley Forge, Pa.: Judson Press, 1978), p. 72.
[266] Hall, 'Erasmian Influence', 154.
[267] Bergston, p. 74.
[268] Balthasar Hubmaier, 'On Free Will' in *SAW*, pp. 117 – 20. According to Hubmaier, the spirit thus remained sound. The flesh, however, has received the

still room, then, for human cooperation in the redemptive process, since 'God gives power and capacity to all men in so far as they themselves desire it'.[269] Like Denck and Erasmus, Hubmaier ruled out the possibility of any kind of divine coercion in these areas, since He desires only those who willingly come to him in response to the bidding of His Word.

In dealing with the complicated question of God's will with regard to the salvation of all men — something which soon became a subject of intense interest for the English freewillers — Hubmaier observed two aspects of the divine plan. As far as God's infinite power and freedom are concerned, it is evident that He possesses an 'omnipotent and hidden will' which 'the Schools . . . called a plenary power or will of God'.[270] Yet he also detected references to 'a revealed will of God' in the Scriptures, according to which God desires that all men come to faith in Christ. The Schoolmen referred to this facet as God's 'ordinary will', since it operates 'according to the preached Word of Holy Scripture'.[271] When these two aspects of God's will are confused, the Scriptures do not harmonize and error can follow. When the correct distinction is made, things quickly fall into proper perspective.

Hubmaier went even further and divided the revealed will of God into two portions as well, maintaining that 'an attracting and repelling will' could be discerned. Under the former, all men are mercifully drawn unto Christ for salvation, since Christ died for all mankind. According to the latter, however, men are left to their own desserts when they choose to reject God's provision in Christ. Thus, God 'is withdrawn from those who withdraw',[272] as God permits men to 'be as they wish to be'.

Once again, Hubmaier's dependence upon Erasmus seems quite pronounced in this area. Erasmus had concluded that 'Dei voluntas . . . est principalis causa omnium quae siunt', since none can resist His will and He may do as He pleases. Erasmus also stated that God's will and His foreknowledge are one and the same, since He sees the future and allows certain things to occur without special intervention. For Erasmus this was akin to a permissive will rather than an active

sentence of death and stands condemned, while the soul became essentially fleshly through Adam's sinfulness. In regeneration, therefore, the soul comes once more under the control of the spirit, or even further, actually 'becomes spirit', so that it can now distinguish between good and evil 'just as well as though it were in paradise'. Hubmaier, pp. 118, 124.

269 *Ibid.*, p. 129.
270 *Ibid.*, p. 132.
271 *Ibid.*, p. 133.
272 *Ibid.*, pp. 134 – 5.

one, but it did not mean that all things occur out of necessity. This is because God also possesses a *ordinatae voluntati* or *voluntati signi* which men can and do resist.[273] This will is related to a *sententiam generalem* which applies in most situations, whereby *liberum arbitrium* remains in the possession of men.[274]

It is thus abundantly clear that the views of both Denck and Hubmaier, as outstanding representatives of early Anabaptist thought, reflect the basic patterns of Erasmus's theological distinctives. And it must not be thought that this influence was confined to representatives of Anabaptism in Switzerland and Germany, as a considerable Erasmian impact was also made on the Dutch wing led by Menno Simons. Menno's writings as a whole amply attest to his familiarity with and dependence upon the scholarship of Erasmus.[275] Thus Hall writes: 'It was especially on the question of the freedom of the will that these men followed Erasmus, and in the following centuries the Dutch clergy were to a large extent led away from a Calvinistic or Lutheran doctrine of predestination into a more liberal standpoint which has its roots clearly in the influence of Erasmus.'[276]

Yet another important link in the chain of freewill thought in Dutch and German Anabaptistic circles was Melchior Hoffmann, who has been described as 'the most creative leader in shaping the early theology of anabaptism in North east Europe'.[277] In his attitude towards grace and predestination, Hoffmann followed both Erasmus and the general Anabaptist outlook in upholding the freedom of the will and the universal dimensions of the atonement. Indeed, his very object in arguing for the celestial flesh of Christ was to preserve the nature of His 'guiltless suffering' whereby He paid for the sins of every man[278] and opened the door to salvation. As a result, it is only the will of man which prevents God's desire to have all men come to Himself from being fully realized, for it has always been possible for men to perform His will if they so wished.[279]

---

[273] Erasmus, *Opera Omnia*, pp. 1231 – 2; 'On the Freedom of the Will' in *Luther and Erasmus: Free Will and Salvation*, trans. and eds. E. G. Rupp and A. N. Marlow, *LCC*, No. 17 (Philadelphia: The Westminster Press, 1969), p. 67.

[274] Erasmus, *Opera Omnia*, p. 1237: 'On the Freedom of the Will', p. 78.

[275] See *The Complete Writings of Menno Simons*, c. 1496 – 1561, ed. J. C. Wenger, trans. Leonard Verduin (Scottdale, Pa.: Herald Press, 1956), pp. 138, 248, 695, 802. Perhaps this influence of Erasmus upon the Dutch Anabaptists and the Dutch clergy in general is all the more appropriate given the fact that Erasmus himself was a Hollander.

[276] Hall, 'Erasmian Influence', 150.

[277] Horst, p. 171. Horst refers to Hoffmann's belief in Christ's 'single divine nature', which reminds one of Harte's criticism during one phase of the King's Bench dispute. See below, pp. 164 – 5.

[278] Melchior Hoffmann, 'The Ordinance of God' in *SAW* pp. 198, 186.

[279] *Ibid.*, pp. 197 – 8.

Hoffmann also seems to have agreed with Erasmus and the Anabaptists in his interpretation of the falling away passages in Hebrews, as he allows that those who have at one time surrendered themselves to Christ and have then forsaken Him cannot be restored.[280] At the same time, Hoffmann seems to indicate that such a fate cannot befall one who is truly regenerate, since these are maintained throughout life by the 'true rebirth'. Those who have 'died in the Lord' are unable to continue in sin and cannot fall at any time. Thus, they struggle through to the end to receive their election.[281]

Evaluating the possibilities

With these lines of ideological transmission and patterns of continental dissemination established, it is now possible to turn to the events of Edwardian and Marian England in a further search for direct and indirect channels of influence on the origins and growth of the English freewill movement, especially as seen in the Kentish conventiclers.

It has been shown that Englishmen of every rank and station were to have easy access to the *Paraphrases* of Erasmus by the middle of Edward's reign, but that the views of Erasmus as presented in the *Paraphrases* ran somewhat against the growing Calvinist persuasion noticeable in many theological circles in the realm, and were by no means as radical in tenor as those attributed to the Kentish sectarians in the Edwardian depositions. Furthermore, when we later include in our discussions certain developments associated with the Marian and early Elizabethan years, we shall see a degree of radicalism and systematization which went far beyond the simple biblicism of Erasmus in many respects.[282] Thus it would seem that whatever Erasmian influence may have reached the Kentish radicals either came in the early stage of their intellectual development through familiarity with the *Paraphrases* when they tended towards Scriptural literalism and unsystematic rationalism, or was transmitted to them indirectly by means of the more radical (and controversial) continental Anabaptists.

The latter possibility suggests numerous potential avenues of mediation, the most obvious being the multitudes of Dutch

[280] *Ibid.*, p. 199.
[281] *Ibid.*, p. 201.
[282] See below, chapters 7 and 8.

immigrants who settled in the south-east of England as a result of religious persecution in the homeland and long standing economic ties through the cloth trade. As already observed, numbers of these Hollanders were espousing Anabaptist tenets in England, and some suffered martyrdom in various parts of the realm in 1535.[283] As a result of the ensuing royal proclamation against the spreading Anabaptist influence, some men of this persuasion are known to have actually fled the English scene and gone over to Holland where they met an equally gloomy end.[284] The case of Joan Bocher of Kent, however, who was burned for her radical opinions on the Incarnation during the Edwardian era, does not necessarily offer prime evidence of a continuing, continental Melchiorite tradition in the south-east, since we have already observed a native strand of thought espousing the same doctrine in the early stages of the sixteenth century. It does indicate something of the frustration experienced by the authorities in seeking to eradicate these heresies, whether of native or continental inspiration. Thus the last Dutch Anabaptists to be executed in England (in 1575) were still firm in their rejection of orthodox Christology.[285]

Undoubtedly, there were many opportunities for association between the English natives and the Hollanders who espoused Anabaptist beliefs. But what of direct links between continental Anabaptism and the Kent-Essex conventiclers? Perhaps the most promising potential in this regard involves the Robert Cole of Faversham who (assuming he is the man of the same name in the radical ranks) may have been deeply involved in direct trade encounters with the Netherlands prior to his adoption of freewill tenets.[286] These trade links may have served to introduce Cole and his associates to Anabaptist beliefs, or may even have been a front for further illicit activities following initial contacts back in England. His subsequent adherence to the Reformed faith does not in any way lessen the likelihood of Anabaptist influence during the formative stage in his career. Calvin's marriage to the widow of a former Anabaptist should be enough to convince any sceptic of the fluid nature of religion in the sixteenth century.

---

[283] See above, p. 30.

[284] See above, p. 32.

[285] Thieleman J. van Braght, *The Bloody Theater or Martyrs' Mirror of the Defenseless Christians*, trans. J. F. Sohm (Scottdale, Pa.: Herald Press, 1968; orig. pub. 1660), p. 1008 – 9. At the beginning of Elizabeth's reign, further problems relating to Dutch Anabaptist views arose in connexion with the ministry of a Dutch Reformed pastor, who was relieved of his position in his London congregation for harbouring those deemed guilty of espousing radical perspectives. See Theodorus Petreius, *Catalogus Haereticorum* (Cologne, 1629), p. 82, and also p. 214 below.

[286] See above, p. 57 and pp. 74 – 5.

Apart from the possible example of Cole, there is little in the way of evidence which immediately suggests definite, direct connexions between continental Anabaptism and the freewill puritanism of the Kentish conventiclers, excepting perhaps the possible involvement of Henry Harte in continental radicalism shortly after the Münster disaster.[287] Nevertheless, it would seem probable that such ideas on the continent would be more than likely to find their way into the radical discussions in England in at least an indirect way, and continental Anabaptism can therefore be seen as yet another in a series of inputs which together helped create the English freewill movement by 1550. In addition to the Anabaptist alternative to the problems of sin and grace, we should include the native tradition of dissent and independence which was particularly pronounced in the south-east of England; the *Paraphrases* and personal influence of Erasmus on the English intellectual climate; and the availability of the Bible in English.

---

[287] See above, pp. 47 – 8. Leonard Trinterud defined Puritanism in its simplest sense as 'the Protestant form of dissatisfaction with the required official religion of England under Elizabeth', although he noted that 'the notion of the pure primitive church, and the conviction that purity of reform must extend to practice as well as to doctrine, were common in the writings of Cranmer, Ridley, Coxe and other Edwardine leaders'. It is thus particularly in this latter context that the term puritanism has been applied in the present study, since the freewillers displayed a radical approach to both doctrine and practice from the earliest point – in fact, prior to the Elizabethan era when 'Puritanism' was closely associated with Calvinist theology. See L. J. Trinterud, ed., *Elizabethan Puritanism* (Oxford: University Press, 1971), pp. 5, 9. See also his study, 'The Origins of Puritanism', *Church History*, XX (1951), 37 – 57. For Elizabethan Puritanism, see Patrick Collinson, *The Elizabethan Puritan Movement* (London: Jonathan Cape, 1967) and Peter Lake, *Anglicans and Puritans?: Presbyterianism and English Conformist thought from Whitgift to Hooker* (London: Unwin Hyman Ltd, 1988) and *Moderate puritans and the Elizabethan church* (Cambridge: Cambridge University Press, 1982). That puritanism and Anabaptism came to be closely linked in England is clear from a manuscript item in the Fairhurst Papers at Lambeth Palace Library entitled 'The Anabaptists. of theire proceedings. The manner of all schismatiks and of their Puritan slanders'. The document consists of a series of notes, at least a part of which are taken from the works of Bullinger. Fairhurst, MSS 2006, fols. 250 – 253b.

4

The King's Bench Prison Dispute

The changing religious climate

Between the events surrounding the Bocking affair and the renewal of controversy in the prisons of London in 1554, the royal authorities continued to demonstrate great concern over the state of rebellion in the realm. This is clearly evident from the concentrated efforts made to define orthodox doctrine and unmask underground associations. For instance, in May 1551, a series of commissions was issued to the English nobility in each county (headed by Edward, duke of Somerset) for the purpose of investigating all reported cases of treason, insurrection, rebellion, 'unlawful assemblies and conventicles' and numerous other crimes 'whatsoever they be'.[1] Sir Thomas Cheney was chosen to head the inquiry for Kent and Canterbury, with Lord Chancellor Rich, Lord Darcy and Sir John Gate selected for supervision in Essex.[2] Then, in September 1552, Thomas Cranmer received orders from the Privy Council 'to examine the sect newly sprung up in Kent',[3] and was furnished with a book containing appropriate examinations.

Although the name of this sect was not stated, the freewill conventiclers were probably intended. The Council must have come

---

[1] Strype, *EM*, II, 2, 201 – 3. I have been unable to find reference to these commissions in the *CPR*, the *APC*, or the *L&P, Domestic*. I have located a commission dated 18 January 1551, ordering prominent divines 'To enquire of heresies throughout the king's dominions, admonishing and receiving back into the flock such heretics as prove penitent but committing those who continue obstinate in their errors to the secular power; and to punish persons who oppose the Book of Common Prayer'. An editorial summary mentions the existence of a 'long preamble of the duty of christian kings and especially of one who bears the title Defender of the Faith to preserve the purity of religion now threatened by doctrines of anabaptists and libertines'. See *CPR, Edward VI* (London, 1925), III, 347.
[2] Strype's account suggests that these commissions were renewed one year later (obviously not involving Somerset by this date). See Strype, *EM*, II, 2, 208.
[3] *APC*, IV, 131.

to appreciate the movement in Kent as an illegally constituted sect in its own right as a result of their investigations of the previous year, and decided to take further action. Cranmer's instructions were to be delivered by a man and woman with whom he was to converse at length and thus become better informed about the subject. He was further directed to take appropriate steps through his commission to ensure that 'theese errours be not suffred thus to over spred the Kinges faithfull subjects'. It is possible that 'theese errours' were the views of the conventiclers which were regarded as fully Pelagian by the royal officials.

More formal instructions were forthcoming in October the same year, this time addressed to Cranmer, Ridley, and 'other worshipful persons in Kent'.[4] According to Strype, these divines were to examine and punish 'erroneous opinions, as it seems, of the Anabaptists and Arians'. It was admitted that these latter types were now appearing despite severe treatment on previous occasions. Since the relevant commission sat at Ashford in the Weald, it is entirely possible that this was the very setting for the gathering of the various undated depositions against the Faversham bloc examined above.[5] The Council must have hoped that the dissenters' activities would be curtailed after dealing personally with some of their number early in 1551, but when news of further problems reached their ears the following year more radical measures were deemed necessary.

If such was indeed the case, then Cranmer himself must have attended the hearings and listened to the depositions regarding Harte and his comrades. The inclusion of Ridley as a commissioner is intriguing and was perhaps due to his familiarity with Kent and his theological expertise.[6] Evidently there were numerous papal supporters amongst the appointees, and these attempted to make trouble for sincere gospellers through their positions. On 8 October 1552, the Councillors sent notice to Rich, requesting that he 'cause the Commission for thexaminacion of heresies to be sealed and returned with speed'.[7] They also asked that Cranmer, who was about to leave for Kent, remain behind for several days of consultation.

Undoubtedly the spiritual climate in Kent was a priority item at this stage, and on 28 October Northumberland suggested sweeping changes in the administration of the county. These included the

---

[4] Strype, *EM*, II, 2, 19 – 20.

[5] See above, pp. 52 – 4.

[6] The information which Ridley may have gathered at this time may have served to link the freewillers' activities with continental Anabaptism in his mind permanently. He also may have been familiar with Harte as a result of these developments. See below, Chapter 5.

[7] *APC*, IV, 138.

recommendation of John Knox for the Bishopric of Rochester so that he might serve as 'a whetstone to the Archbishop of Canterbury and a confounder of the Anabaptists lately sprung up in Kent'.[8] Knox, who in December 1551 had been selected as one of six royal chaplains,[9] had been serving mostly in the Newcastle area in the north as one of the King's itinerants at a rate of £40 per annum.[10] He also seems to have been sent to Kent on at least one occasion, perhaps to preach against the Anabaptist freewillers.[11] He ultimately refused Rochester, and also turned down the living of Alhallows when it was offered to him by Cranmer and the Council in April 1552.[12] His selection for duties in Kent indicates the Council's displeasure with Cranmer's policies, and also suggests that the Kentish freewillers, who were being generally viewed as Anabaptists, were presenting the Council with quite a dilemma.

Other measures, aimed at establishing religious order and unity throughout the realm as a whole, included the publication of articles of uniformity in May 1553. The Forty-two Articles were the product of a synod of ecclesiastics held in London during the winter of the previous year; they were intended to help reduce contention over doctrinal matters by removing the errors created by the papists and the sectarians.[13] There also existed a list of Forty-four Articles which dealt with church rites and order.[14] Other reform items were planned thanks to Edward's personal involvement in the matter, but the young king succumbed to illness before most of them could be put into effect.[15]

When Mary Tudor was proclaimed Queen on 19 July 1553, the religious gears were immediately thrown into reverse as Mary purposed to lead the nation back to Rome. The first signs of an impending reign of terror were soon fearfully discerned, when, on 28 July, three prisoners, including Dr Rowland Taylor of Hadleigh, were placed in the custody of the sheriff of Essex by order of the Council.[16] Further rumblings occurred on 5 August, two days after Mary's triumphant arrival in London. Bonner was granted his

[8] R. Lemon and M. A. E. Green, eds., *Calendar of State Papers, Domestic, Edward VI, Mary, Elizabeth* (London, 1856), I, 46.
[9] Strype, *EM*, II, 1, 521 – 2.
[10] *Ibid.*, 2, 275.
[11] W. Stanford Reid, *Trumpeter of God: A Biography of John Knox* (New York: Charles Scribner's Sons, 1974), p. 100.
[12] Strype, *EM*, II, 2, 69 – 74.
[13] *Ibid.*, 256, 278.
[14] *Ibid.*, 2, 25.
[15] See *Ibid.*, 104 – 7, and II, 1, 589 – 91, for other points in the royal platform.
[16] *APC*, IV, 421. Taylor had been named Scory's successor at Canterbury in May 1550, and was given the Archdeaconry of Exeter in April 1552. Strype, *EM*, II, 2, 262.

release from the Marshalsea, and Gardiner and Tunstall were freed from the Tower.[17] Gardiner was immediately brought into the Council and made Lord Chancellor of the realm.

A most significant event for both the Marian purge and the predestinarian controversy took place on 16 August when John Bradford was arrested at a private residence in Fleetstreet and imprisoned in the Tower along with Jean Veron and one other man.[18] Hugh Latimer's apprehension followed about 13 September, and Cranmer's one day later. Nicholas Ridley's presence completed the inner circle of Edwardian divines who were now imprisoned.[19]

Two days after the arrest of Bradford and Veron, the Queen issued her first proclamation dealing with religious affairs.[20] Although the stated intent of the measure was to allay any fears concerning radical changes in religion, it placed a ban on reading and preaching in all parishes, whether public or private. All men were to refrain from interpreting 'the word of God after their own brain in churches and other places both public and private', and severe restrictions were placed upon printing.[21] Another plank in the Marian platform was completed early in September with the exoneration of Bonner and his restoration to the see of London. The Queen's examiners decided that the said bishop had been wrongfully deprived under Edward by Cranmer and Ridley, and he was granted his former privileges in addition to generous allowances 'for his evil and unjust handling'.[22]

As the summer of 1553 faded into the autumn, the Marian changes continued relentlessly, and no one could be considered exempt from the scrutiny and zeal of the royal persecutors. On 20 November, the Council received four men of Coventry in the Midlands indicted for 'lewde and sediciouse behaviour' on All Hallows Day.[23] Two of the accused were weavers, and one of these, John Careless, was destined to play a leading role in the drama of the prison upheavals soon to follow.[24] Careless and another prisoner were initially committed to

[17] Foxe, VI, 537.
[18] *Ibid.*, 538.
[19] Strype, *EM*, III, 1, 77.
[20] Hughes and Larkin, II, 5 – 8; Strype, *EM*, III, 1, 38 – 40.
[21] Hughes and Larkin, II, 6; Strype, *EM*, III, 1, 39; Foxe, VI, 390 – 1.
[22] Strype, *EM*, III, 1, 35 – 8.
[23] *APC*, IV, 368; James Gairdner, *Lollardy and the Reformation in England* (London: Macmillan and Co., 1913), IV, 339 – 40. Coventry had perplexed ecclesiastical authorities for decades. A deeply entrenched Lollard movement was discernible here in the late fifteenth century, and it evidently maintained ties with other communities as well. Thomson, pp. 104 – 5, 114 – 115.
[24] See especially chapters 6 and 7 below.

the Gatehouse, while the rest were sent to the Marshalsea until further notice.

Other signs of the reversal in royal policies were seen during the second session of Mary's inaugural Parliament which began sitting around 23 October and continued until 6 December.[25] The general purpose of the session was to abolish the overt Protestantism of the Edwardian measures and return worship to the practices of Henry's latter days.

A period of grace was granted until 20 December, by which time uniformity in divine services was to be rigidly established. At the same time, marriage negotiations between Spain and England were proceeding and reached a conclusion in the early days of 1554. Philip of Spain was to enjoy kingship in both realms and lend a hand in English governmental affairs, but the appointment of the officers in both church and state was to be Mary's prerogative alone.

Despite these seemingly favourable terms, apprehension grew steadily throughout the realm, culminating in the armed resistance of early February. The only serious threat was mounted in Kent under the leadership of Sir Thomas Wyatt, who was apparently more upset by the prospect of a Spanish king than the alterations in religion.[26] As is well known, the revolt was quickly extinguished, yet the affair served notice that there was considerable and widespread dissent. It also tended to complicate the judicial system since now there were political rebels to deal with in addition to dangerous heretics. The Queen continued with her religious policy, apparently undaunted by any fears or doubts about her programme. She chose this moment to proclaim against those foreigners in the realm who were continuously infecting her subjects with 'malicious doctrine and lewd conversation'. All who had encouraged Englishmen 'to this most unnatural rebellion against God and her grace' were to quit the realm within twenty-four days on pain of severe punishment. Only approved ambassadors, merchants and denizens were to be excepted. Thus, the great movement of divines to the continent was fully set in motion by an expression of the royal will. Foxe estimated that some eight hundred persons, both native and foreign, eventually repaired to points abroad.[27]

---

[25] Strype, *EM*, III, 1, 83–4.
[26] See above, pp. 61–2 regarding the relationship between Wyatt's revolt and Kentish radicalism.
[27] Foxe, VI, 429–30.

Proceedings in prison

Meanwhile, those who could not take advantage of the period of grace to flee the country awaited developments in prison. On 10 March 1554, Cranmer, Ridley and Latimer were escorted from the Tower and eventually taken to Oxford via Windsor, where disputations were to be held between Catholic and Protestant divines on the nature of the sacrament of the altar.[28] During this same period, on 24 March, Bradford was conveyed from the Tower, where he had been held with the eminent trio, and taken to the King's Bench prison in Southwark. The King's Bench was but one of five well-known prisons in the area, the others being the Marshalsea, the Borough Compter, the Clink and the White Lion.[29] Located on the east side of Borough High Street, both the King's Bench and the White Lion were intended for use by the head of state, and the city received only the revenues arising from the pertinent quit rents.[30] As of 1550 they were generally exempt from city supervision.[31] Apparently the King's Bench site extended some hundred yards backwards from the street and ended in a ditch. St George's Church was nearby, and the greater portion of the parish was designated as the 'Rules of the King's Bench Prison'. By this practice, those debtors who could produce sufficient securities 'against their escape' and who could pay a chamber rent to the Keeper were permitted to live outside the confines of the common gaol, although the precise limits do not appear to have been defined. The destitute were forced to reside in the central facility, which greatly resembled a human pigsty.

As for the court to which the prison normally pertained, the King's Bench acted as the central court for English criminal offences, but was a court of first instance only for the shire of Middlesex, as it sat in this locality.[32] In the days of Queen Mary, however, the King's Bench, along with the Marshalsea and other prisons within range of the capital, served to house prisoners adjudged guilty of all manner of crimes and persuasions,[33] and the institutions began to swell under

[28] Representatives from both Oxford and Cambridge were appointed to engage in the exercise.
[29] David Johnson, *Southwark and the City* (Oxford: University Press for the Corporation of London, 1969), p. 286.
[30] *Ibid.*, p. 116.
[31] *Ibid.*, pp. 334, 404.
[32] Elton, *Policy and Police*, p. 295.
[33] For a sampling of earlier indictments involving Kentishmen see R. Virgoe, ed., 'Some Ancient Indictments in the King's Bench Referring to Kent, 1450 – 52' in *Documents Illustrative of Medieval Kentish Society*, ed. F. R. H. Du Boulay, Kent Records. No. 18 (Ashford: Kent Archaeological Society, 1964), 214 – 65. The Marshalsea and the Fleet were eventually superseded by the King's Bench as the central debtors' prison

the onslaught. A good number of the more esteemed divines were held in the King's Bench by the early spring of 1554, with Bradford acting as something akin to a spokesman for a group comprised of himself, Rowland Taylor, John Philpot and Robert Ferrar.[34] On 6 May 1554, John Hooper, formerly Bishop of Gloucester and Worcester, addressed himself to this quartet, warning them of a planned disputation expected to be held at Cambridge. He urged his comrades to prepare themselves for examination and share any planned strategies, even though the result of the exercise was really a forgone conclusion.[35]

The result of this correspondence was a detailed confession of faith drawn up by the orthodox prisoners in the King's Bench, the Marshalsea, Newgate and the Fleet. The prisoners wished to demonstrate their unity before their captors and also to declare the doctrines for which they were willing to stand.[36] They defied the authorities by asserting that they were now unwilling to dispute with them by any means other than 'by writing', unless they were given an audience by the Queen and Council or the Houses of Parliament. It is clear that the prisoners were afraid of having their oral remarks altered by the papists and set forth 'for their fantasies, to the slandering of the verity'. They also encouraged their fellow-Englishmen to remain obedient to the laws of the land rather than condescend to 'mutter against the Lord's annointed'.[37] Besides Hooper and the four divines in King's Bench, the document was endorsed by eight others, including John Rogers, Laurence Saunders, Edward Crome and Miles Coverdale.[38]

Of the condition of these stalwarts throughout the spring of 1554 we know very little, although Strype claimed that the King's Bench

in 1842, when the Rules were done away with and the prison was renamed the Queen's Bench. David Johnson, p. 335.

[34] Philpot, originally from Hampshire, studied at New College, Oxford, and travelled extensively in Italy before returning to England and being appointed Archdeacon of Winchester under Ponet. Prior to this, Philpot had occasionally fallen out with Ponet's successor in Winchester, Stephen Gardiner. This did not place Philpot in a favourable light once Gardiner was installed as Chancellor of the Realm. Ferrar, appointed Bishop of St David's in Wales in 1548, was deprived earlier in 1554 after a stormy career. Foxe, VII, 605 – 6; VI, 66.

[35] Foxe, VI, 664. Hooper hoped to appeal the decision of the learned, and perhaps gain a hearing before the Queen and Council or even parliament.

[36] Strype, *EM*, III, 1, 221.

[37] Foxe, VI, 550 – 2.

[38] *Ibid.*, 553. Rogers had been made lecturer in divinity and prebendary at St Paul's Cathedral in 1551. Coverdale had been named Bishop of Exeter in the same year, while Saunders had received a licence to preach at the beginning of Edward's reign. Crome, a graduate of Cambridge, had been arrested for preaching without a proper licence and put in the Fleet on 13 January 1554. *NIDCC*, pp. 853, 267; Foxe, VI, 612 – 17; *DNB*, V, 138 – 9.

prisoners 'had tolerable fair usage, and favour sometimes shown them'.[39] He mentioned a garden where the detained were permitted to walk occasionally; this may have been situated between the prison and the ditch. The prisoners were well thought of by their supervisors, and something of an underground ministry to the needs of the persecuted seems to have developed even during the early days. The most active of these aides were two men previously implicated in the Kentish conventiclers' movement, Robert Cole of Faversham and John Ledley of Ashford. Cole, along with his wife and children, was persecuted in his home-town,[40] being nearly apprehended by his most feared opponent there, Master Petit, a Kentish justice. Cole chanced to meet Petit 'in a narrow lane, not far from Faversham', but somehow managed to get past him without being recognized.[41]

Cole must then have made his way to London, perhaps accompanied by Ledley and his wife. At some stage it was reported to Bonner that they were residing at an inn 'at the sign of the Bell in Gracechurchstreet' along with their wives and one William Punt, bachelor.[42] It is impossible to know the exact date of their arrival, but presumably it was during 1554. It was further reported that Cole and Ledley were 'great counsellors' who resorted 'much unto the King's Bench, unto the prisoners, about matters of religion'.

The third member of the party, Punt, was described as an author of 'devilish and erronious books of certain men's doings'. It was also said that he conveyed them 'over' to the continent, where he caused them 'there to be imprinted, to the great hurt of the ignorant people'. On one occasion, Punt had been observed reading a book 'against the sect of the Anabaptists' on the Thames, apparently being in the process of smuggling books 'to the value of a barrel-full'. Furthermore, it was made known that Cole and Ledley had given assistance to Punt in the conveyance of the books. They had gone over to the continent at the same time concerning 'questions of religion, to the learned that were over, to know their counsel in those matters, and so to turn back again upon the same'.[43]

Thus, it seems clear that ties were soon established between the imprisoned Protestant reformers and their comrades who had fled to various parts of the continent and that Cole and Ledley were serving as messengers. This suggests that much transpired between the two

[39] Strype, *EM*, III, 1, 223.
[40] Foxe, VIII, Appendix, No. VI.
[41] Foxe, VIII, 790.
[42] *Ibid.*, 384. This document was listed under 1557 by Foxe, but this was evidently the date of the deposition and not of the offence itself.
[43] *Ibid.*

parties, most of which will never be known. The rather staggering consideration for purposes of this study, however, concerns the involvement of these two freewillers from Kent, now apparently serving the interests of the Reformed camp on both sides of the channel.[44] Since their activities involved smuggling, it would seem reasonable to conclude that Cole's apparent activity in shipping produce from Faversham may indeed have served to forge some kind of link with continental ideologies. The difficulty in interpreting his involvement in these affairs of Marian England is, of course, compounded by his former association with the Kentish freewillers in 1551 and the apparent reversal in his views by the time of the King's Bench developments. Were his early sympathies directed towards the continental Anabaptists, and did these foster his freewill theology? And what is the significance of his importing of books, one of which was a refutation of Anabaptism?

Although one could well wish that the answers to these and other questions about Cole were self-evident, the facts which are available do present something of a possible chain of events. Cole's suggested involvement with the continent during the latter stages of Henry's reign may have served to whet his appetite for the doctrines of the Reformation, be they Anabaptist or Reformed after the Zwinglian or Calvinist type. His views at that time, presumably, were not systematic, and his zeal for biblical truth led him into fellowship with similar seekers from Kent who began to hold meetings in various localities until the royal crackdown. The forceful personality and views of Henry Harte of Pluckley may have proved crucial at this stage in Cole's development.

At some point following the Kentish depositions taken at Ashford, Cole must have been positively influenced by adherents of the Reformed faith. His conversion may have occurred prior to his close call in Kent at the hands of Petit, although it is more likely to have taken place sometime later, probably in the London area. It is certain that Cole had made the switch by 1555, since he was then receiving correspondence from Bradford as an adherent to Reformed ideas.[45] It is likely then, that the change had taken place somewhat earlier. Ledley had abandoned his Pelagian views by this time too, and the two made an effective team in bridging the gap between the exiled and the imprisoned.

---

[44] Hereafter, the term Reformed will normally indicate those Protestants of a Calvinist persuasion.
[45] See Bradford, II, 133. It is possible that the smuggled book against Anabaptism was a composition by either Calvin or Bullinger, since both Reformers had written along these lines.

One may go a step further here and suggest that the major reason behind Cole's sudden reversal, as well as Ledley's, was probably the counsel of Bradford and others of similar persuasion in the prisons. In fact, their case would seem to mark the beginnings of a definite pattern discernible during these days, as the Reformed prisoners embarked on a steady campaign of reclaiming the English freewillers for the cause of truth. In time, this process of reclamation on the part of the orthodox Reformed element in England did more to retard the development and dissemination of freewill ideas in the realm under the middle Tudors than the Edwardian and Marian royal repressions. Thus, although Cole and Ledley may have been the first to be diverted from error to truth, they were by no means the last, as will be clearly seen.

In addition to being entrusted with heavy responsibilities abroad, Cole and Ledley were probably also involved in the underground Protestant congregation which, according to Foxe, came into being in London about the time of 'the first entry of queen Mary's reign'.[46] Cutbert Symson, whom we have identified as another likely conventicler, became a deacon of this church when John Rough returned from exile to assume the pastoral duties. Rough was in turn succeeded by another faithful emissary of the Reformed prisoners, Augustine Bernhere, who was also Hugh Latimer's Swiss aide. The final pastor during the Marian regime, Thomas Bentham, was later assisted in his ministry by the same Robert Cole. Cole's faithful service during these days of upheaval undoubtedly accounts for his later notoriety as a Church of England minister at Bow Church in London.[47]

Although Cole and Ledley stand out on the list of those giving aid to the prisoners during these days, there were certainly other supporters who offered what assistance and succour they might. One of these was the Knight-Marshal of the King's Bench prison, Sir William FitzWilliams, and his wife. He received correspondence from Bradford and translated one of Ridley's works from Latin into English.[48] Furthermore, there were numerous faithful women who kept in touch with the persecuted, including Lady Vane from Holborn, Mrs Wilkinson and Mrs Warcup, each of whom was very close to Bradford's heart.[49] The visitations of the ladies also permitted more isolated groups of prisoners to keep abreast of developments in other quarters. In some cases, liberties were frequently granted to the

[46] Foxe, VIII, 559.
[47] Bentham later became Bishop of Coventry and Lichfield. Foxe, VIII, 559.
[48] Strype, *EM*, III, 1, 224.
[49] *Ibid.*, 226 – 7.

accused, so that joint prayer and periods of devotions were rather common.[50]

Meanwhile, proceedings aimed at eliminating opposition to royal policy continued in Kent and Essex. While the country awaited the arrival of Reginald Pole as papal legate *a latere*, Robert Collens was named as Pole's commissary for Canterbury and Nicholas Harpsfield, archdeacon of the diocese, was granted power of absolution respecting all repentent communicants. Another key official in Kent, Dr Richard Thornenden, suffragan of Dover, was given a more limited power of absolution, perhaps owing to his rather unstable behaviour and tendency to shift with the times.[51] Pole himself did not arrive at Westminster until November 1554, when, as Cardinal Pole, he was received with much fanfare.[52] Just prior to this, in September, a royal directive had been sent to the Kentish justices 'for the speedy administration of justice in the punishment of offenders there'.[53] It would seem that commissioners in Essex needed no such incentive for on 19 August the Council had stated its gratitude to Sir Henry and Edmund Tirrell and Anthony Broune for 'their travails in the well ordering of the shire'.[54] On 6 September Bonner had begun a systematic visitation of the diocese of London in order personally to ensure that clerics with Protestant leanings were summarily removed.

The prominence of Bradford and the reclamation process

During this period of continuous persecution, if not sooner, discord hit the prisons of London and Southwark, especially the King's Bench. Since the net of the Marian authorities drew in all sorts of heretics and malcontents, it should not be surprising to find considerable variance in opinion amongst the residents. To suggest, however, that controversy over the finer points of Reformation theology would develop into bitter contention amongst brethren which nearly defied control would be virtually unthinkable –

[50] *Ibid.*, 223.
[51] *Ibid.*, 211. He also displaced the incumbent of Adisham, John Bland, who was burnt for his faith at Canterbury during the next year. See above, pp. 43, 75 – 6 regarding Bland's activities in Kent. Thornenden occupied his living and even served as one of Bland's judges. Strype, *EM*, III, 1, 213.
[52] *Ibid.*, 248.
[53] *APC*, V, 76.
[54] *Ibid.*, 63.

particularly when it is remembered that the participants had a common enemy, Rome. The sources nevertheless leave no doubt but that this did indeed happen, issues under discussion slowly rising to prominence during the latter stages of 1554. By January of the next year the conflict was full-blown and seemingly desperate.

The first signs of unrest can be detected in Bradford's correspondence with two supporters during the summer months of 1554. On 23 July, he received letters from Mistress Coke in which she evidently expressed her fears about the doctrine of election and the question of final perseverance. Bradford sought to give comfort and prescribe a suitable remedy concerning her 'temptations of election',[55] reassuring her that salvation was wholly dependent upon the grace of God and hence, nothing in man. He stated that Adam had been 'created to life', and he viewed the fall of man as an event which illustrated divine 'glory and election'.[56] Apparently Bradford was then suffering from a severe bout of fever, but he promised to write again when he had recovered. Similarly, Bradford wrote to another acquaintance, Mistress Joyce Hales, on 8 August. She was also experiencing difficulties with some basic Reformed doctrines. The assurance of personal election was now eluding her, and she sought for some confirmation of her chosenness.[57] Bradford reasoned that the spiritual desire within her should satisfy and 'certify' her conscience, that God would be pleased to give that for which she longed. He reminded her of her former confidence on the matter when they had discoursed face to face, and added his own certainty of her standing. He allayed her doubts about the immutability and omnipotence of God, stating that if He had chosen her, as He undoubtedly had, she could never 'perish'. He warned her not to rely on emotion, and added that her 'hope' would be restored.[58]

Thus, Bradford was engaged in an extensive pastoral ministry even amidst the sufferings and confines of prison. The relatively recent reception of Reformed theology throughout the realm during the days of Edward VI, followed almost immediately by the incarceration or flight of many of its most gifted exponents and expositors, had clearly created something of a vacuum at the native level as far as leadership was concerned. Some devout believers, such as these women, merely expressed personal doubts and problems related to the doctrines involved. Others, however, not only expressed misgivings about the basic outlines of Calvinism, but became rather vehement in their

---

[55] Bradford, II, 101.
[56] *Ibid.*, 103.
[57] *Ibid.*, 112.
[58] *Ibid.*, 113 – 14.

opposition. Still others were undoubtedly caught in between and exposed to the reasoning behind both the Genevan and the freewill positions.

Bradford and Henry Harte

Bradford, being of a moderate temperament and full of the under-shepherd's concern, sought to reclaim all wanderers from the error of their ways, at least all those whom he gauged to be not overtly malicious or pernicious. At approximately the same time as he was addressing the distressed women he also turned his thoughts towards an individual for whom he had high hopes, even though this unnamed person was then dabbling in freewill concepts. Bradford had loaned this man some materials which he felt would be of spiritual benefit to him, and in return had recently received three letters in addition to his previous literature – one from the earnest seeker; one from Cutbert Symson whom Bradford now referred to as 'Brother'; and one from the Kentish activist, Henry Harte. He had not yet read Symson's letter because he was confident that no answer would be required. As for Harte's piece, Bradford confessed that he had not examined it either, but stated that he hoped to reply to its contents shortly and 'to have the hands of all prisoners in England . . . subscribe to the condemnation of them all of error'.[59] He then qualified his remark, indicating that he had not meant each and every prisoner in the realm indiscriminately, but only those 'that be of any learning'.

The reference to Harte's work in the plural suggests that the controversial item was in fact a series of articles or statements rather than a formal letter. Evidently Bradford had also sent a list of his own thirteen articles to his anonymous contact and could not understand why these were not sufficient to satisfy any and all opposition. He suspected that his correspondent was guilty of 'calumnation' in his obstinate stance, and rejected any suggestion that his own articles were contradictory. Instead, it was his detractor who was at variance with himself, declaring on the one hand that the will of God is fixed and changeless, and on the other that He often changes His workings 'at the prayers and peevishness of Man'.[60] As for the question of condemnation, Bradford simply stated 'that damnation cometh from

[59] *Ibid.*, 128.
[60] *Ibid.*, 129.

the justice of the Lord on the wicked, through their own just desserts'. Bradford also indicated that he would have more to say on the subject on a later occasion, and expressed his belief that John Philpot's 'book' would contain some answers for the enquirer.

It seems as though Bradford was still suffering from his fever at this point and had to curtail his reply, but he added a lengthy afterthought the next day. Once again he felt constrained to stress the immutability and omnipotence of God, stating that 'his will indeed is always wrought'.[61] He would not allow for any kind of synergism with regard to salvation, since to include human cooperation at this level was to deny the efficacy of grace alone. Bradford suspected that his acquaintance and his fellows were 'adversaries to grace by maintaining free-will', even though they endeavoured to appear otherwise by means of devious semantics. Bradford did stress the need for human involvement in the performance of good works, however, since God was pleased to join His providence with man's input in striving together.

As Bradford drew his postscript to a close, he referred again to 'Harry Hart's errors', adding that he had by then read them and hoped to deal with them when he had cleared up some other matters. He must therefore have read Harte's materials since the previous evening. Obviously, Harte was not the recipient of Bradford's comments on election on this occasion. Neither was it the reformed Robert Cole nor Nicholas Sheterden of Kent, since Bradford sent a letter to these two 'friends and brethren in the Lord' during this same period,[62] perhaps immediately after his previous effort. He still complained of his sickness which had thus far prevented him from replying to his 'father Hart'.[63] Once again, the topic of his letter to Cole and Sheterden was divine election and predestination – clearly the topic of the hour amongst the prisoners and their associates.

Evidently these two Kentishmen had written to Bradford recently, and although he had not yet read their letter personally, he had been informed about the subject matter. Since it was centred on election, he urged his friends to examine their hearts for signs of true faith, stating that when it is found, it ensures ultimate salvation and deliverance. If such faith were not found, however, or if there was uncertainty about its presence, he advised that the matter should not become a subject for disputation until his readers should become 'better scholars in the school-house of repentance and justification'.[64]

---

[61] *Ibid.*, 130 – 1.
[62] *Ibid.*, 133.
[63] *Ibid.*, 135.
[64] *Ibid.*, 134.

Once this 'grammar-school' is passed, one can then proceed to 'the university of God's most holy predestination and providence'. He also cautioned against questioning the will and purpose of God, adding that men must submit in fear and trembling 'as to that which can will none otherwise than that which is holy, right and good, how for soever otherwise it seem to the judgement of reason'. Thus, reason must be dethroned, since divine justice is far above it, and idle curiosity and speculation only leads to presumption.

Bradford closed his letter by assuring his brethren that Philpot, who seems to have been acting as Bradford's assistant, would probably write to them more specifically, as would Bradford himself if necessary after he had dealt with Henry Harte.[65] Once again Harte's prominence in the episode is unmistakable, and Bradford must have been reasonably familiar with him by this time as Harte was probably visiting the King's Bench frequently. In a deposition later passed on to Bonner, Harte was said to have been residing 'at the bridge-foot, in a cutler's house'. The cutler's name was Curle, and Harte was accompanied during this period by one John Kempe.[66] Harte was referred to as 'the principal of all those that are called free-will men' by the 'Predestinators', and it was known that he had composed a list of thirteen articles – the same number as Bradford's – which became a charter for the members of his company. His companion, Kempe, was described as 'a great traveller abroad into Kent', although his doctrine was evidently more difficult to discern than Harte's.

Bradford's reply to Harte's 'erroneous' theology was apparently given in the form of a treatise which was begun on 11 October 1554, although it was actually dedicated or directed to Joyce Hales in her distress.[67] Bradford also sent a copy of his work to Cranmer, Ridley and Latimer in Oxford in January of the next year.[68] The original title was 'A treatise of predestination with an answer to certain enormities calumniously gathered of one to slander God's truth', and it was written in two major parts.[69] In the dedication, Bradford explained something of the background to the tract, reminding Mrs Hales that it was by her doing that he 'was first brought in talk or debating of this matter'.[70] He then recounted how he had received a

---

[65] *Ibid.*, 134 – 5.
[66] Foxe, VIII, 384.
[67] Bradford, II, 195.
[68] *Ibid.*, 169 – 70.
[69] This work is also referred to as the 'Defense of Election' in the Parker Society's edition.
[70] Bradford, I, 309.

'bill' from an unnamed individual which contained 'horrible "enormities" ' or conclusions which the writer had drawn concerning the Reformed approach to election and predestination.

Bradford marvelled that anyone could compose such a monstrous piece of writing and sought to answer its most critical parts in the latter part of his own treatise, 'not leaving out one tittle of every word' which the author had written. The 'bill' of enormities had been personally signed by the author and addressed solely to Bradford, thus indicating that Bradford was by then clearly recognized as the leader of the Reformed prisoners. Bradford advised Mrs Hales that if his own tone was much harsher than was customary for him this was to be attributed to the gravity of the situation which actually required even greater censure than he was providing. He was obviously most perplexed that men who appeared 'godly' in their outward appearance should be so concerned to subvert his beloved doctrine of election which enhanced human dignity, established Christ's kingdom and dethroned man's 'wisdom, power, ableness, and choice'. To have confidence in God's election was, for Bradford, the 'whole sum' of all duties and responsibilities which the Almighty required of His people.[71]

Following the formal dedication, Bradford proceeded to enlarge upon his own doctrinal perspective in detail in the first section of the tract. From the writings of the Apostle Paul, Bradford presented the following 'proposition':

> That God the eternal 'Father of mercies', 'before the beginning of the world', hath of his own mercies and good will, 'and to the praise of his grace and glory', 'elected in Christ' some, and not all the posterities of Adam, whom he hath predestinate unto eternal life, and 'calleth them' in his time, 'justifieth them, and glorifieth them', so that 'they shall never perish' or err to damnation finally.

Bradford went on to illustrate this basic proposition in eight specific points and then turned to answer his 'calumnious calumniator'. Apparently the author, who must have been Harte, had found six fallacies in Bradford's views and had conveyed 'The enormities proceeding of the opinion, that predestination, calling, and election, is absolute in man as it is in God.'[72] Bradford listed each objection methodically and gave his responses to them individually. As might be expected from a writer like Harte, the articles gave evidence of a

---

[71] *Ibid.*, 308.
[72] *Ibid.*, 318.

biblical rationalism and simplicity in their attempt to uphold the responsibility of man in choosing to receive God's offer of salvation. The detractor stressed the inherent contradiction involved in universal justice without universal mercy, and saw this perspective to be in opposition to God's general declaration of love and mercy towards His whole creation. It also detracted from Christ's glory as the Light of the world and limited the 'virtue' of His blood, since it was recorded in Scripture that He came to taste death for every man and had become the propitiation for the sins of the entire world.

In his third point, Bradford's opponent suggested that moral responsibility was undercut by an exaggerated picture of man's powerlessness to choose.[73] He knew that man was responsible for his sins, however, since the Scriptures affirmed it and presented man with a choice between the path of life and the path of death. This gift of choice operates in accordance with God's prior knowledge of all things, His predestinating activity and His election of all men unto salvation in Christ.[74] To deny this is to deny the 'power and omnipotence' of God and to cast doubts upon His wisdom and judgements.

The fifth enormity cited dealt with the matter of the covenant, which Harte believed would be annulled if Christ was not 'a general Saviour to all men' and if man's capacity to choose was not straightforward or real. He also declared that 'no man is lost of God . . . if they come to destruction wholly and clearly ignorant', as Christ clearly taught that each man is individually responsible for that which he has been given in this life. All must give 'a just account' on the day of reckoning.[75] The final enormity brought the issue down to the practical level, as Harte pointed out the futility of the exercise of excommunication in the local church when false opinion prevailed, since 'such as they call good they say are predestinate, and those that they call evil may (some say of them) be called: now how they be, nor when they shall be called, say they, that it cannot be known'.[76] Moreover, only those who 'think, or rather imagine' themselves to be predestinate can know of this calling, and their declaration must of necessity be respected. Discipline in the church is thereby threatened, according to Harte, since any particular individual may be destined for salvation and thus be exempt from severe chastening.[77]

[73] *Ibid.*, 319 – 20.

[74] *Ibid.*, 321.

[75] *Ibid.*, 323.

[76] *Ibid.*, 327.

[77] Harte's concern for order in the church is reminiscent of the position of the Swiss Brethren in the 1527 Schleitheim Confession.

Harte closed his short statement with an appeal to the possessors of 'true judgement', and especially to the judgement of the Holy Spirit. He was severely taken to task by Bradford, of course, who accused Harte of appealing 'anabaptistically to the Spirit without the scripture'.[78] Earlier, he had criticized Harte's emphasis on the universal dimensions of the atonement, accusing him of desiring 'to save devils and all' through his 'generalities' and denial of free grace.[79] As for the apparent difficulties involved in harmonizing the universal salvific will of God with His activity in showing mercy and hardening according to His purposes, Bradford sagaciously deferred further inquiry until the next life, when, he believed, 'no contradiction shall be seen in God's will'.[80] He also expressed the hope that his opponent might yet be enlightened and see the folly of his position. With this end in mind, Bradford decided not to identify him in this instance.

Despite Bradford's refusal to name his detractor at this point, it emerged in his subsequent correspondence with the Oxford trio. In a letter sent in mid-January 1555, he informed his companions that he was including 'a writing of Harry Hart's own hand', so that they might 'see how Christ's glory and grace is like to lose much light'.[81] There were others who raised similar objections during these days, however, and Bradford described them as 'curious heads' in the final part of his October treatise.[82] He pointed to the literary ineptness and lack of theological understanding which was typical of these 'ignorant persons', and chastised the freewillers in general for reversing theological truth.[83] He condemned the base rationalism of his opponents as extreme presumption and arrogance, reminding his readers that the Scriptures descend 'to our capacities as much as may be in many things', so that believers may confidently rest assured in the wisdom, majesty and power of God.

Although this was Bradford's principal written contribution to the predestinarian controversy, it was only one of several discussions concerning the doctrine of election which came from his pen.[84] Though perhaps something of a moderate, Bradford was clearly

[78] Bradford, I, 329.

[79] *Ibid.*, 323.

[80] *Ibid.*, 324.

[81] Bradford, II, 120.

[82] Bradford, I, 330.

[83] The freewillers aversion to higher learning can be accounted for much more easily in the light of such charges on the part of the Reformed theologians.

[84] He also wrote 'A Treatise of Election and Free-will' at some unknown point, as well as 'A Brief Sum of the Doctrine of Election and Predestination', which is also undated. See Bradford, I, 211 – 20.

coming to be recognized as the leading authority on the Reformed faith in the London area at the time, and there can be little doubt that his writings had considerable impact upon those to whom they were addressed. Yet he began to encounter even stiffer opposition in the King's Bench itself throughout the remainder of 1554. He had been in the habit of meeting his freewill detractors face to face in the jails, sometimes at his own inconvenience and expense.[85] But the dispute grew so bitter that he finally in a letter to the freewill inmates announced that he was suspending his visits as of 1 Janaury 1555. They had apparently been accusing him of slandering the church through incorrect doctrine during his encounters with them, and they particularly objected to his views on the perseverance of the elect. For his part, Bradford accused the group of supporting one view when in dialogue with him, and then adopting another in reality. Thus, they would deny that human perseverance was a cause of salvation with their lips, but would 'in deed . . . do otherwise'.

Bradford countered that perseverance was a necessary effect of salvation by grace, not a cause, else it would be grace no more. He also affirmed that 'once God's child indeed, and God's child for ever'. Furthermore, man needed to feel certain about the presence and reality of divine grace within, since out of this persuasion flows 'all godliness to God and man'.[86] Those who seek to undermine this assurance in either themselves or others are serving the purposes of Satan, and Bradford solemnly warned the freewillers about the consequences of their continuing 'obstinacy' − if indeed they were offending with full awareness and not from ignorance. He prayed that God would deliver them from such activity.

Bradford's hopes were evidently realized to a considerable degree, as an anonymous letter appeared during these troubled days, apparently written by a recently converted prisoner who had thrown off the trappings of freewill doctrine and accepted Bradford's tenets. This letter was appropriately addressed to the convert's former associates with the intention of encouraging them to follow in the writer's footsteps. Written in a warm and magnanimous vein, it referred to the ills besetting the English realm and considered that one reason for the 'calamity' was immoderate behaviour among the professors of the Gospel.[87] He lamented that many of them had fallen because they 'were not sound in the predestination of God . . . but . . . were rather enemies of it'. Clearly, the battle for England was heating up.

---

[85] Bradford, II, 165.
[86] *Ibid.*, 166 – 7.
[87] Strype, *EM*, III, 2, 325.

It is evident that the writer included himself among those who had held defective views and expressed regret that he had ever participated in bitter railings against those who taught the 'undoubted truth' regarding divine election. He was sorry that he had aggressively campaigned for the cause of 'that error of freewill', yet he knew that God had been merciful in showing him the truth about his base nature and the emptiness of freewill because he had acted in ignorance.[88] He also reminded his readers that others were being similarly enlightened during those days, as God had graciously 'dealt with many' of their number who were all very well known in their circles. In fact, these 'brethren' had originally been jailed for holding to the doctrines of 'Pelagianism' — doctrines which they subsequently came to 'detest and abhor'.

It is significant that this writer appealed for unity among the gospellers on the basis of common hostility towards Catholicism, and declared that freewill doctrines were error in the same category as the papal interpretation of the sacrament. It is also noteworthy that the prospect of his imminent execution acted as a whip to stir him up to extol divine election and predestination to his comrades. Bradford and his colleagues had clearly provided excellent teaching on the fine points, as he recounted how the faithful 'preachers' who had been his 'prison fellows' had reconciled the truths of the Apostles Paul and James for him for the first time.[89] Thus, he had come to see that faith justifies man before God, while good works justify man before the world.

It is also clear that this unnamed writer had lost some of his former friends when his theology changed, but he expressed gratitude for the new ones which God had provided. He even mentioned 'Ledley and Cole' as two of his new-found comrades — men who had also escaped from 'wallowing in the mire' of freewill thought.[90] He then proceeded to espouse a moderate Reformed interpretation of divine redemption.[91] Fundamental to his position was the conviction that all the elect people of God will be kept from falling away eternally, since each one is being conformed to the image of Christ.[92] Those who

---

[88] *Ibid.*, 326 – 7.

[89] *Ibid.*, 328.

[90] *Ibid.*, 329.

[91] *Ibid.*, 331. He held that Christ was ordained by the Father only with the fall of Adam in view, so that a remnant of Adam's descendents might be spared and kept according to divine wisdom. The author was also very careful to interpret the universalist passages of Scripture according to his overall framework, confining the fullest extent of the propitiatory work of Christ to the elect only, and not to all men indiscriminately.

[92] *Ibid.*, 330, 333.

endeavoured to take advantage of this security by engaging in licence merely proved themselves to be reprobates and the objects of divine wrath.

In drawing his letter to a close, the writer hoped that encouraging news would be forthcoming from the freewillers' camp. Apparently some such news had recently been conveyed to him by his 'brother Robert Cole', who had given a favourable report of their progress to the Reformed prisoners. Thus, efforts to reclaim the lost for the cause of Gospel verity were obviously continuing at full speed.[93]

Not all the news transmitted to the predestinarian party during these days could have been encouraging, however, as a stiff pocket of resistance continued to operate both within and outside the prisons. Another anonymous letter from the same episode and attributed by Strype to Henry Harte gave no evidence whatsoever of discouragement among the freewillers' ranks.[94] The document was addressed to several persons – an unnamed 'especial good friend', a porter named John Smyth and his wife, one Thomas Dodmer and several others. Since Dodmer was expected to be in London at that time, it is probable that all the addressees were London residents. The mention of a porter suggests some public establishment, which could mean anything from a prison worker to a minor office-holder in the church – or possibly even an employee at the 'alehouse in Cornhill' where dissenters were known to lodge while in London.[95]

The author displayed a comprehensive grasp of the Scriptures, as he warned his 'fellows' of the need to be separate from the world's evil-doers.[96] Since God dwells within His own people, they must have no part with infidels, but must instead 'come out from among them'. He wrote to his readers with the same urgency noted in Harte's earlier tracts, and spoke of those who were now 'past repentance' through their ignorance. He deemed the present to be a 'miserable time', so that the need to be watchful and ready was prevalent. Sounding much like Erasmus or the continental Anabaptists, he argued that the keeping of God's commandments was well within the scope of man's abilities, for God does not require that which is impossible for man to perform. He is 'not so unreasonable' as to command that which man cannot possibly attain.[97] If God summons men to come to Himself for rest, they must be able to do so freely since He desires only free and willing hearts. Even the irrational

---

[93] *Ibid.*, 334.
[94] *Ibid.*, 1, 413.
[95] Foxe, VIII, 384.
[96] Strype, *EM* III, 2, 321.
[97] *Ibid.*, 322.

beasts have been given certain capacities for use in keeping with their natures. Man, being far superior to animals and even celestial bodies such as the sun and the moon, is required to do all things by means of his 'freewill'. This means that reason must be employed 'reasonably', or else the human plight actually becomes worse.[98] Thus, the day of final judgement is reserved for mankind and not for irrational beings. Another theme presented by the writer which indicates the influence of Harte was the stress upon God's universal salvific will. He desired that men should repent and live instead of passing on to destruction. The writer stated unequivocally that 'it was not God's will that man should come to nought' since He had 'created man to be undestroyed'. Those who persist in sin, therefore, cannot blame God for their misery since they are rejecting His provision of life. True believers, meanwhile, ought to perform the works of God and keep His commandments rather than proclaiming their inability to do so. When they desire to do His will and observe His counsels in actuality, they may expect God's help in producing the kind of fruit which leads to eternal rewards.[99]

[98] *Ibid.*, 323.
[99] *Ibid.*, 324 – 5.

5

The Oxford Connexion

While the relentless efforts of Harte and his associates caused repeated difficulties in the King's Bench, Bradford began the new year with a more earnest appeal to the learned divines imprisoned at Oxford. Around 18 January 1555, he wrote an informative letter to Cranmer, Ridley and Latimer, enclosing 'a little Treatise' which he had written himself, and 'a writing of Harry Hart's own hand'.[1] The treatise was undoubtedly his work on election, while Harte's material must have been the 'enormities' previously examined. Clearly, Bradford's chief correspondent at Oxford was Ridley. Bradford had evidently before this received many items for his perusal through that faithful assistant of Latimer's, Augustine Bernhere, who acted as a messenger between the worthies at London and Oxford.

On this occasion, Bradford asked that Ridley and the others examine the contents of his work and send their 'approbation' according to their judgement. He related that all the prisoners in the vicinity of the King's Bench had generally endorsed his tract, but were awaiting the approval of their Oxford cohorts before giving fuller signification. Anticipating some surprised reactions to his request from Oxford, Bradford spoke of the intensity of the prison contention:

> The matter may be thought not so necessary as I seem to make it: but yet, if ye knew the great evil that is like hereafter to come to the posterity by these men, as partly this bringer can signify unto you, surely then could ye not but be most willing to put hereto your helping hands.[2]

Thus, early in 1555, Bradford was alarmed by the potential still remaining for the freewillers' cause; he feared that they might actually carry the day and leave their offensive imprint on the English Church for years to come. He included Harte's handiwork so that Ridley and his associates might the more readily perceive the

---

[1] Bradford, II, 170 – 1.
[2] *Ibid.*, 170.

impending danger and be spurred into preventive activity. Referring to the freewillers' views, Bradford bemoaned their co-mingling of the 'effects of salvation . . . with the cause'. He added that if the matter was not settled promptly, more damage would 'be done by them, than ever came by the papists', since their lives commended them 'to the world more than the papists'.[3] At the same time, he warned that they were 'plain papists, yea, Pelagians' in the realm of soteriology. They also condemned 'all learning' in their mistaken zeal. Bradford besought his readers to turn their attention towards the refutation of these opinions.

In order to stress the urgency of this request for aid, Ferrar, Taylor and Philpot added their signatures to Bradford's letter. Hesitancy on the part of other prisoners in the London area may indicate some degree of apprehension on their part: they may have felt that the Oxford trio might not totally agree with Bradford. As Bishop Laurence observed, Bradford's choice of words in seeking their approval is somewhat restrained,[4] and he may have sensed that complete endorsement would not come easily. Still, the need for earnest appeals was definitely impressed upon Bradford's mind.

As for the initial response from Oxford, it appears that Ridley was the only one to take any action, although it may have been decided that he should serve as spokesman for the others. He seems to have been corresponding with Bradford on a regular basis even prior to this occasion. In fact, it is quite likely that Ridley had written to Bradford immediately beforehand – perhaps a day before receiving Bradford's plea via Bernhere or even earlier on the same day.[5] In this piece, Ridley expressed his concern over Bernhere's absence, as his return to Oxford was by then long overdue.[6] Ridley's anxiety was compounded by the fact that Bernhere had been entrusted with the writings which Bradford had mentioned in his supplication to the Oxford reformers. Apparently Ridley had no copy of these and had been loath to let them go, but he did so in the light of Bradford's previous letters. The works, which Ridley referred to as his 'scribblings *de abominationibus sedis Romanae et Pontificum Romanorum*',[7] were evidently written in Latin and extremely precious to Ridley as he awaited to be led 'in certamen cum antiquo serpente'.

---

[3] *Ibid.*, 170 – 1.
[4] Richard Laurence, ed., *Authentic Documents Relative to the Predestinarian Controversy* (Oxford, 1819), pp. xiii – xxiv.
[5] *Ibid.*, p. xxvii.
[6] Miles Coverdale, ed., *Certain most godly, fruitful, and comfortable letters of such true saintes and holy martyrs as in the late bloddye persecution as gave their lyves* (London: John Day, 1564), fol. 67. RSTC 5886.
[7] *Ibid.*, fol. 67.

Ridley's fears were soon relieved with the arrival of Latimer's aide on or about 19 January with Bradford's letter and Harte's material as well. Bernhere seems to have written a report of his journey and immediately sent it to Ridley in prison. He apologized profusely for his extended absence, but assured Ridley that his delay was most justifiable.[8] He regretted that he had not had time to copy Ridley's 'book' as he had hoped, but added that he had brought all the writings back to Oxford in case Ridley had need of them. If Ridley would permit him to have them again, he would gladly copy them out most speedily. He urged Ridley to preserve all his works and assured him that he would have them printed 'beyond the seas' where he would have the assistance of 'learned men' should Ridley be ultimately delivered from his present misery.

Bernhere also mentioned that unprecedented 'turmoilings' were now occurring in London and that things were at present going badly for the 'godly ministers' there. He remarked that the 'best tragedy to describe it would ask a great deal of time' and promised to brief Ridley on any details with which he was unfamiliar. Given Bradford's eagerness to impress the gravity of the situation upon the minds of the Oxford men, it is probable that Bernhere was making reference here to the predestinarian controversy. He closed by announcing his hasty departure on the following morning and requested that Ridley reply at once.

This the learned master undoubtedly did, welcoming Bernhere back to Oxford with gratitude to God.[9] He had examined the items which Bernhere had brought from London and was returning them to the Swiss so that the other divines on the circuit might peruse them too. Ridley had received Bradford's correspondence which included a generous sum of money, but added that he would not accede to the request for a reply to the freewillers as he had not yet 'done that, for diverse dangers' to his personal 'scribblings'. He was anxious lest harm should befall any prisoners who should cause an item to be set forth under his own name at that time, and he recalled how he had warned Hooper about hastily attempting it.

Thus Ridley was clearly fearful of composing a treatise in aid of the Reformed prisoners when first asked to do so, lest the authorities take reprisals against both him and his fellows. He wanted to see how Latimer and Cranmer reacted before proceeding but he did promise that he would 'also think of the matter to do the best' that he could.

---

[8] Nicholas Ridley, *Treatises and Letters of Dr. Nicholas Ridley* (London: The Religious Tract Society, n.d.), p. 235.
[9] Bradford, II, 172.

As for Henry Harte and his 'scribbling',[10] Ridley felt that time could be spent more profitably than in refuting such drivel. He also affirmed that Cranmer knew Harte better than the other prisoners in Oxford,[11] and that he had heard how Harte had been 'often monished' and presumably renounced some of his 'follies' only 'to fall in them again'. Ridley closed his letter to Bernhere by informing him that he had written to Bradford the previous day and brought Bernhere up to date on his writing ministry at Oxford. He also instructed Bernhere to burn his current letter after reading it.

Ridley wrote to Bradford himself around 20 January,[12] since his earlier letter had been sent just prior to Bernhere's arrival and so had contained no response to Bradford's request for some apologetical work on behalf of divine election. In this document, Ridley expressed his gratitude for the financial assistance, and assured Bradford that he had made a speedy examination of the contents of his letter. In the hastiness of the moment owing to Bernhere's impending departure, he 'noted nothing but a confused sum of the matter' and had not heard from the others regarding their impressions. As for Bradford's request, which had been amplified by Bernhere, Ridley now promised to give the matter due thought and consideration despite the constant supervision which made consultation with the other prisoners difficult.

Then, in a rather puzzling statement, Ridley added: 'I have answered him in a brief letter; and yet he hath replied again: but he must go without any further answer of me for this time.'[13] In the original edition of the printed letters of the Marian martyrs, Coverdale, the editor, inserted that Ridley was here referring to Henry Harte. This would suggest that Ridley had sent him a brief letter soon after Bernhere's return and that Harte had already responded. Were this conjecture true, Ridley's letter to Harte and Harte's reply could have taken no more than two days, since Ridley did not receive the initial request from Bradford until about 18 January. As Laurence pointed out, for this to be possible Harte must have been staying in the vicinity of Oxford.[14] Although Laurence thought this farfetched, it is possible that Harte was visiting other prisoners in the area in connexion with the predestinarian controversy in London, or may have followed Bernhere to Oxford in hopes of discoursing personally with the Reformed leaders in the light of Bradford's request. It is rather unlikely that Harte himself was

[10] *Ibid.*, 172 – 3.
[11] See above, pp. 44 – 6.
[12] Bradford, II, 173 – 5.
[13] *Ibid.*, 174.
[14] Laurence, pp. xxxiii – xxxiv.

imprisoned in Oxford, although this would make sense of the time factor.[15] The only other plausible interpretation, one which is perhaps to be preferred, is that Bernhere, not Harte, was the recipient of the recent letter, that Bernhere had replied, but Ridley could not answer before Bernhere's departure from Oxford. This harmonizes the account smoothly, although it is rather intriguing to imagine that Ridley may have written personally to Harte at this time, or perhaps even before he had received Bradford's request. At any rate, the crucial point is that Ridley promised not to drop the issue entirely despite his wariness; he even seemed to encourage hopes that he would compose the desired tract in time. In this vein, he wrote: 'Austin's persuasions may do more with me in that I can think I may do conveniently in this matter, armed with your earnest and zealous letters, than any rhetoric either of Tully or Demosthenes, I ensure you thereof'.[16]

In subsequent correspondence with Ridley, Bradford apparently lamented over the lack of immediate response to his urgent appeal and traced the deterioration of circumstances in London to Ridley's procrastination.[17] Ridley again replied, this time relating that he had now 'in Latin drawn out the places of the scriptures, and upon the same noted what I can for the time'.[18] He declared that he was most 'fearful' in approaching such weighty subjects, and did not dare go much beyond that which the text of Scripture stated in itself as it led him 'by the hand' through the mysterious waters. He also wrote confidently of the ultimate defeat of heresies which would 'never be able to do the multitude so great harm'. He referred to former days when such errors had arisen only to be ably and soundly 'confounded' by the servants of God so that the masses were either preserved from error or corrected promptly.

Thus, Ridley did not seem to share Bradford's alarm at the spread of freewill thought and dissent in the south-east during the Marian years, perhaps because he was removed from the London scene and sealed off from most contacts with the outside world at Oxford. Yet, at the same time, he did undertake to make a response based largely upon the biblical texts dealing with election. He evidently had a good deal of time to spend on such literary labours and was thankful for the privilege that was his in proclaiming the glory of God to other men, even though such works might not 'come to light' for some time. He

[15] It is my belief that Harte was not imprisoned at any stage during the Marian reaction.
[16] Bradford, II, 174.
[17] *Ibid.*, 214. According to the Parker Society edition, mid-April of 1555 is the probable date of this correspondence.
[18] *Ibid.*, 214.

was probably counting on Bernhere to succeed in having them published after his death.

As for the subject of election and Ridley's response to Bradford's promptings, we are left with something of a riddle when considering Ridley's brief reference to his annotations. Coverdale was convinced that Ridley was deeply concerned with the topic of election in this specific context, 'whereof he afterward wrote a godly and comfortable treatise remaining yet in the hands of some, and hereafter shall come to light, if God so will'.[19] Gloucester Ridley later utilized Coverdale's information, but added that he had never seen a reference to the treatise's publication, nor even come across it in manuscript form.[20] Laurence therefore stressed that Ridley's work must have been unsympathetic to the predestinarian party in the King's Bench, if indeed there had been a formal tract at all. Otherwise, why should the Reformed exponents have refrained from printing a work by so eminent a theologian which would be greatly beneficial to their cause if supportive of their position?

Yet Laurence apparently failed to take notice of Ridley's extreme apprehensions about having materials published under his own name, and his scepticism regarding the existence of such a work has not been echoed by more recent experts. For example, Jasper Ridley stated that Ridley wrote a treatise on biblical predestination within a short time of his letter to Bradford of 20 January 1555, and that the item was lost over the years. He affirmed that 'there is no reason to doubt that in it Ridley expressed, in a more forceful and brilliant style, the opinions which Bradford had put forward in his treatise'.[21] Thus, Jasper Ridley believed that Ridley's opinions would not only be compatible with those of Bradford, but would be presented even more powerfully and eloquently.

But what of the precise nature of this missing link, this 'comfortable' treatise which Ridley supposedly composed? Until now, the substance of the document has remained a complete mystery. Yet in recent years, with the revision of the catalogue of manuscripts deposited in the Lambeth Palace Library, an item has come to light among the Fairhurst Papers which satisfies many of the necessary contextual conditions.[22] This treatise, which bears neither name nor date but which has been identified as being written in a

---

[19] *Ibid.*, 214.

[20] Gloucester Ridley, *Life of Bishop Ridley*, p. 554, quoted in Laurence, p. xxxvii.

[21] Jasper Ridley, *Nicholas Ridley*, p. 363. Ridley was obviously referring to Bradford's 'Defense of Election.'

[22] See E. G. W. Bill, ed., *A Catalogue of Manuscripts in Lambeth Palace Library* (Oxford: Clarendon Press, 1972, 1976), II, 203.

sixteenty-century hand, is a theological work in Latin written as a refutation of certain Pelagian errors revived by the Anabaptists of the author's era. It is entitled *Responsiones ad argumenta Anabaptistarum et novorum Pelagianorum quibus nittuntur necessariam doctrinam de aeterna Dei electione et praedestinatione, ab ecclesia excludere et errores Pelagiani et Celestini jam pridem ab ecclesia damnatos ab inferis suscitare.*[23]

The treatise consists of answers to seven problems raised by Anabaptist freewillers and includes their arguments, supposedly as stated by the radicals themselves. Since Harte was fond of using lists and forming confessions, it is possible that these relate to yet another in his series of statements — something which he could have sent to Ridley during their alleged correspondence or even delivered personally early in 1555. The language and arguments of the 'responses' clearly belong to an able scholar of Ridley's calibre, and it has already been observed that he had a penchant for writing in Latin and had even made jottings on this very subject in that tongue.[24] It is quite possible, therefore, that a fuller work was composed by Ridley when time permitted and was based upon his preliminary notes. As noted earlier, Ridley, took full advantage of his imprisonment by engaging in an extensive writing ministry, and was later described by Fuller as 'the profoundest scholar' among the Marian martyrs.[25] He certainly had had many opportunities to observe Anabaptism in Kent and Essex in the past, and had probably come to identify the Kentish conventiclers with this continental sect at the time of the commission's hearings at Ashford in 1552.[26] He was also known to have studied the Waldensians with great interest.[27] Thus, Ridley would consider himself to be well-qualified to undertake a refutation of the alleged Anabaptist views concerning election and predestination which were seen as revivals of Pelagian and Celestinian errors.

[23] London, Lambeth Palace, Fairhurst Papers, MSS 2002, ff. 94–106. In English translation this would be: 'Replies to the arguments of the Anabaptists and new Pelagians in which they strive to exclude from the church the necessary doctrine concerning the eternal election of God and predestination, and to resurrect from the dead the errors of the Pelagian and Celestinian which were long ago condemned by the church.' This title bears some resemblance to a piece written by Thomas Cottesford in 1555, entitled: 'An Epistle written to a good Lady for the comfort of a friend of hers, wherein the Novatians error now revived by the Anabaptists is confuted, and the sin against the Holy Ghost plainly declared.' The subject matter of this piece was falling from grace and the unpardonable sin, however, and there is no evidence that Cottesford ever wrote a treatise in Latin. See Horst, pp. 175, 190–2.
[24] See above, pp. 126, 129–30.
[25] Thomas Fuller, *The Church History of Britain* (Oxford: University Press, 1845) IV, 195.
[26] See above, p. 104.
[27] Coverdale, fol. 72.

Anabaptists: revivers of ancient heresies

As for the contents of the treatise itself, the first argument presented by the Anabaptist dealt with the basis of election. He sought to maintain that election would be impossible unless some distinction or variable is observed either in the One who elects or in the creatures who are the objects of election. This is so because 'different results cannot emerge except from different and opposite causes'.[28] Thus, there must be some basis for 'choosing and rejecting' men either within God Himself or within human beings.

The Reformed respondent assured his readers that God acts only according to His predetermined plans, and all His actions have a definite purpose. Moreover, the scope of His activity is so comprehensive and orderly that 'neither the wicked nor the devil nor sins can be excluded from predestination'.[29] Predestination does not depend upon the individual creatures themselves, however, but must be seen as an eternal 'work of God' which 'must be placed in the divine mind' alone. He may choose to have mercy upon some and He may choose to pass others by and leave them in their misery as a demonstration of His hatred of evil. He does not, however, cause these men to sin by pouring His malice out upon them, since all men are evil through natural conception. This proves, then, that there is no variation in God's ways whatsoever. Nor is there any discrimination made 'in those things which are chosen'.[30] God's will is the primary cause of all things, and it is unthinkable that any human contribution could determine His choice. Thus sin, which is the 'reason' for condemnation, is not in any way the 'cause' of divine reprobation. For if this were so, then no man could be chosen since all are conceived in sin.

After answering the major premise contained in the Anabaptist argument, the respondent moved on to some subsidiary aspects. He denied that God had made some men 'good' but created others 'evil', since all His creation had been described as 'good'. Although God knew that man would become evil 'by his own free will', He did not create them in order that they might be lost.[31] In the same way, 'God does not hate His own work, but the corruption of His work'.[32] Once

---

[28] Fairhurst, MSS 2002, fol. 94a. I would like to acknowledge an incalculable debt to Mrs Diana Burnett for assistance in transcribing and completely translating this document.
[29] Fairhurst 2002, fol. 95a.
[30] *Ibid.*, fol. 95b.
[31] *Ibid.*, fol. 96b.
[32] *Ibid.*, fol. 97a.

again, His hatred of men is not the cause of reprobation, but rather the result of His judgement according to His will.

These matters were further explored in response to the second Anabaptist argument which endeavoured to demonstrate the consistency of God's declared will regarding human salvation. He simply could not desire that all men should choose the way of life and at the same time create some men for the purpose of destruction. The respondent answered by recognizing a distinction within the will of God. He argued that by the 'will of design' or 'signified' will, God willed that none should perish.[33] This aspect of His will set forth the universality of His grace, since 'He poured out His great blessings to all indiscriminately'. As a result, virtually all men experience 'a certain inner prodding' from time to time, which is nothing other than the work of God in provoking men 'to good living'. There is another side to His will, however, which may be termed the 'will of the well-pleased' or the 'permissive' will of God. Under this operation, God desires that sinners who persist in lawlessness should come to destruction. This distinction is necessary because it upholds God's sovereign control of all things so that He performs 'nothing against His own will'. He is, therefore, not willing to save all men 'absolutely and efficaciously', else none would ever be damned. Nevertheless, according to His 'signified' will He would rather have men repent and live eternally.[34]

Subsequent arguments and replies were likewise concerned with the universal dimensions of grace and redemption. In fact, arguments three and four were cases allegedly set forth by the Anabaptists in order to advocate universal redemption by Christ. In the third it was argued that Christ had liberated those who had been 'subject to slavery'.[35] Those who have been liberated, then, are also redeemed, thus implying that all were redeemed by Christ without exception since all had been under the yoke of slavery to sin. Similarly, in the fourth argument, it was stated that Christ had even redeemed those who ultimately rejected Him and returned 'to their own vomit'.[36]

These arguments were disposed of by the respondent with little fanfare, as he once again employed a crucial theological distinction. According to this, Christ's sacrifice of Himself was 'sufficient' to redeem all from eternal death since it was of infinite worth. Yet it is clear that His death has not been 'efficient' for all since not all men appropriate or 'apprehend it by genuine faith'.[37] There is no

[33] *Ibid.*, fol. 99a. The Latin term was *voluntas signi*.
[34] *Ibid.*, fol. 97b.
[35] *Ibid.*, fol. 98a.
[36] *Ibid.*, fol. 99b.
[37] *Ibid.*, fol. 98b.

automatic application of Christ's death to all men, since faith is 'a gift of God' not given to everyone.

As for the important relationship between Adam and Christ, the second Adam, the respondent stressed that all men are of the posterity of the first parent simply through partaking of humanity. For the original Adam 'wrapped up his entire race in damnation'. In order to enjoy the benefits of Christ's restorative work, however, one must 'be faithful'. Those who reject the grace of God in Christ 'have extinguished God's light' and the benefits extended to them, thereby denying the One who 'redeemed all sufficiently'. In this sense, it is proper to say that these are guilty of denying Christ 'by whom they had been redeemed'.[38]

The fifth argument sought to establish that God had indeed granted sufficient salvific grace to all men without exception, since all men are redeemed by Christ's work. Relying heavily upon Augustine, the respondent continued to distinguish between the efficacy and the sufficiency of the atonement, and also upheld the difference between the 'signified' and 'permissive' divine will. God's mercy, then, is not 'offered equally to all'[39] in terms of redemption, even though there is a sense in which He calls all men 'generally' by means of 'promises and threats'. Here again dualism became the basis for the solution to the apparent problem, since this general call does not make men 'apt to be moved' in the restricted salvific sense.[40] Esau was not motivated in the ultimate sense, even though it was not beyond God's power to do so. Pharaoh's case is yet another example of this 'passing over' process, since God did not choose to 'soften his heart or take away the hardness'. God did not desire Pharaoh's repentance after His 'efficacious' will, but only provoked him to change his heart according to his 'signified' will.[41]

The Reformed expositor was at this point concerned with answering some specific Anabaptist objections to his position. He denied that men were reduced to the status of 'blocks of wood and stones' through his interpretation, claiming that men do act but only through the motivation and prompting of the Spirit of God.[42] Only God can produce in man a 'willingness to believe' and do that which is truly good. Moreover, when the Anabaptists refer to the Apostle Paul's statement concerning God's desire for universal repentance, it must be understood that Paul was speaking in terms of all 'races of

[38] *Ibid.*, fol. 99a – b.

[39] *Ibid.*, fol. 101b.

[40] *Ibid.*, fols. 100b – 101a.

[41] *Ibid.*, fol. 101b.

[42] *Ibid.*, fol. 102a. Such a charge had been made earlier in the century by the continental radical, Hans Denck. See above, p. 96.

individuals, not individual men'.[43] This suits the theme of Paul's message exactly, as he urges that special prayers be made for rulers so that all nations will be included in the proclamation of truth.[44]

Furthermore, when reference is made to Peter's remarks on God's patience in waiting for all men to come to repentance, this must be understood solely in terms of His 'signified' will since He saves only those whom He has chosen eternally 'in Christ'. Nor must Peter's exhortation to make one's 'calling and election sure' be interpreted as the Anabaptists do, for they 'infer' from these words that 'the security of . . . election and calling depends upon good works'.[45] Those who are 'preordained to life' through the eternal 'hidden plan' of God, however, are indeed chosen for the purpose of purity and holiness; but the acquisition of this purity is not dependent upon human initiative in the performance of good works. Instead, 'perpetual tenure of the calling, by His pure grace, follows' and the elect are thereby strengthened in the true faith as they live in a godly manner.[46]

The sixth argument was something of an extension of this latter discussion, as it was stated that faith was prior to election in the redemptive process. God's choice thus falls upon those who obtain sanctification and who believe in the revealed truth of God.[47] The respondent pointed out that salvation rested solely upon God's 'eternal election', and that the 'signs' of this election ought not to be confused with the 'causes'. Since individual men cannot look directly into God's mysterious plan in order to be sure of their salvation, God sets before men certain 'signs and tokens' of their election in order to foster trust in His activity. The only 'legitimate proof' of election, then, can be found 'within'. If He has sanctified His people and brought them to faith through the Spirit's working, they may confidently rest in their election; for true faith and the Spirit's grace in regeneration and sanctification are the proofs or signs of their 'eternal election'.[48]

Finally, the seventh argument attempted to prove that men might enter into and fall out of divine election according to their deeds. When an offending person is excommunicated properly by the Christian community, it follows that he is expelled from the Kingdom

---

[43] Fairhurst 2002, fol. 102b. The biblical reference is to I Timothy 2:4. This interpretation seems to have been favoured by Erasmus on occasion as well. See above, p. 91.
[44] Fairhurst 2002, fol. 103a.
[45] *Ibid.*, fol. 104a. Cf. II Peter 3:9 and 1:10.
[46] *Ibid.*, fol. 104a – b.
[47] *Ibid.*, fol. 104b.
[48] *Ibid.*, fol. 105a.

of God and falls from the election as well.[49] In this way, 'the elect can err and reprobates can be chosen and incorporated into the church of Christ'. In rejecting this hypothesis, the author of the 'responses' stated that the fundamental aim behind the act of excommunication was to bring the wayward ones 'to their senses' through discipline. Personal well-being is therefore uppermost in the mind of the church. Restoration, not separation, is the prime goal, and it does not follow that those who are excommunicated from the fellowship of the church are thereby 'thrown out of Christ and the eternal election of God'.[50]

Having concluded the presentation of, and formal replies to, the seven Anabaptist arguments, the respondent drew his treatise to a close stating:

> These are the things which seemed to me must be replied from the holy scriptures, and from the opinions of the holy fathers, in answer to the frivolous and foolish arguments of the Anabaptists: If however they should have others, let them bring them out into the open, and let them wait patiently for an explanation.[51]

At no point does this work provide evidence of personal vindictiveness or bitterness on the part of the author. Instead, his concern was genuine and his tone altogether in keeping with that of a gentleman scholar — as Ridley was known to be. He was clearly a first-rate theologian,[52] and the Latin employed was of a quality which would be expected of a churchman of Ridley's learning and position. Indeed, Ridley preferred to write in Latin at various points during the latter stages of his life.[53] Furthermore, the apologetical nature of this work would seem most appropriate for Ridley in style and in approach, as he composed important works against the doctrine of transubstantiation and the veneration of images at other times. He also tended to employ a very structured format in certain of his works, most notably in *A Determination Concerning the Sacrament made at Cambridge* in 1549. It was in this particular work that Ridley listed his arguments consecutively in a most orderly fashion. A similar

---

[49] *Ibid.*, fol. 105b.

[50] *Ibid.*, fol. 106a.

[51] *Ibid.*, fol. 106a.

[52] For example, his observations regarding a distinction within the divine will is somewhat reminiscent of the Scholastic reasonings on the subject. See the comments on this by Hubmaier in *SAW*, pp. 132–3.

[53] It will be remembered that Sir William Fitz-Williams, the Knight-Marshall of the King's Bench, was known to have translated one of Ridley's Latin works. See above, p. 112.

methodology was utilized in his treatise against the worship of images and gave evidence of Ridley's capabilities as a highly-systematized thinker and writer. Then too, Ridley's condemnation of the separatist tendencies of the Anabaptists and Novations at his trial proceedings[54] is extremely similar to the anonymous author's association of the Anabaptists with Pelagians and Celestinians as far as their views on redemption and grace were concerned. In both cases, there was a clearly marked tendency to link the later radicals with the ancients.

It is indeed difficult to imagine that the English Reformed exponents would find anything objectionable in this treatise, anything which might stop it being published and distributed.[55] Instead, it would seem more likely that this work, if written by Ridley as either a complete treatise or perhaps a draft version on the subject of predestination in keeping with his expressed hopes,[56] was kept under wraps by the author and his followers because of his fear of reprisals on the part of the Catholic authorities. This would clearly explain Coverdale's guarded reference to the tract, for it is in any event most improbable that one as deeply involved in the English Reformation movement as Coverdale would be misinformed on the existence of such a key work. Thus, given the subject matter and scholarly style, it seems reasonable to conclude that the 'responses' were a part of the attack upon freewill doctrine in mid-century England, written by Nicholas Ridley while he awaited execution in Oxford in 1555, and that he was moved to perform this task by Bradford's request for help in controverting the English freewill radicals led by Henry Harte and his fellows.

Lesse and Scory: Augustinianism further revived

It should be noted that many of the basic themes of this anonymous work were evidenced in other quarters of the realm during the mid-Tudor years. For instance, the author's determination to prove that the Reformed faith was in keeping with the teachings of the Apostolic

[54] See below, pp. 145 – 6, for Ridley's trial. For the Cambridge tract on the sacrament, see *The Works of Nicholas Ridley, D.D.*, ed. Henry Christmas, Parker Society, No. 39 (Cambridge: University Press, 1843), pp. 167 – 79. For his treatise on image worship, see pp. 81 – 96.
[55] Laurence seems to leave open the possibility of suppression in his introduction to *Authentic Documents*, p. xxx – vii.
[56] See appendix 1 for further consideration of possibilities in this area.

church and patristic period, and hence not an innovation as the
Anabaptists maintained, was also clearly seen in the revival of interest
in Augustine's works. Two new translations of his basic writings on
predestination and perseverance were forthcoming, once again
indicating that these matters were seen as most critical by the English
Calvinist leadership. Nicholas Lesse of London translated both *A
Work of the Predestination of Saints* and *Of the Virtue of Perseverance to the
End*, and these were published in 1550.[57] Then, in 1556, they were
again published, this time in a translation by John Scory, the former
Bishop of Chichester.

Lesse, who dedicated his labours to the Duchess of Somerset, noted
in his introduction that there was at that time 'a corrupt sort of
heretics' in England imposing limits upon the omnipotence of God.
Some of these were content to question the certainty of His
predestinating activity, while others went even further and denied the
existence of any form of predestination whatsoever. They were thus
'stout defenders of free will'. Furthermore, these fanatics were all the
more dangerous because they spoke 'with godly words, such as a man
would think did come from the mouth of god himself with outward
religion, and sanctimony of life'.[58] This gave them an outer
appearance of holiness, which Lesse believed enabled them to deceive
even prudent men, not to mention those who were 'simple and
unlearned'. Accordingly, Lesse had taken it upon himself to prove
that the doctrine of predestination was no 'new doctrine, but such as
the old church hath alway firmly believed and constantly defended'.
The 'venemous beasts' which were responsible for this erroneous
perspective were 'the anabaptists and freewill masters' who were 'so
much the more dangerous as their mischief is cloked with a double
face of holiness ten times more religious to seem . . . than were the
superstitious and arrogant papists'.[59]

Despite his rigorous denunciations, Lesse was obviously an astute
theologian, as he distinguished between the views of the sixteenth-
century freewillers and the ancient Pelagians. Whereas the latter had
denied that the source of faith was divine grace, the Anabaptists and
freewill men accepted this truth. They erred, however, in asserting
that the power and merits associated with good works are dependent
upon man's consent in receiving them.[60] Not only did they

---

[57] Nicholas Lesse, ed. and trans., *A Worke of the predestination of saints wrytten by the famous
doctor S. Augustine/Of the vertue of perseveraunce to thend* (London, 1550), sig. A. i. My
quotations from Lesse have modernized spelling.
[58] *Ibid.*, sig. A. i – ii.
[59] *Ibid.*, sig. A. iii.
[60] *Ibid.*, sig. A. iv.

undermine the omnipotence of God, but they also sought to bring about 'the utter confusion and subversion of whole common-wealths'.[61] This made them 'a more pestilent sect' than the papists had ever been, since at least the Catholics had been concerned about social order and justice. The freewillers were harmful to both body and soul no matter 'how holy a pretense soever' they may have had.

Whereas Lesse had been mainly preoccupied with Protestant sectarians, Scory was equally concerned with Catholic distortions. He referred to the 'Papistes and Anabaptistes' who had 'revived agayne the wycked opinions of the Pelagians, that extolled mans wyll and merites agaynst the fre grace of Christe'.[62] The purpose of his introduction was to demonstrate that 'the true catholike Church of Christe' had been manifested in the English Church during the days of Henry VIII and Edward VI,[63] and that the 'religion' which had prevailed then was not an abominable innovation but a true reflection of the ancient church.[64]

---

[61] *Ibid.*, sig. A. vi. Note the nationalist implications of Lesse's remarks.

[62] John Scory, ed. and trans., *Two bokes of the noble Doctor and B. S. Augustine thone entitled of the Predestinacion of saintes, thother of perseveraunce unto thende*, The English Experience, No. 32 (Amsterdam: Da Capo Press, 1968: orig. pub. 1556), sig. A. ia. Once again, it is worth noting the similarity between Lesse's wording and the anonymous treatise which may well have been Ridley's. It is also striking that Scory had been appointed Bishop of Rochester in April 1551, and had thus held Ridley's former post for a time. Scory had also served as chaplain to both Ridley and Cranmer. Furthermore, Scory's acquaintance with some forms of Anabaptism was at first-hand ever since his dealings with Joan Bocher in April 1550. At the time of the publication of his translation of Augustine's works, he may have been residing in Geneva, evidently still trying to live down his recantation before the Marian authorities in 1554. His condemnation of the papists along with the Anabaptists may have been calculated to win friends among the Reformed adherents both in England and abroad. Strype, *EM*, II, 2, 261, 269; II, 1, 335; Garrett, pp. 285 – 6.

[63] Scory, sig. A. viib – viiia.

[64] *Ibid.*, sig. A. iiia. Scory's opponents had claimed that they alone should be considered true 'catholics' and had tried to exclude those who, in Scory's opinion, were the legitimate descendents of the historic faith.

6

Reconciliation: attempted and thwarted

Shortly after his crucial correspondence with Ridley, Bradford was brought before the highest officials in the land and charged with seditious behaviour.[1] After rejecting Gardiner's offer of mercy, he was returned to prison under the care of the under-marshal of the King's Bench. This time Bradford was to be more restricted in his activities, as the Lord Chancellor directed: 'he is of another manner of charge unto you now, than he was before.'[2] Under these new strictures, Bradford was not to confer privately with other prisoners or write any letters. On 30 January, he was arraigned in St Mary Overy's Church along with Taylor and Saunders.[3] Hooper and Rogers had received similar pronouncements the day before. All were sentenced to die at the stake.

During these days of turmoil, Bradford addressed himself to the needs of his cell-mates as best he could and kept abreast of new developments in the predestinarian controversy. The ban on letter-writing was clearly not enforced, and he wrote to Robert Cole and pleaded for unity among the brethren in order to avoid further dissension. He advised: 'If love may appear in all our doings, and that we seek one another with a simple and a single eye in God's sight, doubtless all prejudice, whereby we are letted to see manifest things, will be had away, and we will take things spoken and alone in the best part.'[4]

Bradford was also engaging in detailed correspondence with John Careless, the Coventry weaver, who was being drawn into the vortex of the King's Bench problem. Because of Bradford's strict confinement Careless was evidently assuming the role of predestinarian apologist, and his activity increased steadily throughout the remainder of 1555. On one occasion, Bradford wrote to Careless concerning one Skelthrop who had abandoned his freewill tendencies recently and adopted Reformed views. Bradford wanted to be remembered to him, and trusted that he would give such a clear evidence of right

[1] Foxe, VII, 149. The date was 22 January 1555.
[2] *Ibid.*, 152.
[3] Strype, *EM*, III, 1, 331.
[4] Bradford, II, 215.

doctrine through his conduct 'that his old acquaintance' would be convicted of their waywardness.[5] It is worthy of note that this same Skelthrop was probably the last prisoner involved in the King's Bench episode to be released. When the jails were emptied on the accession of Elizabeth in December 1558, a 'Robert Seulthroppe' was found within the confines of the same prison and released.[6]

At the same time as he remarked on Skelthrop's change, Bradford urged Careless to convey discreet 'salutations' to one Trewe and his company as well.[7] Bradford hoped that God had appointed a similar time for their conversion. They were obviously still within the freewill camp. Another Reformed prisoner in the King's Bench, John Philpot, was now also receiving frequent dispatches from Bradford. He was instructed to 'go on for God's sake to seek unity in Christ' among the disputants,[8] but was warned not to confront the dissemblers in an inflammatory manner. Instead, it would be far better to let them run their course in order to increase their judgement or speed their conversion.

Bradford also told Philpot that Cole had written to him in search of support against the freewillers. In response to Cole's request, Bradford now planned to write to the said Trewe, along with one Abyngton or Avington, and stated that Philpot would be shown these letters in due time. He was dealing with yet another prisoner as well, one 'Master Gibson', who had been jailed 'upon an action of thousands pounds'.[9] Since Gibson was also a freewiller, Bradford hoped to see him turn to the truth before his execution date. Apparently Bradford was given the opportunity to confer with Gibson twice each day. Thus, Careless and Philpot were now working closely together under the constant supervision of Bradford in opposition to freewill radicalism.

Bradford followed through on his commitments to write to the freewillers – perhaps the same day as his condemnation, on 30 January. Referring to his adversaries as his 'beloved in the Lord', Bradford stated that he might never have another opportunity to communicate with them, as his writing instruments could be taken away from him at any time.[10] He also enclosed a monetary gift to the men, since Trewe and Avington had apparently accused him of

---

[5] *Ibid.*, 243.
[6] John Strype, *Annals of the Reformation and establishment of Religion* (Oxford: Clarendon Press, 1824), I, 1, 55.
[7] This was John Trewe, Kentish radical and apparent leader of the moderates in the freewill party in the King's Bench dispute.
[8] Bradford, II, 243.
[9] *Ibid.*, 244.
[10] *Ibid.*, 180.

withholding their share of past donations. Evidently some funds had been entrusted to Bradford on the understanding that all of the prisoners would share in the distribution, but the freewillers were suspicious of improper handling of the money. Accordingly, Bradford enclosed 13s. 4d. with the promise of more should the need arise. He closed graciously in the following words:

> Though in some things we agree not, yet let love bear the bell away; and let us pray for one another, and be careful one for another; for I hope we be all Christ's. As you hope yourselves to pertain to him, so think of me; and, as you be his, so am I yours.[11]

Despite Bradford's sincerity, his letter and gesture did not produce the desired effect. Coverdale later commented that Trewe and Avington were 'sore offended' at Bradford's remarks, since he had 'said he had hindered himself to further them, as though he had thereby upbraided them'.[12] Consequently, they promptly returned the letter, and in the process, evoked yet another from Bradford, probably within twenty-four hours of his first effort. Bradford attempted to soothe the ruffled feelings of his antagonists and assured them of his financial integrity.[13] He claimed that he had not meant to upbraid them at all, but merely wanted to gain their 'weal'. In closing, he asked that they 'rather bear than break' in the light of God's merciful pardon.

As if these bothersome accusations were not enough, Bradford received repeated visits from some of the Marian persecutors during the month of February. Bonner himself came to see him on 4 February, and Nicholas Harpsfield followed on the 15th and 16th.[14] Since his condemnation, Bradford had been removed from the King's Bench and was awaiting his execution in the Compter in the Poultry.[15] On 23 February he was visited by both the Archbishop of York and the Bishop of Chichester.[16] Clearly, he was viewed as an eminent divine by friend and foe alike. Meanwhile, the first of the Marian martyrs, John Rogers, suffered on 4 February.[17] Bishop Hooper followed him to the stake later in the same month.[18]

---

[11] *Ibid.*, 180.
[12] Coverdale, fol. 475.
[13] Bradford, II, 181.
[14] Foxe, VII, 165, 168 – 74.
[15] *DNB*, II, 1066.
[16] Foxe, VII, 174 – 8.
[17] Strype, *EM*, III, 1, 332.
[18] *Ibid.*, 282.

On the day of his second examination by Harpsfield, Bradford wrote again to the disputants in the King's Bench controversy and included members of both sides in his greeting.[19] Of the predestinarian leaders he mentioned Ledley, Cole, Sheterden and Middleton — all former Kentish freewillers now supporting the Reformed doctrines. The current freewillers were represented by Henry Harte, whose name headed the entire list, John Kempe, John Gibson, John Barry and John Lawrence. Kempe and Gibson were travelling companions of Harte, while Barry and Lawrence, who hailed from Essex, had become embroiled in the controversy as messengers and aides to the imprisoned freewillers.[20]

In addition to these key individuals, Bradford mentioned several secondary figures who had not been as prominent in the struggle to date. These were Roger Newman, Richard Prowde and William and Richard Porrege. The latter were probably brothers and may have come from the Sandwich area in Kent, as Richard appears to have served as a Jurate there under Elizabeth.[21] William Porrege, along with the Kentish tanner Thomas Sprat, was known to be another of the Reformed messengers to the continental exiles. He evidently made the crossing between Dover and Calais on numerous occasions and once was nearly apprehended by Kentish officials while en route to Sandwich.[22] Porrege was later ordained by Grindal in January 1560.[23] Similarly, Richard Prowde of Faversham was ordained priest by the same divine just two months after Porrege and became an outspoken minister in Buckinghamshire.[24] Nothing further is known of Newman, although John Newman, the Maidstone 'pewterer' who was martyred during those days, may have been a relation.[25]

Besides these men who were especially addressed, Bradford included 'all other that fear the Lord and love his truth, abiding in Kent, Essex, Sussex and thereabout.'[26] As he awaited his executioners, he asked his 'dearly beloved' to consider the matters which had made for 'some controversy' among them more seriously,

[19] Bradford, II, 194.
[20] I am assuming that Bradford meant John, not William, Lawrence, and that a further error was made in inserting William, not John, Kempe, Also, Barry's name appears as 'John Barr'. Although a John Barrett was a Bocking conventicler, Barry is more likely here (unless they were one and the same person). Gibson was surely the 'Master Gibson' referred to above, p. 141. Names were clearly a problem for Bradford at the time. See the editor's note in Bradford, II, 194. See pp. 159 – 63 below for a detailed account of the role of Barry and Lawrence.
[21] Garret, p. 258.
[22] Foxe, VIII, 576 – 8.
[23] Garrett, p. 258.
[24] *Ibid.*, p. 262.
[25] Foxe, VII, 329, 335.
[26] Bradford, II, 194.

particularly those relating to the issue of predestination. He expressed his confidence in the integrity of his 'little Treatise' on the subject, and warned his readers again about the folly of presumptuous inquiry into secret things. He also asked them to regard each other in a generous and sincere light. After a digression on the relationship between law and Gospel and the outer and inner man,[27] Bradford assured the disputants that his counsel, if followed, would certainly put an end to 'all controversies for predestination, original sin, free-will' and the like. He reiterated his conviction that they were all true saints, despite the continuing doubts about his motives and sincerity which some of them entertained. Apparently some were still suggesting that he was upholding his doctrine in order to secure material gains or, rather curiously, to spread 'desperation'. As a proof of his love, he had not permitted copies of his treatise on predestination to be taken overseas, so as to keep the matter within the local setting and ensure that the offending participants would not come to public disgrace.[28]

As February wore on and Bradford's period of grace was extended, many rumours circulated concerning his status in an attempt to demoralize the other Protestant prisoners. One such report, which came to Ridley at Oxford, claimed that Bradford had been fully reconciled to Catholicism and was on excellent terms with Gardiner.[29] Nothing could have been further from the truth, of course, even though Bradford was being pressured from several quarters. On 21 March, he was visited by Dr Hugh Weston, Dean of Westminster and Archdeacon of Essex. Weston later presided at Cranmer's trial.[30] Then, on 30 March, one of Bradford's comrades, Robert Ferrar, went bravely to the stake. Cutbert Symson, now a trusted supporter of the Reformed cause,[31] received the death sentence on 25 May and awaited execution.[32] Two other ex-freewillers from the original Kentish conventicle, Nicholas Sheterden from Pluckley and Humphrey Middleton of Ashford, were condemned on 25 June. Sheterden, who had undergone a lengthy examination at the hands of Harpsfield and Collens, had handled himself with distinction in adversity. The discussions centred mainly on the topic of transubstantiation.

During the course of his ordeal, Sheterden made passing reference to 'the error of the Anabaptists, which deny that Christ took flesh of

[27] *Ibid.*, 196.
[28] *Ibid.*, 197.
[29] Coverdale, fol. 66.
[30] *DNB*, XX, 1272.
[31] Foxe, VII, 26.
[32] Strype, *EM*, III, 1, 347.

the Virgin Mary'. He gave evidence that he wanted no part of such doctrine, and in doing so served to confirm the popular but not altogether accurate association between Anabaptist radicalism in England and the doctrine of the celestial flesh of Christ.[33] Sheterden was also examined by Gardiner and Richard Thornenden, suffragan Bishop of Dover.[34] He and Middleton, along with two other Kentishmen, were burned at Canterbury on 12 July after being held in Westgate for some time. A third member of the original Kentish cell, George Brodebridge of Broomfield, suffered likewise at Canterbury on 6 September along with several other men from the county. It is not clear whether Brodebridge ever abandoned his radical views on election and freewill, as he was examined only on the standard articles which dealt with auricular confession, the real presence in the sacrament, and other matters pertaining to Catholic worship. Each of these items was firmly rejected by Brodebridge who maintained that a priest could not even effect the forgiveness of his own sins, much less someone else's. He also viewed the Eucharist as a memorial of Christ's death in the Zwinglian sense.[35] It is likely that Brodebridge's widow followed him to the stake in June 1557.[36]

Meanwhile, Bradford's time had finally come. On 1 July 1555 his execution took place at Smithfield.[37] Ridley had noted his friend's approaching death in a letter to Bernhere some time beforehand, expressing his admiration for Bradford and his gratitude for the privilege of knowing him.[38] Bradford had evidently continued to rely on Bernhere's services up to the end and had urged the messenger to be 'merry' in expectation of Bradford's early departure to a better kingdom.[39]

Ridley and Latimer were spared until the following October when, on the 15th, they suffered for heresy at Oxford.[40] Ridley had evidently carried his strong aversion toward Anabaptism to the grave, as the subject was broached on at least two occasions during his formal examinations. In one instance, he was reminded of the gravity of causing schism within the church and of separating from the fellowship of the same. His accuser mentioned that Ridley had been 'reported to have hated the sect of the Anabaptists' and had always 'impugned' them in his dealings with them. How could he then, in all good conscience, separate himself from the Catholic Church?

[33] Foxe, VII, 307.
[34] *Ibid.*, 310 – 12.
[35] *Ibid.*, 383.
[36] *Ibid.*, VIII, 326.
[37] Strype, *EM*, III, 1, 355 – 6.
[38] Coverdale, vol. 73.
[39] *Ibid.*, fol. 470.
[40] Strype, *EM*, III, 1, 361.

Ridley responded by stating his conviction that the Roman mass was not true communion, thus implying that his position was justifiable. The Anabaptists, however, along with the Novatians, constituted a different case entirely. He declared:

> The sect of the Anabaptists, and the heresy of the Novatians, ought of right to be condemned, forasmuch as without any just or necessary cause they wickedly separated themselves from the communion of the congregation, for they did not allege that the sacraments were unduly ministered, but, turning away their eyes from themselves, wherewith according to St. Paul's rule they ought to examine themselves, and casting their eyes ever upon others, either ministers, or communicants with them, they always reproved something for the which they abstained from the communion, as from an unholy thing.[41]

Here, Ridley echoed the earlier sentiments of both Calvin and Zwingli, who had accused the continental radicals of unjustifiable schism and excessive spiritual presumption.[42]

In the second reported case, Ridley was again defending his stance with respect to the Catholic Church. The Bishop of Lincoln charged that Ridley, in the days of Edward VI, had once encouraged Gardiner to staunchly defend the Eucharist against the Anabaptists. How could he now oppose the said sacrament of the English Church which he had once exhorted others to maintain? Ridley then clarified the issue, explaining that his major concern at that time had been to see Gardiner come to a proper understanding of justification by faith. In the face of resistance, Ridley had also urged Gardiner to 'be diligent in confounding' the Anabaptists, who were then rising up against 'the sacrament of the altar'.[43] Ridley further explained: 'In this sense I willed my lord to be stiff in the defence of the sacrament against the detestable errors of the Anabaptists, and not in the confirmation of that gross and carnal opinion now maintained'.[44] Thus, in explaining his attitudes toward the doctrines and practices of the English Church during these years of religious fluctuation and instability, Ridley left behind his final comments on the shortcomings of the Anabaptist movement.

[41] Foxe, VII, 411.
[42] For the issues at stake between the radicals and Calvin and Zwingli see Williams, pp. 138, 597.
[43] Foxe, VII, 522 – 3; Cf. Strype, EM II, 1, 107 – 8. See above, p. 49, regarding Ridley and Gardiner and some Kentish Anabaptists.
[44] Foxe, VII, 523.

The next reformer involved with the predestinarian controversy to bear the rigours of examination was John Philpot, formerly Archdeacon of Winchester and now an inmate in Bonner's 'coalhouse'. On 2 October 1555, Philpot was brought before the Queen's commissioners at Newgate Sessions,[45] and went through the first of at least sixteen formal inquisitions. Philpot had undoubtedly become a key member of the predestinarian party, as he had been a resident of the King's Bench during the early days of his confinement.[46] His closest friend since the death of Bradford was John Careless, the weaver from Coventry, with whom he carried on a steady correspondence. As indicated, the Reformed cause was depending more and more upon Careless's leadership and Philpot served as a close adviser. Philpot was kept closely informed of Careless's recurring problems with the radicals in the King's Bench,[47] and urged him to be steadfast against the 'arrogant and self-will-blinded scatterers' there. He also explained that such 'sects' were necessary in order to test and beautify the faith of the righteous.

Philpot carried on Bradford's plea for unity and charity among brothers. Presumably, this charity did not have to be extended to outright heretics, as Philpot was once found spitting upon an Arian he had encountered who was attempting to 'pervert some of his own heresy'.[48] He was also involved in the defence of infant baptism in the prisons, as he was asked to furnish an apologetical basis for the doctrine amidst considerable debate on the subject.[49] He argued that the practice was rooted in the Scriptures and used in the primitive church, and stated that its abuse in the Catholic Church did not destroy its validity. Nor did the Anabaptists succeed in undermining it, even though they were 'an inordinate kind of men stirred up by the devil, to the destruction of the gospel'.[50] These Anabaptists were full of lies and innovative fantasies, since they declared 'the baptism of children to be the pope's commandment'.[51]

Ironically, Philpot was falsely associated with Anabaptism himself during one of his private conferences with Bonner.[52] Bonner's accusation came in response to Philpot's reluctance to swear an oath at the giving of his testimony. Philpot vehemently denied that he was

---

[45] *Ibid.*, 606.
[46] Strype, *EM*, III, 1, 437.
[47] John Philpot, *The Examinations and Writings of John Philpot*, ed. Robert Eden, Parker Society, No. 34 (Cambridge: University Press, 1842), p.247.
[48] Strype, *EM*, III, 1, 435.
[49] Philpot, pp. 271 – 84.
[50] *Ibid.*, p. 274.
[51] *Ibid.*, p. 280.
[52] Foxe, VII, 646.

an Anabaptist and explained that he refused simply because Bonner was not his ordinary. He was then accused of other enormities, such as maintaining that God was 'the author of all sin and wickedness'[53] – perhaps an allusion to Philpot's predestinarian position. Philpot's examinations continued throughout November and the early part of December, his condemnation coming on 16 December and his execution two days later.[54]

The account of John Trewe

With Philpot gone, the Reformed prisoners had lost yet another spokesman, and the burden of leadership continued to fall increasingly upon the shoulders of John Careless as the new year dawned. Such leadership was crucial, for at this very point one of the freewill radicals in the King's Bench composed his personal account of the controversy.[55] The author, John Trewe of Kent, had been apprehended in his native county 'for dissuading not to come to the church'. His ears were then cut off as punishment for his behaviour.[56] It is possible that Trewe had been one of the original Faversham conventiclers, and further that his family may have come from Sussex originally since he refers to the county in personal terms during the course of making an analogy.[57]

Although it cannot be determined exactly when Trewe entered the King's Bench, it is evident that he made his presence felt from the beginning. As a leader of the freewillers, Trewe became something of a target for the Reformed group and reported in his opening remarks that he had been the victim of numerous slanders and hurts at the hands of those who had been 'the beginners of this lamentable contention'.[58] He had been reluctant to set forth his case, however, in the hope that his opponents would mend their ways so that concord could be established. Such agreement had seemed likely on several occasions, particularly during the Christmas season of 1555.

---

[53] *Ibid.*, 646. When his fellow prisoners likewise refused to swear and testify falsely against him, they were also described as Anabaptists by the taunting Bishop.
[54] *Ibid.*, 628 – 85. See especially 678 – 85. Cf. VIII, 333.
[55] This account is one of the items printed by Laurence from the original Bodleian MS, 53, fols. 116 – 26. See Laurence, 'John Trewe . . . signifieth the cause of contention in the King's Bench, as concerning sects in religion, the 30th of January, Anno Dom. 1555', pp. 37 – 70. The date as listed at the beginning of the tract was based on the old calendar. Hence, it should read 1556 according to current usage.
[56] Foxe, VIII, Appendix, No. VI.
[57] Laurence, p. 42.
[58] *Ibid.*, p.37.

Yet negotiations had ultimately broken down, and Trewe was reported to have been responsible for the failure. He now felt compelled to write his apologetic so that no further evil might be spoken against him by ignorant persons and so that the blame might be placed where it was due.

As Trewe began to unfold his story he made rather astounding revelations regarding the origins of the predestinarian controversy. The most critical of these indicated that the battle began over a difference in opinion concerning the normal Christian lifestyle and not over the questions of election and freewill themselves. Trewe was upset with his Reformed cell-mates over the manner in which they spent their many idle hours, particularly 'by their use of gaming', which in Trewe's view did much damage to the weaker consciences in the prison. He and his comrades had felt it was their duty to 'gently admonish' their fellows and urge them to abandon their pastime in favour of redeeming the time during such evil days. They also encouraged their companions to mourn over England's miserable plight and pray for persevering strength in the face of adversity, since 'these sharp storms of persecution, the which (through this our sloth) was like to drive many one from God unto the devil'. Thus, Trewe saw the nation as being directly under the judgement of God at that point owing to its spiritual declension. He and his compatriots were in a state of mourning 'for the great misery that is fallen on this land, and for the lamentable perplexity that many of our weak brethren (that were not able to bear the cross) were in'. Though his anxiety was undoubtedly sharpened through the rigours of forced confinement, perhaps coming close to the point of loss of perspective, there is no doubt that Trewe and his colleagues were most sincere in their concern for their country and her languishing people, nor that Henry Harte and others of similar persuasion would be in complete agreement about both the diagnosis and the cure of the spiritual malaise.

Not surprisingly, the gaming faction was not at all convinced by these supplications, and attempted to justify their conduct through the usage of Scripture. This effort was stoutly resisted by Trewe's party which brought forth other passages that suggested a different interpretation. As time went on, Trewe and his mates were accused of being 'justifiers' of themselves since they were piously devoted to prayer and fasting.[59] They answered that their 'justification came by faith in Christ's death and bloodshedding' and stated that they had purposed not to be among those who would fall from steadfastness during the coming persecutions. Their opponents replied that 'none

[59] *Ibid.*, p. 38.

of them that God ordained to be saved, could be driven from him by persecution, nor yet by any other occasion or means'.[60] This was due to divine election and predestination which had occurred prior to the world's foundation, so that none of the chosen ones could ever be lost. Trewe's group believed this doctrine to be false, since to them it encouraged licence and libertinism. They even felt they could see this demonstrated before their eyes, as they observed that 'many did fly to their utter destruction, by means of the said false doctrine'. At this point in the proceedings, Trewe's delegation asked their opponents to account for the many Scriptural warnings and injunctions against participation in sinfulness if none of the elect could ultimately perish.[61] The Reformed exponents replied that the threats and warnings were made in order to instil a proper fear toward the performance of evil in the elect, and not to raise fear about everlasting destruction. Trewe's company once more objected. To them, this was similar to stating 'that the words of the/ Holy Ghost doth no more good, than a man of clouts with a bow in his hand doth in a corn field, which will keep away the vermin crows awhile, but when they know it what it is, they will fall down beside it, and devour the corn without fear'.[62]

Trewe and his fellows were also alarmed by the Calvinist interpretation of reprobation. Trewe could not accept the suggestion that God had created some men for damnation, and that their plight could not be avoided by any means. This appeared to be showing 'partiality', since God had thereby chosen some for salvation while others were arbitrarily selected for damnation. How then could man's moral responsibility be upheld, and how could one escape referring to the Creator as the author of sin and evil? For 'he that maketh a thing only to do evil is the cause of the evil'.[63] Yet the supporters of election and reprobation made 'much of God' and His justice in their conversation,[64] even though He appears to offer salvation to men who can never receive it. How then can He be grieved over the death of the wicked and yet bring their destruction to pass at the same time?[65]

Evidently Trewe and the other freewillers also resented the Reformed camp's support of higher learning. They had clearly been

[60] *Ibid.*, pp. 38 – 9.
[61] *Ibid.*, p. 39.
[62] *Ibid.*, p. 40. Others in the predestinarian ranks seemed to stress that the situations related to the warnings were merely hypothetical, so that there was little or no possibility that the end in view would ever be actualized. The freewillers believed that this position did much harm to the church, and also belittled the glory of God.
[63] *Ibid.*, p. 42.
[64] *Ibid.*, p. 43.
[65] *Ibid.*, p. 44.

irritated by the assertion that only 'great learned men could have the true understanding of the word of God'. At the same time, Trewe noticed how intolerant his opponents became at the constant proddings of the freewillers. He accused his adversaries of 'defacing, displacing, and washing away' pertinent biblical texts, and could never support their position and maintain his personal integrity; for all would be dependent upon divine foreordination, and nothing upon 'God's assistance in our perseverance'.[66]

Trewe continued his account by referring to another basic tenet of the Reformed prisoners – one which he had not yet clearly dealt with, even though he had alluded to it at several points. This concerned the extent of Christ's atoning death. Trewe regarded the suggestion that Christ had not suffered 'for all men' as horrendous, since to him it made Christ and His work seem inferior to the 'first Adam'. He was also concerned lest men be lost in despair in their anxiety over their standing, not knowing whether Christ actually died for them or not. Trewe saw the Reformed position as something of a paradox at this point, in that it seemed to undermine the very certainty of election and salvation which it allegedly sought to establish. Thus, 'none of them' could be 'certain' (if they believe their ancient writers) 'before their end, whether Christ died for [them] or not'.[67] According to Trewe, he and his fellows figured 'they did in effect destroy the thing they in words went about to build most strongly', that being the certainty that Christ's atoning death was 'for them'. Instead of adopting the paradox, one should establish '[that he] is in the state of salvation, and one of God's elect children, and shall certainly be saved' through repentance and faith, and by remaining faithful unto the end. This synergistic interpretation was too much for the Calvinist supporters in the prison, however, and they began to decry the freewillers as heretics and refused to eat with them or even exchange greetings. The freewillers were thus gradually ostracized, lest they have opportunity to spread their views among other prisoners. Yet the Reformed group campaigned vociferously in support of their own cause. Trewe also suspected that certain monies had been unjustly withheld from the freewillers during this period.[68]

At this point in his narrative, Trewe felt it necessary to number the predestinarian 'enormities' comprehensively, so that they would be impressed upon his readers' minds. These he gathered in a total of twenty-three points, many of which simply repeated earlier claims.

[66] *Ibid.*, p. 45.
[67] *Ibid.*, pp. 45–6.
[68] *Ibid.*, p. 47.

He highlighted the horrors of reprobation,[69] the belittling of Christ's atonement,[70] and the futility of moral effort and fostering of anxiety.[71] He argued that human 'experience' was sufficient 'to confute' the opposition's argument at one point, even 'if there were no Scriptures written' to effectively do the same. He seemed to be arguing then, that the predestinarian position went against nature in a most fundamental and unthinkable manner, almost as if to say that one would be better off not being born than brought into such a horrendous state of affairs. Sounding like Harte, he warned of the impending judgement of God upon the nation's toleration of error,[72] and bemoaned the fact that many simple persons were being discouraged from reading the Scriptures in their revulsion against the predestinarian explanations.[73] The fact that the predestinarians were alleging 'that no simple man without the tongues can truly understand' the Scriptures was obviously not helping the freewillers to see eye to eye with their rivals either. Nor was the atmosphere improved when, as Trewe soon recounted, the Reformed bloc issued a threat that the freewillers 'were like to die for it, if the Gospel should reign again, affirming, that the true church might shed blood for believers' sake'.[74] Thus, if moral suasion and argumentation was inadequate during the controversy, there seemed to be precious little reluctance to adopt the tactic of intimidation.

Following his doctrinal summary, Trewe continued with his narrative of events up to January 1556, relating that his colleagues were still willing to forgive their opponents despite all that had transpired. In fact, they had recently made a generous overture to the Reformed prisoners and had been received with warmth at first. The predestinarians had agreed to desist from proclaiming their views, but, according to Trewe, they quickly broke their promise and began slandering the freewillers and racking the Scriptures. There was heated disagreement over the question of baptism, as the freewillers would not agree that children might be lawfully baptized 'in the church of the Antichrist'.[75] Yet another cause of renewed disruption was a public lecture given by the predestinarians, in which they maintained that 'play and pastimes' were fit for Christian men since all things cleansed by God were approved for His people.

[69] *Ibid.*, pp. 48 – 9.
[70] *Ibid.*, pp. 49 – 50.
[71] *Ibid.*, pp. 50 – 52.
[72] *Ibid.*, p. 51.
[73] *Ibid.*, pp. 53 – 4. This seems to have been a constant theme of the south-eastern radicals.
[74] *Ibid.*, pp. 56 – 7.
[75] *Ibid.*, p. 55. Thus, the issue was not the propriety of infant baptism itself.

Evidently the games which the prisoners were accustomed to play included 'bowls, dice, and cards', and Trewe observed that participation was not possible 'without many idle words'.[76] As Knappen has pointed out, puritanism and ascetecism were not yet bedfellows as far as the predestinarian party was concerned,[77] and it seems somewhat ironic that the forerunners of the mature Puritan movement should have been criticized for such idleness. Undoubtedly the plight of being incarcerated would lend itself to these occupations, although as already seen, the prisoners were sometimes granted generous liberties by sympathetic captors so that certain worthwhile activities could be pursued in confinement. It must have been this factor which lay behind Trewe's rationale and prompted his irritation.

With the sudden turn of events, the freewillers began to lose all hope of reconciliation and decided to withdraw voluntarily from their opponents. Shortly after this, on a date not specified by Trewe, a number of prisoners were unexpectedly released from confinement. Included in this group were Cutbert Symson, now a leader in the Reformed camp, Thomas Upcher or Upshire of Bocking, and Richard Woodman from Sussex.[78] Woodman, an iron-maker, received only a temporary reprieve, as he ultimately suffered for his obstinacy in June 1557.[79] Foxe relates that Woodman had been first arrested in the spring of 1554 and had then spent over a year in the King's Bench before being transferred to Bonner's 'coalhouse' for another eight weeks.[80] Then, on 18 December 1555, he was delivered from the 'butcher's hands' along with four other men and directed to prove himself to be a full member of 'the true catholic church'. He was known to have written a confession of faith while in the King's Bench, and had endorsed the validity of infant christening even when performed by 'papistical ministers'.[81] Perhaps it was this admission which helped secure his release.

---

[76] *Ibid.*, p. 56.

[77] Knappen, p. 150.

[78] Laurence, p. 57; Foxe, VIII, 333.

[79] Foxe, VIII, 377.

[80] *Ibid.*, 334.

[81] Burrage, I, 54. He was rearrested in spring 1557, apparently with the compliance of his family, and went through an arduous series of examinations at the hands of the persecuting authorities. During his initial imprisonment in the King's Bench, he wrote a confession of faith which seems to touch on some of the matters mentioned by Trewe in his treatise. Woodman firmly expressed his disagreement with certain Anabaptist views, perhaps in an effort to clear himself from any speculation regarding involvement with the freewillers. He also stated his belief that children who were baptized by Catholic priests were 'truly baptized notwithstanding that the minister be a popish heretic'. This would confirm Trewe's account, in that the Reformed group came to the same conclusion in their deliberations. Foxe, VIII, 332 – 77; Burrage, I, 27, 54.

Woodman's role in the prison dispute seems to have diminished following his deliverance. The same could not be said of Upcher and Symson, however, as they both remained active and vigilant in the Reformed cause. Trewe mentioned that Symson had approached the freewillers at this time, probably just prior to Christmas Day 1555. Symson made a plea for 'unity in the truth', something which the freewillers also desired but only on certain conditions.[82] The predestinarians were to refrain from propagating their views as they had promised before, although the freewillers conceded that they might retain their beliefs privately. The 'order' of this proposed unity was placed in the hands of Symson and the others, and while the necessary approbations were being solicited from the rest, temporary peace and harmony prevailed. Before the treaty could be brought to a fitting conclusion, however, a delegation from the Reformed party approached the freewillers on or about 22 December and announced that a communion service was planned for Christmas Day. The freewillers were welcome to participate if they so desired, but if not, the Calvinists would proceed on their own. At first, the radicals were reluctant to commit themselves, as Trewe explained:

> We answered, that we would gladly receive with them, but we would have the unity thoroughly established first, lest we did receive it to our damnation; for we take the communion to be (as it is) a thing of great efficacy and bond of peace, perpetual love, and perfection, that men should well examine themselves, whether they were in perfect love, and through God's gift and assistance able to keep the promise they make by receiving thereof.[83]

Despite their caution, the radicals were anxious not to cause offence in the light of this gracious request. In order to expedite negotiations, they asked the Reformed prisoners to declare them all to be orthodox Christians, since the predestinarians had previously branded them as heretics. The Reformed side agreed, provided that Trewe's company would return the favour and recognize the Calvinists to be rightful members of the universal Church. Here a snag developed as the freewillers maintained that they had never 'slandered' the predestinarians. Hence there was no need for a declaration on their part. Following another period of uneasy negotiations, reconciliation was finally attained without formal written declarations, and on the following day the Reformed delegation returned with a statement of faith for both sides to sign.

[82] Laurence, p. 57.
[83] *Ibid.*, p. 58.

Trewe was ecstatic at the thought of concord, and even tried to overlook some perceived weaknesses in the articles so that his comrades would commit themselves and sign the document. This they did, despite Trewe's personal reservations. Within a short time, however, Trewe's conscience began to trouble him because he had consented. He then lapsed into despair and sickness. After a few hours had passed, the man whom Trewe described as 'the chief of their company', John Careless, came to visit him to learn the reason for his depressed state. When he heard, he attempted to allay Trewe's fears. Being unsuccessful, he promised to consult Trewe's colleagues about having Trewe's name deleted from the statement if the others remained affixed. Careless then left Trewe in the hope that he would change his mind by the morrow and went to visit Trewe's comrades.[84]

Careless must have been greatly alarmed at the reception he then received. Trewe's mates had also become dissatisfied with the articles, but agreed to support yet another confession if Trewe would approve it. On the next day, 24 December 1555, Careless returned to check on Trewe's state of mind and found him in even greater despair, since the communion service which he had rashly agreed to attend was just one day off. Careless was clearly disturbed at Trewe's plight, and assured him of his love even without the presence of written articles. This gave Trewe a measure of relief, and Careless persisted in seeking formal agreement with the more moderate freewillers. But these men went to Trewe immediately and asked for help in drafting a suitable confession. Trewe consented warily and rendered the desired service. When Careless was shown the final draft, however, he protested against the 'heresies' it contained and refused to sign. Thus Trewe's worst fears were realized, as Careless 'brake off the unity' and then attributed the blame to Trewe.[85]

Careless also began to pronounce written slanders against the freewillers in a 'book', even though the radicals still wanted reconciliation. They were particularly accused of holding Melchiorite views on the atonement of Christ. Trewe wrote that it was being reported that the freewillers denied 'that Christ was come in the flesh, and that he passed through the blessed Virgin Mary, as saffron doth through a bag'.[86] Trewe affirmed, however, that his company abhorred that 'detestable opinion'. In doing so, it seems as if they were clearly dissociating themselves from a basic characteristic of

---

[84] *Ibid.*, p. 61.
[85] *Ibid.*, p. 62.
[86] *Ibid.*, p. 63.

Dutch Anabaptism — and also of native English nonconformity.[87]

Further proof of the orthodoxy of the moderate freewillers was offered in a series of articles which Trewe attached to his treatise as the concluding section. He stated that he had not done so with malicious intent, but only to clear the air surrounding the affair so that the horrible doctrines of his opponents might be fully exposed and many men spared ruination.[88] The first two articles were critical in the light of previous accusations, as Trewe affirmed the traditional doctrine of the Trinity in the initial one and examined the Person of Christ in the second. He declared that Christ, the 'eternal Son' of God, was the means whereby believers are brought to their inheritance as the sons of God 'through Election'. It was also stated that Christ 'took so much flesh and blood and nourishment of the blessed Virgin Mary, as any child doth of his mother'. Moreover, in Christ are seen 'two perfect natures, the Godhead and manhood . . . perfectly joined together . . . never to be divided'.[89]

The third article in Trewe's confession endorsed the ancient faith of the Church as set down in the Apostles' Creed, while the fourth stressed the grace of God in the work of redemption to the exclusion of all human merit. Christ's offering of Himself was sufficient for the sins of Adam and 'all and singular of his posterity's sins' as well. Those who repent and persevere to the end shall no doubt be saved. Fifthly, the responsibility of man to keep the perfect law of God was stated. This precluded participation in 'vain gaming' and communications with false sects. He also warned against presumptuous inquiry into God's secrets, and expressed sorrow on behalf of his supporters for the offences committed during the contention. They promised never to engage in such divisive activities again with the help of God.[90]

The sixth article contained the prisoners' somewhat surprising acknowledgement that true religion had prevailed in England under Edward VI, as the sacraments had been properly administered and the Scriptures adequately expounded.[91] The last item was a final plea for unity, even if it meant that some matters had to remain

---

[87] Again, it appears that Trewe represented a moderate segment within the freewill party in denying these tenets, although it is perhaps difficult to imagine that Careless would have raised the issue without some justification.

[88] Laurence, p. 64.

[89] *Ibid.*, pp. 65 – 6.

[90] *Ibid.*, p. 67.

[91] *Ibid.*, pp. 67 – 8. It would seem that Trewe could not be legitimately accused of being an Anabaptist if he genuinely approved of the sacramental system under Edward VI. Of course, his opinion may not have been accepted by all of the Kentish freewillers, since some appear to have distanced themselves from the established Church prior to the middle of Edward's reign.

unresolved. Clearly, neither side was benefiting from the debate and the glory of God was being severely denigrated. Trewe also hoped that where their views were defective each side would be made to see the truth. Far from playing the role of the irresponsible separatist, Trewe, like Harte, was genuinely concerned about the welfare of the church of Christ in his native land. He seemed to be saying that he repudiated Calvinist doctrine because its implications were unacceptable and indeed dangerous. Furthermore, they were demoralizing and dehumanizing. They gave evidence of a different human spirit than that possessed by Trewe and his fellows, and also reflected a depressing view of life and the world where everything was uncertain and potentially frightening: where a man could not be sure whether he was loved by his Creator or not, where God did not operate according to accepted human standards of equity and justice, and where it was acceptable for some men to have an eternal advantage over others without reference to anything in either the chosen or the rejected.

At the end of these articles twelve signatures were affixed. These were the moderates among the freewillers who were willing to achieve concord at the expense of further doctrinal definition.[92] Most of them were secondary figures in the fray, with the exception of Trewe himself and two of his co-signatories. The second signatory, Thomas Avington, was known to have been a turner from Ardingly,[93] and he played a key role in the freewillers' programme until his execution at Lewes on 31 May 1556. The third man to sign, Richard Harman, came from Westhothlegh in Sussex and had been committed to the King's Bench on 27 May 1554, 'for his leude and sedytious behaviour' there.[94] Harman was probably a Merchant Adventurer with connexions at Cranbrook in Kent and seems to have been apprehended for Lutheran leanings at Antwerp back in July 1528. At the time of his arrest he was corresponding with Thomas Davy, a clothier from Cranbrook, who advised Harman to hold fast to the truth with patience. Davy was also concerned about the suppression of the Gospel in the vernacular — a subject with which the Faversham radicals could readily identify. Another of Harman's correspondents at that time was James Andrews, who also seems to have been a Cranbrook clothier.[95] Andrews was eventually imprisoned in the

[92] *Ibid.*, pp. 69 – 70.
[93] Foxe, VIII, 151.
[94] *APC*, V, 28.
[95] The relatively high incidence of clothiers involved in this type of activity in this part of the Weald is reminiscent of the situation at Bocking, where once again two local suppliers were implicated. The opposition to the suppression of the Scriptures in the vernacular is also highly significant and opens the question of the relationship between

Fleet for heresy.[96] The subject of his letter to Harman had been the New Testament,[97] obviously a topic of crucial importance then, especially since Warham's order of 3 November 1526 to search for Tyndale's translation and other works deemed heretical. Just how and when Harman became identified with radical activity in Sussex is unknown, but his early association with Kent and the continent provides another fascinating illustration of how the cloth industry and the spread of nonconformist ideas went hand in hand during the Tudor years.

Of the remaining nine persons who signed Trewe's confession, at least one, John Saxby of Colchester, was eventually released from prison after making a moderate submission to the English Church in 1557.[98] Two others, John Jackson and Cornelius Stevenson, had been jointly involved in a previous incident when Stevenson allegedly defected from the freewillers' ranks.[99] Thomas Read was probably an associate of Avington, as the two were executed together in Sussex in June of 1556.[100] In addition, one of the subscribers was a woman. Her name was Margery Russell, but there are no further clues as to her career and identity.

The discussion continues: Barry and Lawrence

With the air supposedly cleared as far as the moderates in the freewill camp were concerned, the onus appeared to be upon the Reformed party to issue some sort of rejoinder. This pressure may have prompted a statement of faith drawn up by a King's Bench inmate, John Clement, who was described by Foxe as a wheelwright.[101] His work, 'A Confession and Protestation of the Christian Faith', was evidently intended to express the mainstream Reformed orthodoxy of the remaining predestinarian prisoners in the light of various heresies then rife within the realm.[102] Clement appears to have been a

economic prosperity and the growth in independent thinking in the south-east during these years.
[96] Peter Clark, *English Provincial Society*, p. 31.
[97] *VCH*, II, 65.
[98] Foxe, VIII, 310.
[99] See below, p. 166.
[100] Foxe, VIII, 151.
[101] *Ibid.*; Strype, *EM*, III, 1, 586.
[102] Strype refers to those who denied 'original sin, the doctrine of predestination and free election', and the baptism of children to the detriment of the realm, so that even 'true professors' of the Gospel were suspected of scandalous activities.

concerned, articulate layman who helped to continue the Reformed tradition following the martyrdom and flight of the more learned worthies. Unlike many of his contemporaries, Clement died within the confines of the King's Bench itself and was buried behind it on 25 June 1556.

Clearer efforts to defend the Calvinist view of predestination, perhaps partly in response to Trewe's claims, were also forthcoming from the pen of Augustine Bernhere. Bernhere, while continuing to support the underground Protestant congregation in London, wrote at least two treatises on election.[103] The second of these drew forth a reply from the two Essex freewillers serving as messengers to their party in prison – John Lawrence and John Barry.[104] The latter was described as a servant to Lawrence at Barnehall in Essex, which may have been located between Bocking and Colchester on Marks Tay.[105] As already noted, these men were likely included in Bradford's address to the south-eastern disputants,[106] and they were assisted in their labours by Lawrence's brother-in-law, John Jeffrey. This trio used to reside 'at an alehouse in Cornhill' when they came to London.[107] They were once described as being the 'greatest' among the radical troublemakers, being most effective 'in persuading the people'.

The alehouse in Cornhill was evidently something of a focal point for nonconformist activity, as allegations were made against other dissenters who resorted frequently to the same establishment. Many of these were originally from Colchester, and it was said that three of them were residents of the King's Head tavern there when not in London.[108] This tavern was obviously a meeting-house for religious

---

[103] Oxford, Bodleian Library, Bodleian MSS, 53, fols. 103 – 16, 126 – 38.

[104] *Ibid.*, fols. 138 – 40.

[105] Foxe, VIII, 384. Although the precise location of Barnehall is difficult to determine, a portion of land on Marks Tay was sold by one John Lawrence on 8 November 1555. The Lawrence family was evidently quite prominent at the time, which may account for Barry's servitude. Another possible location would be the village of Barnes, situated slightly to the east of Chelmsford and south of the road to Colchester. Philip Morant, *The History and Antiquities of the County of Essex* (Chelmsford, 1816 rep.; orig. pub. 1768), II, 204.

[106] See above, p. 143.

[107] Foxe, VIII, 384.

[108] *Ibid.* These three had been 'preachers' under the previous reign. One of them, 'Master Pulleyne', eventually fled to the continent and joined Knox's congregation in June 1557. Here, he was a collaborator on the Geneva Bible, and was one of the last exiles to return to England following the death of Mary. Upon his return, he was arrested near Colchester in 1559 for unlicensed preaching. At this time, he was found in the company of John Dodman, a man who had previously been listed in the party of Lawrence and Barry at the Cornhill alehouse. Pullain had once served as rector of nearby St Peter's prior to his deprivation in 1555, and was appointed Archdeacon of

activists in the Colchester area, and it was undoubtedly the same 'inn' where Barry argued with the continental radical, Christopher Vitel, over the divinity of Christ around Michaelmas 1555.[109] Vitel had been proclaiming many unique tenets since his arrival in England and his reputation spread quickly. Barry and two female supporters were soon at the scene ready to defend the divinity of Christ. Vitel, however, clearly won the day due to his superior debating skills, astonishing many in the tavern by his constant 'babbling'. His encounter with Barry is most significant in connexion with the King's Bench controversy, for it underscores the orthodoxy of the by now moderate freewill party — at least as far as the doctrine of the Trinity is concerned. It also demonstrates that issues other than election and freewill were worth fighting for among the English radical forces.

Barry's major contribution was his work with Lawrence in response to Bernhere, presumably early in 1556. Their reply is important to the study of English freewill thought before Arminius because of its rationality and assertiveness, as it gives evidence of a growing sophistication in freewill fundamentals. Apparently the freewillers had left 'a writing' earlier with Bernhere or his companions at Bartholomewtide, and the two sides had also had a personal encounter. As a result of these developments, a reply from Bernhere on the matter of reprobation had been expected. When his treatise arrived, Barry and Lawrence could only marvel at Bernhere's importunity in presenting his case.

Bernhere had obviously accused the freewillers of holding to some form of universal salvation, as they were reported to believe that 'God

---

Essex by Grindal in 1560. Dodman, who came from Hadleigh in Suffolk, may have accompanied Pullain to the continent, and was later given the livings of East Mersea and Bentley in Essex. The relationship of these men to Barry and Lawrence is far from clear, although they all seem to have resorted to the same alehouse on a regular basis. Apparently, news of a subversive kind could always be obtained at this establishment, as well as at its counterpart in Colchester. Garrett, pp. 262 – 3, 145; Foxe, VII, 738.

[109] William Wilkinson, *A Confutation of Certaine Articles Delivered Unto the Family of Love*, The English Experience, No. 279 (Amsterdam: Da Capo Press, 1970; orig. pub. 1579), RSTC 25665, sig. iiiiz; Strype, *Annals*, II, 2, 284. For a recent evaluation of Vitel's career in England, see Martin, 'Christopher Vitel: an Elizabethan Mechanick Preacher', *Sixteenth Century Journal*, X (1979), 15 – 22. According to Martin, Vitel was the leader of the Family of Love in England throughout the 1570s. The Familists had originated on the continent around 1540 under the leadership of the radical, Hendrik Niclaes, who in turn had apparently looked to the Davidjorists for inspiration. Joris himself had been prominent at the 1536 Bocholt Conference, but shortly thereafter began to withdraw himself from public contact and concentrated upon mystical pursuits. Similarly, Niclaes was prone to pantheistic speculations, and was said to have claimed to be deity incarnate. Thus, it is significant that Vitel was found arguing about the deity of Christ on this occasion with the freewillers, for the incident serves as an

hath generally chosen all men to salvation'.[110] Accordingly, none could ultimately perish, since all were included in the election of God. Barry and Lawrence, however, were most offended by this accusation, as they did not believe that ungodly men could be included in the decree at all as long as they remained in their sinful condition. In fact, the majority of people seemed to fall into this undesirable category and were thus excluded from 'the election'.[111] They advised Bernhere that he might have 'spared' the time and effort expended on behalf of his cause. It was true that they accepted the universal choosing of all men 'in Christ' prior to creation, but this was dramatically altered by the sin of Adam, whereby all men fell 'to damnation and condemnation'.[112] Since that point, only 'those that be sanctified by the spirit and believe the truth' are to be reckoned as being among the elect of God.[113] .

The freewillers were further disturbed by Bernhere's discussion of the two-fold will of God, as he had distinguished between God's 'revealed' will and His 'secret will' in order to prove his case against them. Barry and Lawrence could not fathom how any man could presumptuously refer to the contents of a secret divine will when by definition it was not revealed. Yet Bernhere had boldly asserted that it was God's secret will that Adam should lapse into sin, even though He did not wish men to perish according to His revealed will. This seemed to make the Creator of life the 'author of synne' and deny biblical truth. Thus, they asked in disgust: 'Who can abide the hearing hereof?' To them, Bernhere was 'unreasonably learned' and going beyond the bounds of the sacred writings.

Bernhere's position was all the more reprehensible to his critics because he had placed the electing activity of God in eternity prior to creation and the fall and thus, 'not of late'. According to his theory, God had evidently chosen some for salvation while the rest were left to be 'reprobated' as a display of His justice. However, this did not make sense in light of Bernhere's declaration that man was not

---

indication that the freewillers wanted nothing to do with Familist speculations. For more on David Joris, see Horst, pp. 54, 76. On the Familists see *NIDCC*, 368 – 9.

[110] Bodl. MSS, 53, fol. 138a. By universal salvation or universalism, theologians generally mean the belief that all men will ultimately have a full share in divine salvation, so that none will be eternally lost. Thus, any form of punishment is of a temporary nature only. By way of contrast, a belief in God's universal salvific will indicates that one is convinced that divine salvation is intended for all men, and that none are excluded from the opportunity of responding to divine grace by virtue of the universal dimensions of the atonement of Christ. On universalism, see *A Dictionary of Christian Theology*, ed. Alan Richardson (London: SCM Press Ltd., 1969), p. 352.

[111] Bodl. MSS, 53, fol. 138a.

[112] *Ibid.*, fol. 139b.

[113] *Ibid.*, fol. 138a.

created for destruction, and the freewillers could see no logic in his position. They even expressed willingness to listen to his postulations if he could demonstrate them clearly from the Scriptures, but he had obviously not been able to do so to their satisfaction. Still, they suspected that he would go on looking and eventually 'bring one' if he was able to 'find it'.[114] Failing this, he could be expected to contrive a proof-text and claim that it was 'in the Greek tongue' — evidently a tactic which Bernhere had already made use of in his 'book'. Hence, he stood opposed to all 'English translations', since they did not conclusively support his case.

Barry and Lawrence then took the offensive and argued that man's creation in the image of God ruled out the possibility of any kind of eternal reprobation. Here they agreed with Bernhere that the *imago Dei* involved man's original state — 'righteous, holy, prudent and beautiful with all manner of good gifts'.[115] Therefore, destruction came upon men universally through the sin of Adam so that all were then headed for condemnation. Yet God had provided His Son 'to die for all of adam's posteritie'.[116] Now, God 'effectually' calls all men unto Himself through His Word, so that all men might receive 'eternall Lyfe' through the shedding of Christ's blood.

The freewillers also took exception to the way in which Bernhere had likened them to the 'papists' and 'pelagians', while he referred to his own cohorts as 'most godly lerned' men. It was almost as if Bernhere felt that the Reformed leaders surpassed even the 'prophetts' and the 'apostles'. This evaluation was highly suspect to the freewillers, since they had observed the behaviour of these men and decided that they were 'not verie wholesome' if they could display 'no better fruits'. Thus, they were not at all impressed by the lives of Bernhere's colleagues and seemed to associate their questionable, carnal life-styles and attitudes with their apparently erroneous doctrinal position. And yet Bernhere would speak of them only in the loftiest, most glowing terms because of their great learning.

Clearly resentful of these claims to superior intelligence, Barry and Lawrence challenged Bernhere either to prove his case regarding reprobation from the Scriptures, or else to leave them free to make more profitable use of the time — for the freewillers had a 'conscience' about the way they spent their time, while their opponents showed that they had none by spending many hours discussing their notions without ever coming to the heart of the

114 *Ibid.*, fol. 138b.
115 *Ibid.*, fol. 139a.
116 *Ibid.*, fol. 139b.

matter. In drawing to a close, they asked for direct Scriptural proofs for several key points: namely, that God had not elected all men prior to creation; that God had reprobated 'some people before the world'; that Christ had not been sacrificed for all of the descendants of Adam; that God did not call all men unto salvation through His Word and that the call was not effectual; and finally, 'that Adam, David, Solomon, Mary Magdalene and the thief being in their abominable sins, were also in Christ and in the election'.[117] They also taunted Bernhere mercilessly, stating that it would not save them to come to his opinion if they were already among the reprobate. Neither could they perish if they were among the elect.[118] Still, they asked him to remember that they bore no personal animosity toward him, but merely rejected his doctrine. Indeed, their motive in writing to him was love itself, since they hoped that he would change his mind and escape the wrath of God.

Despite the blatant signs of doctrinal propagandizing, this rebuttal by Barry and Lawrence was extremely significant. Not only did it give further insight into the inner workings of the negotiations at a critical stage; it also demonstrated that the freewillers had before the death of Mary begun to formulate a mature alternative to Genevan theology. Devoid of the alleged absurdities and crudities of the early Kentish conventiclers, the arguments of the radicals were by now being presented in a more sophisticated manner. While the social origins of the freewillers were betrayed by their resentment toward the Reformed party's usage of New Testament Greek in order to prove their points, it is nonetheless quite clear that the overall quality of their campaign had greatly improved, so that their formal challenge for Scriptural proofs was undoubtedly taken quite seriously. Indeed, Bradford's earlier alarm at the movement's potential seems to have moved closer to realization at this point, as the radicals began to articulate a systematic platform of beliefs which provided something like a preview of seventeenth-century Arminianism. This platform involved the rejection of several tenets crucial to the Reformed position, including the unconditional election of individuals to salvation and the view that the atonement of Christ was limited in its scope. Also implicit in their stance was the conviction that men could fall away from salvation, or even better, fall out of God's election after having been included in it. These points were later refined to an even greater degree by an anonymous writer who was evidently very close to events in the prison.[119]

---

[117] *Ibid.*, fol. 139a – b.
[118] *Ibid.*, fol. 139b.
[119] See below, chapter 7.

Henry Harte's contribution to the fray

Further reaction to the wave of confessionalism, and especially to the articles of faith which had been drawn up for joint approval in the King's Bench, was forthcoming from a rather unexpected quarter by spring 1556. Henry Harte, who had not signed Trewe's statement,[120] chose then to render his personal criticisms of the discussions. He secured a copy of a doctrinal statement written by John Careless and added his comments on the reverse side.[121]

Careless later explained that the confession had been intended for William Tyms, a curate from Hockley in Essex, who had resided in the King's Bench until his transfer to Newgate.[122] Harte managed to intercept the articles, added his own comments, and then sent it on to its original destination. Tyms and the other Reformed prisoners in Newgate received it and subsequently included their impressions of Harte's 'letter' on 21 April 1556.[123]

It is clear from Harte's comments that Careless's confession was virtually identical to the one which concluded Trewe's treatise and which had been signed by the moderate freewillers. Indeed, it is possible that the articles were a joint labour of Careless and Trewe. Harte began by issuing the familiar caution against presumptuous inquiry and added that all true and certain knowledge must be linked directly to the Word of God.[124] He thought it dangerous for each side to regard the others as true believers, for if any errors were upheld for the sake of unity the members would be guilty of bearing witness against themselves. He was also highly critical of the wording with respect of the Person of Christ. He could not comprehend how God could be seen as three eternal Persons according to the first article and still have Christ represented as being 'made one persone forever' at His Incarnation according to the second. He explained:

> In the second article ye saye that god and mane were joyned together in christ into one persone never to be devyded, and in the fyrst ye saye that god was three persons without begynnynge and

---

[120] This lends further support to the hypothesis that Harte escaped detection throughout the Marian years.

[121] Foxe, VIII, 164.

[122] *Ibid.*, 167.

[123] Cambridge, Emmanuel College Library, Letters of the Martyrs, MSS, 260, fol. 87. This document was also printed by Benjamin Evans in *The Early English Baptists* (London: J. Heaton & Son,1862),I, 273 – 5, at Appendix H.

[124] Martyrs, MSS, 260, fol. 87a.

ending so that ye make quaternytye in god if ye holde the
humanytye which our savyour christ toke of the blessed virgyne
marye for a persone and is not.[125]

Do we have here a reference to celestial flesh doctrine, thereby
indicating that Harte partook of incarnational peculiarities? Indeed,
it is extremely difficult to determine the drift of his critique. Perhaps
we shall never know for sure, although the question of defective
Christology would seem unlikely in the light of the moderation and
orthodoxy of his tracts. As for his alleged pronouncements on the
subject of predestination during the early conventicling movement,
one must never forget that informants, then and now, are not above
embellishment when it suits their purpose.

As for the fourth article, which dealt with the nature of salvation,
Harte objected to the treatment of good works and rewards which
were basically empty terms devoid of meaning to the Reformed
exponents. At this point he could not resist a play on words, declaring
his suspicion that 'a carles mane' had been their teacher and had
taught them 'as carles a fayth'.[126] After urging the Newgate prisoners
to keep the commandments, Harte indicated that he had run out of
time in his commentary, and that he would withhold further remarks
until he had heard how his foregoing statements had been received.
In closing, he referred to himself as their 'frynd . . . as far as
charytye' did 'bind' him.

At this point, the Newgate prisoners led by Tyms wrote several
brief denunciations of Harte's comments on the same parchment.
Tyms, by now condemned to die, attested that Harte's doctrine was
'most blasfemose to chryst's death and passyon'. Christopher Lyster,
a husbandman from Dagenham in Essex, added his approval of
Tyms's evaluation and stated further that Harte's beliefs were 'more
to the derogacyone of god's glorye then ever was heard at Anye
papyst's mowth'.[127] Other signatories concurring with these sentiments were Robert Drakes, parson of Thundersley, Essex;[128] George
Ambrose, fuller, Thomas Spurge, fuller, and Richard Spurge,
shearman, all of Bocking parish in Essex;[129] Richard Gratwicke,
probably also from Essex;[130] John Mace, an apothecary from
Colchester; John Harman, tanner, from Colchester; and finally,

---

[125] *Ibid.*
[126] *Ibid.*, fol. 87b.
[127] *Ibid.*
[128] Foxe, VIII, 106.
[129] *Ibid.*, 105 – 6.
[130] Foxe mentions one Roger Grasbroke, *ibid.*, 139.

Simon Joyne, sawyer.[131] Joyne closed the testimonial by stating his utter denial of Harte's 'false oppynyons and slanders report' against his 'faythfull bretherne'.

Tyms was clearly the leader of this group of Essex men, and the fact that several of their number came from Bocking suggests that some were involved with the Kentish freewillers from the beginning of the controversy in Edward's day. Indeed, the parson at Bocking complained that they had not been attending the parish church as required,[132] and they were arrested in the spring of 1555. Once in prison, Tyms had become intimate with Bradford, Philpot and Taylor in the King's Bench.[133] John Jackson, the fourth man to sign Trewe's articles, had corresponded with Tyms shortly after his arrest and informed him of Avington's radical opinions. Tyms was both disgusted and surprised, since he had been previously unaware that Avington 'or any other' had held those views.[134] Other newsworthy items in the correspondence included the tidings that Cornelius Stevenson, another of Trewe's signatories, had changed his stance in favour of the Reformed faith.[135] This event must have taken place before July 1555, since Tyms announced joyfully that he was going to pass the information along to Bradford and the other stalwarts.

Although Jackson questioned the accuracy of Tyms's story, Tyms announced that he had the details of Stevenson's conversion in the man's own handwriting. Tyms would have liked to convey similar news regarding all the 'obstinate' freewillers, but was confident that he had at least discovered the source of their error. This was nothing other than the pride and self-confidence of Thomas Avington who believed 'hys owne wit best' and proved to be completely unteachable. Jackson was also guilty on this score since John Careless had vainly endeavoured to reclaim him for the Reformed cause. Since Jackson was 'so wedded' to his own opinions, Tyms was bent on advising Careless to stop giving Jackson the opportunity to abuse him and spend his time more profitably.[136]

---

[131] *Ibid.*, 138.

[132] *Ibid.*, 106. Originally apprehended for organizing services in the woods around Hockley, Tyms was referred to by Bonner as 'the ringleader' of his fellows, and was regarded as the primary teacher of 'heresies' among them. His case would suggest something of an exclusivist tendency among certain of the Reformed-leaning element in addition to the freewill radicals, unless it be conjectured that Tyms and his associates, like numerous others, went through a later conversion to Reformed theology under the influence of Bradford. Foxe, VIII, 107, 109.

[133] Foxe, VIII,121.

[134] Martyrs, MSS, 260, fol. 27a.

[135] Stevenson is referred to only as Cornelis in Tyms' letter.

[136] Martyrs, MSS, 260, fol. 27a.

Jackson's radicalism was confirmed during his formal examination before Dr William Cook, Recorder of London, on 11 March 1556.[137] Cook accused Jackson of being 'the rankest heretic of all them in the King's Bench', and questioned him at length on the sacrament of the altar. Although a freewiller, Jackson could not be accused of entertaining an underdeveloped appreciation for the sovereignty of God in the practical sphere, as he testified that no one could harm him unless it was permitted by God. His fate is unknown, but these glimpses of his character serve notice of his prominence in the prison controversy in 1556.

During this same period, Tyms received a letter from a close comrade regarding the King's Bench dispute.[138] The writer, who was probably John Careless, spoke about three leaders in the freewill camp. One of these was 'that blynde guyde Kempe', while the others were simply referred to as 'two prating parrotts'.[139] The first was clearly John Kempe, Harte's one-time travelling companion, while the other two were probably Harte and John Gibson. Tyms's friend was livid over the manner in which the freewillers had presumed to instruct one of the Reformed pastors in the fine points of doctrine. The writer promised to expose Kempe's 'detestable doings' for the entire world to see, so that 'the posterytie' would know what a rogue he was in actuality. As for Trewe and his mates, the writer reported that they were now given 'to more contention then ever they were', and hoped that God would 'kepe them from hardenes of harte'.[140]

Keeping Tyms abreast of developments in the King's Bench would be most appropriate for Careless and his colleagues, as they remained behind with Trewe's party after Tyms and his comrades were transferred to Newgate. The writer also referred to Tyms's letter to the freewillers, perhaps meaning the one to Jackson dealt with immediately above. He stated that the radicals' reaction to it was not yet known, but assured Tyms that he and the Reformed group had retained a copy of it and would soon communicate with him again if God should permit. Time must have been running out for Tyms at this point, as he, along with Drakes, Ambrose, the Spurges and one John Cavel, a weaver, were burned for their faith at Smithfield on 24 April 1556.[141] Four days later, six more suffered at Colchester — Lyster, Mace, John Spenser, Joyne, Richard Nicoll and Harman.[142]

[137] Foxe, VIII, 242–3.
[138] Martyrs, MSS, 260, fols. 68a–69b.
[139] Ibid., fol. 69a.
[140] Ibid., fol. 69b.
[141] Foxe, VIII, 105. This was just three days after they had been busy condemning Harte's articles.
[142] Ibid., 138. Foxe lists these martyrs as Christopher Lyster, John Mace, John Spencer, Simon Joyne, Richard Nichols, and John Hamond.

Apparently Richard Gratwicke had been slated to die with his fellows, but managed to escape the ultimate penalty by subscribing to the same confession which Saxby and others from Colchester had accepted.[143] Thus, the controversy dragged on, even though, for a variety of reasons, many of the participants were now removed from the storm centre.

[143] *Ibid.*, 139, 310.

7

'The Careless by Necessity'

With the fortunes of the Reformed camp apparently taking a turn for the worse, John Careless underwent a rigorous examination before Foxe's 'Dr. Martin' on 25 April 1556. The account of this inquiry provides one of the richest and deepest insights into the entire King's Bench episode.[1] It is clear that the Privy Council had been disturbed by the news of disorderly contention in the prison system and had commissioned Martin to discover the causes at once.[2] A moment of supreme embarrassment followed for Careless, as Martin not only played upon his name but also produced the very confession of faith which Harte had intercepted and sent on to Newgate. The Council had already seen it,[3] but must have had some difficulty in understanding its layout. Accordingly, Careless was asked to identify his own handiwork.

When Martin began to go through the articles, however, Careless protested that the handwriting was not his even though the 'tenor' of the piece was in accordance with his 'first drawing indeed'.[4] As for the theology behind the articles, Careless affirmed that he would be willing to change any tenet which could be proven defective. Martin was not impressed, replying sardonically: 'Yea, so you will say all the sort of you, and yet ye be of divers faith.' When Martin then turned the sheet over to where Harte had offered his criticisms, Careless recognized Harte's handwriting immediately since Tyms had already sent him 'a copy' of the contents. Martin recognized that Harte's remarks were 'clean contrary' to those of Careless and demanded to know the identity of the writer.

Careless denied knowledge of both the faith and the hand, however, and stated that he would answer for his own beliefs and not those of another. Martin, perhaps perceiving Careless's deceit, slyly

---

[1] Foxe, VIII, 163 – 70.
[2] *Ibid.*, 166.
[3] *Ibid.*, 168.
[4] This confirms that Harte intercepted a revised draft of the original confession drawn up by Careless, perhaps in conjunction with Trewe, and that the document in Martin's possession likely bore Trewe's handwriting and not Careless's. Careless admitted to drafting the articles, but affirmed that they were not in his hand.

asked if Careless knew 'one Henry Hart'. Again, Careless denied any knowledge of Harte. In his later explanation he wrote:

> But yet I lied falsely; for I knew him indeed, and his qualities too well. And I have heard so much of him, that I dare say it had been good for that man if he had never been born: for many a simple soul hath he shamefully seduced, beguiled, and deceived with his foul Pelagian opinion, both in the days of that good king Edward and since his departure, with other things that I will forbear to name for diverse considerations. But I would wish all men that be godly-wise, to beware of that man, whose opinions in many points are very noisome and wicked: God convert him, or confound him shortly, for his name's sake, Amen.

Martin would not accept Careless's professed ignorance, however, and proceeded to read Harte's commentary. Careless continued his posture, since he did not want Martin to know that Harte, Kempe and Gibson had been active in seeking to persuade the Newgate prisoners to abandon their Reformed perspective.[5] As Martin found Careless obstinate at every turn, he next asked if Careless knew 'one master Chamberlain'. When Careless again replied in the negative, Martin shrewdly remarked: 'No dost? and he hath written a book against thy faith also.' Seemingly desperate to change the subject, Careless returned to Harte's statements.[6] Martin acknowledged that Harte was 'a rank heretic as any can be', but added that Careless was in the same category.

Next, Martin began to probe for the causes of the prison controversy once more. He found it noteworthy that the two sides were so antagonistic toward one another, and yet they were 'both against the catholic church'. Careless was obviously deeply wounded at being classified with schismatics and extremely anxious to hide the contention as much as possible. Martin then referred to Trewe by name and suggested that the doctrine of predestination was one of the sore points in the fracas. Trewe had appeared before Martin at an earlier time and had told him that Careless believed in unconditional election and the horrors of reprobation.[7] Careless said that Trewe had not represented his view accurately and stated that it was not the first time Trewe had lied about him. When pressed to reveal further details of the dispute, Careless maintained that election had been the only topic of discussion and that the controversy had already been

[5] Cf. above, p. 167.
[6] Foxe, VIII, 165.
[7] *Ibid.*, 166.

settled for quite some time. But he later confessed to the readers of his testimonial: 'This I spake to make the best of the matter; for I was sorry that the papists should hear of our variance.'[8]

Martin was not fooled by this claim either; he remained unimpressed when Careless stated that the prisoners had simply taken part in some 'earnest reasonings' which had been interrupted by the action of the prison-marshall in isolating the parties as much as possible. Careless then questioned Martin's authority to examine him on the subject of predestination,[9] but finally granted the following confessional statement:

I believe that Almighty God, our most dear loving Father, of his great mercy and infinite goodness (through Jesus Christ) did elect and appoint in him before the foundation of the earth was laid, a church or congregation, which he doth continually guide and govern by his grace and Holy Spirit, so that not one of them shall ever finally perish.[10]

Martin was evidently not satisfied with this declaration and after questioning Careless on the extent of the atonement,[11] asked him to explain Trewe's position on the matter. Although Careless would not attribute universalism to Trewe, he believed that Trewe's view was the same as that of the Catholic clergy, that is to say, 'that we be elected in respect of our good works, and so*long elected as we do them, and no longer'.[12] The conversation then touched on Arianism, as Martin had heard of two men in the King's Bench who were denying the deity of Christ. Careless lamented over the case, replying that this was the one item above 'all other things' which he had wanted to hide from Martin.[13] There were indeed 'two simple poor men' who had espoused this error, although Careless hoped that they might have been corrected in their thinking by that time.

Shortly afterward, Martin stated that he had other pressing matters to deal with, but affirmed that Careless was one of the most pleasant

[8] Careless was prepared to speak an outright lie to Martin in order to protect the interests of the Protestants in the realm.
[9] Foxe, VIII, 168.
[10] *Ibid.*
[11] *Ibid.*, 169. Martin told Careless that he had been informed that Careless did not believe in Christ's effectual death for all men. Careless briefly asserted his conviction that Christ died 'effectually . . . for all those that do effectually repent and believe, and for no other'.
[12] *Ibid.* This, of course, was not Trewe's position at all, and it raises doubts about Careless's understanding of his opponent.
[13] It is most significant that Christology was a keen issue during these days, and the presence of these individuals suggests that the entire spectrum of theological theories evidenced on the continent was being discussed in England as well.

fellows with whom he had ever discoursed among 'the Protestants'. When Martin attempted to sum up the examination in rather disparaging terms, however, Careless replied:

> There is a thousand times more variety in opinions among you doctors, which you call of the catholic church, yea and that in the sacrament, for the which there is so much blood shed now a-days — I mean of your latter doctors and new writers; as for the old, they agree wholly with us.[14]

With this, Careless and Martin parted company, each respecting the other to a considerable degree. Careless was able to report that he left his examination 'with a glad heart'. With his martyrdom approaching, he seems to have relied heavily on support and encouragement from the outside messengers and the underground congregation with which Bernhere was connected.[15] He seems to have corresponded regularly with Thomas Upcher, who was now free of his bonds and perhaps *en route* to Frankfurt.[16] It is likely that he also kept in touch with Cutbert Symson who served as deacon in the London congregation during the pastorate of John Rough.[17] Described as a wealthy man by an informant,[18] Symson also acted as 'paymaster' for the various London prisons, distributing funds collected for the joint succour of the inmates. He carried a special 'book containing the names and accounts of the congregation' and kept track of those 'that had not paid' their dues.[19] Presumably, Cole and Ledley were still being sent overseas to confer with the English exiles during these days.[20]

Unfortunately for the network, Symson, along with Rough and others, was apprehended at Islington on 12 December 1557,[21] and then subjected to much cruelty.[22] He suffered with two of his

[14] Foxe, VIII, 170.

[15] In one of his letters to the Swiss, he wrote of how Bernhere had been wonderfully preserved from great dangers. Foxe, VIII, 185 – 6.

[16] Coverdale, fols. 580 – 5 and 618 – 20; Garrett, p. 317.

[17] Foxe, VIII, 454. It has been suggested that the congregation had five pastors during the Marian years, and that Rough was the fourth. Bernhere may have served in this capacity prior to Rough, while Thomas Bentham, with aid from Robert Cole, was probably Rough's successor. Symson was apparently one of the deacons under Rough. See White, pp. 10 – 11; Foxe, VIII, 459. Cf. Foxe's 1563 edition, fol. 1700. For more on Symson's identity, see appendix 2 below.

[18] Foxe, VIII, 459.

[19] *Ibid.*, 454. Foxe stated that the size of the congregation varied from about forty to over two hundred during Mary's reign, with a definite increase toward the end. Foxe, 1563 ed., fol. 1700.

[20] Strype, *EM* III, 2, 147 – 8.

[21] *Ibid.*, 444.

[22] *Ibid.*, 455.

associates at Smithfield in the spring of 1558 and was evidently one of the last actors in the King's Bench episode to be martyred. Thomas Avington had been executed on 6 June 1556, in company with several of Careless's friends,[23] while Careless himself died from natural causes in the prison around 1 July 1556.[24] His adversary, John Trewe, managed to escape from the King's Bench during the same month of July with the help of one Robert Crowhurste.[25] Crowhurste was soon recaptured, but, as late as 29 July Trewe remained at large. He may have escaped detection for the remainder of Mary's reign.

John Knox and the anonymous assailant

At this juncture, if not sooner, the controversy in the King's Bench must have begun to subside, as most of the principal disputants had been removed. Indeed, the case might be considered closed were it not for the presence of one further mystery item which emerged during this later period. This was a fully-developed theological treatise which mercilessly attacked the Reformed view of election in a detail hitherto unknown in England. The document, referred to as *The Confutation of the Errors of the Careless by Necessity*, was probably never printed but circulated in manuscript form.[26] It created a stir among the exiled English divines in the late 1550s, and a request for a formal refutation was received in Geneva by November 1559. Since the earliest agitation for a rebuttal seems to have come from Scottish sources some two years earlier, it is probable that the anti-Calvinist work was produced no later than 1557.[27]

The cudgel was finally taken up by John Knox sometime before the fall of 1559,[28] and he included the arguments and statements of the freewiller in their entirety in his point by point response. Indeed, the contents of *The Confutation* are known only through Knox's reply, *An*

---

[23] *Ibid.*, 151.

[24] *Ibid.*, 163.

[25] *APC*, V, 315.

[26] *The Works of John Knox*, ed. David Laing (Edinburgh: Woodrow Society, 1846 – 64), V, 16.

[27] 'The Confutation of the Errors of the Careless by Necessity', *Transactions of the Baptist Historical Society*, IV (1914), 89; Knox, V, 15*. Hereafter this tract will be referred to as simply 'The Confutation'. The Baptist Historical Society merely edited Knox's reply and published the piece as a treatise which hopefully resembled the original.

[28] Knox, V, 15*.

Answer to a Great Number of Blasphemous Cavillations Written by an Anabaptist and Adversary to God's Eternal Predestination. [29]

As for the format and contents of *The Confutation*, it is noteworthy that the author employed a method similar to that previously utilized by both Harte and Trewe. This involved highlighting certain enormities, or in this case, errors, allegedly promulgated by the Reformed camp. In refuting these errors at length, the author sought to establish his central thesis, namely that God had but one will toward man — that he should repent and live — and that those who taught the contrary were encouraging libertinism and licence. Accordingly, the first of the enormities turned upon the subject of the unconditional election of individuals to salvation and the related question of reprobation. The writer believed it to be a 'careless' error to uphold this view on redemption and charged that his opponents used 'unreasonable reasons' to try and sustain their arguments. Indeed, his tract placed heavy emphasis upon the reasonableness of his own position throughout, as he used a common sense, logical approach with clever analogies included alongside the theological content. He could not see how God could create man in His own image for the purpose of destruction, since 'God loveth His own birth, that is man'.[30] Even the 'Careless by Necessity' would refrain from begetting a child destined for everlasting misery. Thus, the 'Careless Men' who taught the 'naughty opinion' that God had created the greater part of the world for destruction were even worse than the 'Atheists', since they pictured Him as 'a cruel man, a tyrant, and an unjust person', when in fact, His mercy was definitely 'greater than His wrath'.[31]

A related portion of the freewiller's case rested upon the assertion that prior to the fall of man, all men had been 'Predestinate to life'.[32] The radical author believed that since all were created in Adam, the first parent, it followed necessarily that mankind had been 'created in one estate, that is, after the image of God to life'.[33] Had things been otherwise, God could be made to appear falsely as a respecter of persons.[34] Even worse, had God issued His decree of reprobation prior to creation and the fall, then death would have been the consequence of His ordinance and not the 'reward of sin' as the

[29] Hereafter, this work will be referred to in the present text as Knox's 'Answer', as published in its entirety in the fifth volume of the Woodrow Society edition of Knox's works.
[30] 'The Confutation', 91.
[31] *Ibid.*, 92.
[32] *Ibid.*, 93.
[33] *Ibid.*, 95.
[34] *Ibid.*, 94.

Apostle Paul maintained.[35] In harmony with Barry's and Lawrence's earlier pronouncements against Bernhere, therefore, the writer maintained that the doctrine of election must not be made to appear contradictory to the doctrine of creation. Instead of permitting the former to supersede the latter, one should focus solely upon predestination to life, which is an unconditional 'free gift of God' given before the world's foundation when no man had done anything worthy of either merit or condemnation.[36]

Not content with these observations, the author decided to examine the Scriptural teaching on election in detail, since he hoped to win his opponents for the cause of truth and believed that they had never really come to grips with the issue as it was presented in the sources. This he proceeded to relate according to his understanding and in the process presented the most articulate and balanced freewill argument to appear in the realm during the early Reformation period. For instance, he delineated three levels of election which he had observed, namely, 'generally, specially, and most specially of all'.[37] The first was concerned with Christ's role as the Light of the world, enlightening all who experience natural birth and bidding them to drink of the water of life without discrimination. The second involved those who respond to the initial call and begin walking on the Christian pathway. At this point, many are offended and turn away, including 'a whole band of Stoics, with their Destiny playing fast or loose, and that of Necessity, which passeth all jugglers' cunning'.[38] Those who maintain that salvation and damnation are 'of mere Necessity' are also found among these.

The third and final type of election applies to those who conform to the principles of the first two and persevere to the end amidst tribulation. These are the especial 'Elect and Chosen' ones, since they obtain that for which they have been chosen through self-renunciation and submission to God. It is most difficult for any who reach this level to 'fall away' or be deceived, since they not only possess spiritual perception but have also begun to experience the benefits of a consistent Christian life. Those who fail to heed the calling of God, however, establish themselves as reprobates through their rejection of the divine will and offer of grace.[39]

As for the delicate matter of divine foreknowledge, the author maintained that God had foreknown all men in eternity and had

---

[35] *Ibid.*, 95.
[36] *Ibid.*, 109.
[37] *Ibid.*, 97.
[38] *Ibid.*, 98.
[39] *Ibid.*, 99.

ordained that they should be like His Son. The will of God must be clearly distinguished from His foreknowledge, therefore, since God does not will all that He sees. For example, He foresees the death of the sinner, but states that it is not His will that he should die. Foreknowledge, then, depends not on the one who has the knowledge, but hinges on 'the thing that is known'. It does not imply necessity at all, since no man is ever compelled to act in violation of his own will. This understanding must be balanced by faith in God's omnipotence, however, as He is free to do 'or leave undone, whatsoever pleaseth Him'.[40]

In handling some of the problem texts of the Scriptures which touched on these issues, the author continued with his conviction that the unconditional aspects of election and reprobation were unreasonable. His major premise at this interval seemed to be twofold: that the nature of God's love as revealed in His Word was incompatible with the Reformed view of redemption, and that the omnipotence and sovereignty of God were not at all threatened simply because His will was not always performed.[41] He conceded that it was possible to make a distinction between the 'will' and the 'permission of God' in order to avoid attributing mysterious things, including evil motives and deeds, to His hidden will. Apparent contradictions are thereby avoided and God's power, justice and immutability are kept intact.[42] In short, this distinction makes it unnecessary to adopt 'the evil opinion of God' propagated by the 'Careless Libertines',[43] whose 'poisoned doctrine' leads to 'abominable absurdities'.[44]

In closing his lengthy treatise, the author gave a description of 'The Properties of the god of the Careless by Necessity' and contrasted these with 'The Properties of the True God'.[45] Whereas the former deity was chiefly wrathful and unmerciful through his awful decrees, the latter was known primarily for His mercy which 'exceedeth all His works'. Whereas the former was not omnipotent since he was bound by his arbitrary decrees, the latter was indeed all-powerful and free since He could do or 'leave undone' all things according to His pleasure. And, whereas the former was known to incite men to do evil and then punish them afterward, the latter tempted no one and abhorred evil in all forms.[46] Not only were these deities to be contrasted, but their children ought to be also. Those of the former

40 *Ibid.*, 100 – 3.
41 Thus, for this anonymous writer, there could be no such thing as irresistible 'grace'.
42 Knox, V, 363.
43 *Ibid.*, 382.
44 *Ibid.*, 363.
45 'The Confutation', 122.
46 *Ibid.*, 122 – 3.

tended toward pride, envy, evil ambition and contention, while those pertaining to the true God resembled their Father in His meekness, patience, consistency and detestation of 'all contentions'.

After presenting his case, the author sought to appeal to all unbiased readers, first asking for a fair decision in the light of revealed truth. Speaking finally to the 'Careless men', he urged them to weigh his words carefully since he had spoken the truth and had written his tract 'of necessity'. With this, his discourse came to an end, and it evidently did not receive a formal reply until Knox's 'Answer' around 1559. Not surprisingly, Knox agreed that *The Confutation* had been written 'by Necessity', since the author was none other than 'the seed of the Serpent' and had to spew forth the appropriate venom.[47] Knox also consistently accused the author of being a devotee of Sebastian Castellio,[48] and further identified his opponent as a representative of the Anabaptist faith.[49]

Despite Knox's predictable reaction, there is no doubt that *The Confutation* represented the most profound challenge to the Reformed position in England during the mid-Tudor era. Although many of the themes were similar to those previously encountered, there was an intellectual refinement and maturity present which easily superseded the earlier efforts at several points. In the first place, the writer displayed a familiarity with classical literature and terminology in his refutation. Besides his comment on the Stoics, he made passing reference to such figures as Plato,[50] Epicurus, Sardanapalus, Venus, Croesus and Tarquinius.[51] He also drew upon apocryphal works related to the Old Testament period to back up his claims at various intervals.

In his logical evaluation of causation and the divine decrees, he distinguished between the principal cause, or '*Causa causae*', and the secondary or 'inferior cause', the '*Causa causata*'.[52] At the same time, he gave evidence of that unmistakable trademark of the south-eastern freewillers since the Edwardian years, namely a deeply entrenched suspicion of higher learning. Like Barry and Lawrence, as well as Harte in his earlier tirades, he asked:

How can such great men beleve, seeing they seek to be praised one of another, and to be preferred for their knowledge in the tongues, and for the multitude of their bookes which they writ? Such

---

[47] Knox, V, 467.
[48] *Ibid.*, 348, 396 – 7, 398, 465.
[49] *Ibid.*, 462 – 3.
[50] 'The Confutation', p. 93.
[51] *Ibid.*, p. 97.
[52] *Ibid.*, p. 96.

learned men are more mete to be in Herodes hall, then in Christes stable . . . If you will have Christ, ye must not go to seke him in the Universities, where you may be praised for your sharp wittes and eloquent tongues; but you must go forth unto him out of the tentes, and suffer rebuke with him.[53]

Although the author expressed his aversion to the learned of the earth, he nonetheless claimed to appreciate knowledge as a divine gift which was good and proper when used aright. Thus, he could actually assert that he did not at all 'despise learning or learned men' without discrimination, since he knew of some who had received 'the truth of this matter' from God and had not become puffed up. This was remarkable, since these humble servants possessed a 'perfect knowledge of the tongues' and were the equal of any of the 'Rabbes' of which the 'Careless by Necessity' might boast.[54] Indeed, it was the adulation given to men of higher learning and wealth by the Reformed and the accompanying spirit of comradeship that proved utterly irksome to the freewiller. He accused his opponents of being respecters of persons who gave preference to the well-to-do, and who were willing to pass over the moral 'vices' of their supporters and patrons in the face of their generosity. Thus, the predestinarians made no ethical demands whatsoever upon such adherents, for they were accepted as 'faithful brethren' on the strength of their liberality and did not have 'to endeavour themselves to bring forth the fruits of lively faith'. But then, why should they make the effort, when membership in the Reformed 'congregation' was considered to be 'the surest token of their Election'? And furthermore, if this approach should prove to be inadequate, then the 'Careless by Necessity' could argue that one's conduct was an uncertain standard by which to measure one's ultimate position with respect to salvation.[55]

Clearly then, the anonymous writer had had contact with learned circles, and even insisted that some men from those ranks supported his views. Yet his association with such men had not removed his basic distrust of advanced learning as an end in itself. He also appeared to identify the Reformed camp with the Edwardian divines who had sought to stifle religious liberty under the previous administration. This was quite understandable to the freewiller, since the 'chief Apollos' of the predestinarians was bent on pursuing a policy of persecution.[56] It was upon this leader that Servetus's blood

[53] Knox, V, 294−5.
[54] *Ibid.*, 294.
[55] 'The Confutation', p. 111−12.
[56] *Ibid.*, 112. This would be an obvious reference to John Calvin.

cried 'a vengeance', along with that of others whom the writer claimed he could mention by name. Evidently, he had Joan Bocher and other radicals in mind at this point, since he added that God had already 'partly . . . revenged their blood, and served some of their persecutors with the same measure wherewith they measured to others'.[57] To make this crime all the more heinous, the predestinarians attempted to justify their conduct by setting forth books wherein it was affirmed that religious dissenters could be lawfully persecuted and executed.[58] The writer reasoned:

> Notwithstanding they, afore they came into authority, they were of another judgement, and did both say and write, that no man ought to be persecuted for his conscience sake; but now they are not only become persecutors, but also they have given, as far as lieth in them, the sword into the hands of bloody tyrants. Be these, I pray you, the sheep whom Christ sent forth in the midst of wolves?[59]

As can be seen, the author had no respect whatsoever for the Reformed exponents, especially since they shifted their stance with regard to religious freedom once they had become part of the ruling elite. What was worse, they were totally oblivious to their perilous predicament and could not see that they had been lulled into a false sense of security and careless living in which one travesty was being heaped upon the next. Once again, this point was reminiscent of earlier phases in the controversy, especially harking back to Trewe's explanation of the origin of the contention where there was a close relationship between the life-styles of the Calvinists and their stance regarding the perseverance of the saints. Within this context, the freewillers regarded themselves as divine messengers whose duty it was to awaken their unsuspecting and inconsistent opponents from their slumber.

Consequently, the radicals continued to preach a rather fluid interpretation of redemption comparable to previous explanations, wherein men moved in and out of God's election of grace according to their level of commitment to Christ at any given moment – a thought totally abhorrent and ridiculous to the Reformed. The anonymous writer also pushed the discussion regarding the nature of God's will through to its logical conclusion, stressing the 'great difference between the will and the permission of God'.[60] In order to

---

[57] *Ibid.*, 112.
[58] *Ibid.*, 112.
[59] *Ibid.*, 112 – 13.
[60] *Ibid.*, 121.

avoid the conclusion that a 'contrariety' exists in God, it was preferable to assert that His will was not always performed by His creatures, and that in many cases what did occur took place only by His consent. At the same time, the writer could not see any threat to God's omnipotence, since it is only through His permission that men have the freedom to go against His will.[61] To those who had scruples in this area, he replied:

> God is goodness itself, his will is always good, yet man is apt to do and may do evill contrary to God's will, notwithstanding God remaineth omnipotent, suffering man to do evill whome he might destroy before he did the evill, if so it pleased him . . . Thus we see plainely that many things be done contrary to the will of God.[62]

With these words, the anonymous writer proved that the freewillers had finally eliminated most of the weaknesses inherent in their earliest pronouncements. It should also be stressed that further indications of maturity and evolution were given at this time by the author's ability to distinguish between the Calvinism then being espoused at Geneva and that which was being offered by the 'Careless by Necessity' on the home front. Since this judgement adds a significant new dimension to the discussion (and is in keeping with what has already been observed in Barry and Lawrence), it is necessary to study his criticism in its totality before evaluating it. He wrote:

> But to what purpose should I thus contend with you that Adam did fall out of the Election, seeing in this ye agree not yourselves; for your congregation which is at Geneva, in the Confession of their faith, say, 'That of the lost sons of Adam, God elected some to life, and the rest he refused.' Either improve their belief, or else confess with them that all the children of Adam were lost by the transgression. If they were lost, then were they out of the Election with their father Adam, from the transgression until the promise was made.[63]

In the first place, it is noteworthy that the author of *The Confutation* recognized that his English rivals were closely associated with their

---

[61] *Ibid.*, 118 – 9.
[62] Knox V, 320.
[63] 'The Confutation', 114.

counterparts at Geneva. In all probability, this closeness was determined by the presence there of numerous English exiles who had sought refuge on the continent following the death of Edward VI. Secondly, and more importantly, it is obvious that the writer was aware that a difference of opinion existed among the various Reformed supporters as far as the fine points of doctrine were concerned. He was evidently sure that those at Geneva, undoubtedly under the guidance of Calvin himself, espoused a more moderate brand of predestinarian theology than that which was being taught by the 'Careless by Necessity'. Whereas the latter seemed to accept that the doctrine of election actually superseded, or at least took precedence over, the doctrine of creation, the former more accurately maintained that God had elected some from among the descendants of Adam and refused to choose others. To hold otherwise would mean that the cause of death within the human race was not primarily the sin of man but rather the prior decrees of God. This being impossible to the freewiller on account of his view of causation, the more extreme concept of redemption had to be stoutly resisted and rejected.

As indicated, this distinction is crucial, since it demonstrates again that the freewill party was now able to discern variations and modifications within the Calvinist party; it also shows that their opposition to the English Reformed divines was buttressed by the conviction that these worthies represented a more extreme form of Calvinism than that which was being adhered to at Geneva. This certainly helps to account for the intense degree of opposition which the south-eastern freewillers exhibited throughout the controversy, and helps to explain why they deemed it necessary to present their fellow countrymen with a viable alternative to the more deeply-entrenched Calvinist tradition which seemed to them to be threatening the spiritual fervor and vitality that existed in the realm during the mid-Tudor period.[64] And, although the freewillers did not succeed in carrying the day as far as the polemics were concerned, they did upset some of the best minds in the realm in the attempt.

As mentioned above,[65] Robert Cooke may be considered to be a possible author of this key work. This thesis was put forward by David Laing in the last century,[66] and no further attempts have so far been made to identify the writer. Laing referred to Knox's personal acquaintance with the unnamed author of the tract and to the

---

[64] It is obvious from the present survey that there were some variations in the English Reformed movement itself; thus, for example, the views of John Bradford appear somewhat more moderate than those attributed to Augustine Bernhere.
[65] See above, p. 63.
[66] Knox, V, 16, 13* – 14*.

apparent reversal in the man's doctrinal position which obviously displeased Knox.[67] Evidently Laing drew his conclusion about Cooke merely from reading Strype's account of his life[68] and from some tentative deductions which made his case seem 'nearly conclusive on this point'.[69] He felt it 'at least highly probable' that Knox had come to know Cooke when the former was at Edward's court in his capacity as royal chaplain.[70] Laing also pointed to Cooke's debate with William Turner over the nature of original sin and saw this to be in keeping with the tenor of *The Confutation* and its author.

This supposition was generally accepted by the anonymous editor of *The Confutation* in the *Baptist Quarterly* in 1914. To Laing's reasonings he added the suggestion that one 'R.C.' was known to have been 'a prominent opponent of John Careless on this very question of Predestination'.[71] Careless was drawn into the matter because of the obvious play upon words utilized by the original author, but the Baptist editor's argument erred since the initials of Careless's opponent undoubtedly stood for Robert Cole and not Robert Cooke. This is confirmed by the admission that 'R.C.' kept company with 'N.S.', another freewiller, who could be none other than Nicholas Sheterden of Pluckley.[72] The alleged animosity between the two Kentishmen and Careless either referred to their pre-conversion days, or else represented a complete misinterpretation of the evidence regarding the prison dispute on the part of the claimant.

Furthermore, there is not a shred of evidence to suggest that Cooke and Careless debated with one another at any time, although something of a case might be constructed in favour of the hypothesis if it could be proven that the Bocking clothier who bore the same name was the author of *The Confutation*.[73] There was also a Robert Cooke of St Michael's Church at Queenhithe who was charged with 'reasoning of the Scripture, and of the sacrament' under the persecutions associated with the Six Articles in 1541.[74] This may indeed have been the Robert Cooke of the Edwardian and Elizabethan courts, as it is certain that this man held controversial views on the Lord's Supper well into the Elizabethan era,[75] but on this information alone it would

[67] *Ibid.*, 16.
[68] *Ibid.*, 16, 13*.
[69] *Ibid.*, 16.
[70] *Ibid.*, 14*.
[71] 'The Confutation', 90.
[72] *Ibid.*, 89.
[73] See above, pp. 51, 63 – 4.
[74] Foxe, VIII, 446.
[75] See below, p. 184.

seem unwarranted to associate him with the Bocking movement.[76] It is quite possible, however, that this Robert Cooke may have been of the well-known Cooke family of Gidea Hall, Essex, whose most noted member in the sixteenth century was Edward VI's one-time tutor, Sir Anthony Cooke.[77] A Robert Cooke who resided in London may have been a cousin of Sir Anthony, as he was definitely the grandson of Sir Thomas Cooke of Gidea Hall and had taken a wife from Essex.[78] Indeed, this man may have accompanied Sir Anthony to London and been introduced to the royal court through him, thereby meeting Knox in the process during the latter's days of favour there. He may then have been offered the position of wine steward in the household of Queen Catherine Parr,[79] as Strype's man was, and taken up permanent residence in London.

This Robert Cooke evidently had considerable musical abilities, but these were overshadowed by his penchant for theological controversy as during his career he argued with such prominent divines as Coverdale, Parkhurst and Jewel. As indicated, his most celebrated opponent was William Turner, physician of both souls and bodies.[80] Around 1550, Turner became concerned about the spread of Pelagianism in England and delivered a lecture 'against two of the opinions of Pelagius: namely against that children have no original sin, and that they ought not to be baptized'.[81] Shortly afterward, Cooke wrote a refutation of Turner's position which in turn prompted Turner to publish a full response to the first item in question, along with a promise that he would later attend to the second. This latter work, published in 1551, followed the format

---

[76] Foxe mentions yet another Robert Cooke from the diocese of Coventry and Lichfield who, in September 1556, gave testimony against a fellow parishioner. Although this man's residence in the vicinity of Coventry is noteworthy in that Careless hailed from the town itself, the nature of the case does not warrant an association with the King's Bench episode. Foxe, VIII, 256.

[77] One of Sir Anthony's daughters became the second wife of William Cecil, while another married Sir Nicholas Bacon. See James McConica, *English Humanists and Reformation Politics* (Oxford: Clarendon Press, 1965), p. 217.

[78] This information was graciously passed on to me by Nancy Briggs, Students' Room Supervisor, Essex Record Office, County Hall, Chelmsford. The source is the pedigrees of the Cooke family of Gidea Hall as contained in the Sage Collection, Nos. 701, 707.

[79] R. A. Houlbrooke, ed., *The Letter Book of John Parkhurst, Bishop of Norwich* (n.p.: Norfold Record Society, 1974, 1975), p. 83.

[80] Garrett, p. 314.

[81] Turner, Sig. A. iiia. See also Horst, p. 115. As noted above, p. 89, Cooke had cited Erasmus as an authority on infant baptism and the early church at the close of his 'booke'. Cooke had referred to Erasmus's opinion that the Apostolic church did not practise the rite, since it had not been 'received' in the Apostles' time. Turner linked Cooke's opinions with the Münsterite radicals. Turner, sig. D. ia, F. ib – iia.

common to that day, in that Turner recorded the arguments of Cooke at various intervals and then replied to the same. According to Turner, Cooke had proven himself to be a genuine Anabaptist: he had denied the efficacy of infant baptism and linked the ordinance to mature faith in believers only.

Another of Cooke's major themes had been the universal offer of divine grace through the death of Christ. He believed that all men were offered the forgiveness of sins, although not all were willing to receive it. Only the 'churche sanctified by faith in the blood of Christ' receives the remission,[82] and only the members of the church qualify for baptism. Those who lack the assurance of sins forgiven receive no benefit at all from baptism, since they do not understand the significance of the divine promise represented therein.[83]

Following this heated exchange, nothing definite is known about Cooke and his activities in London until the Elizabethan years, when details of his whereabouts were discussed by Parkhurst in his correspondence with Rudolph Gualter in 1575.[84] Cooke was still a resident of the royal court and served as a singer in the Queen's chapel. According to Parkhurst, he had come close to losing his position a short while before because of his erroneous opinions, but had sung his recantation to the satisfaction of the authorities. These opinions presumably were related to original sin and the baptism of infants, although, as mentioned, Cooke had also developed some independent thoughts on the nature of the Lord's Supper which he had outlined to Gualter in August 1573.[85]

Although it has been conjectured and is quite feasible that Cooke had come to know Gualter as a Marian exile on the continent, there is no proof of this assertion. And although the thesis put forward by Laing regarding Cooke's authorship of *The Confutation* is reasonable, the problem of insufficient evidence still exists. It simply cannot be proved that Strype's Robert Cooke ever wrote at length on the subject of election, or that he was intimately related to any of the Marian prison events. And, although it may have been possible for Cooke to write the treatise while in exile on the continent, it must be remembered that his name does not appear on any list of English exiles during the Marian years.

---

[82] Turner, Sig. K. iiia.

[83] Although Turner had hoped to devote further attention to Cooke in the future, his flight to the continent in 1553 seems to have curbed his involvement. Garrett, pp. 314 – 15.

[84] Cambridge University Library, MSS, Ed. 2. 34, fols. 21 – 2, 23b; also printed in Burrage, II, 7 – 8, and translated and printed in Houlbrooke, ed.

[85] Hastings Robinson, ed., *The Zurich Letters*, Second Series, Parker Society, No. 54 (Cambridge: University Press, 1842, 1845), II, 236 – 7.

Harte again?

It would seem far more plausible, therefore, to maintain that the author of *The Confutation* must have been an active participant in the controversy itself, that he was in fact, someone well-known to both sides. Given what thus far has been noted concerning the writings and activities of the freewillers, it would seem that only John Trewe and Henry Harte would qualify as being sufficiently competent to write such a highly technical theological treatise. As for Knox's claim that he knew the author of *The Confutation* personally, it is possible that he may have met either Trewe or Harte or perhaps both during the days of his preaching missions in Kent, since he may have dealt with men of their persuasion.[86] As for which of the two dissenters is the most likely, it would seem that Harte should draw the top honours, as nothing more is known about Trewe after his escape from the King's Bench in July 1556. Then, too, Trewe had already composed a major work on the nature of the controversy in January that year. It also seems possible that Harte was to some extent the more radical of the two leaders, especially after the publication of his more moderate treatises in the mid-Edwardian years. This interpretation would coincide neatly with Knox's assertion that the author of *The Confutation* had shifted his stance since the time of their earliest acquaintance.

As for Harte's whereabouts during the denouement of the King's Bench episode, it would seem virtually incontrovertible that he continued to escape detection during the Marian years and died intestate in the early part of 1557. In the deed of administration, dated 16 March, the disposal of his goods was left in the hands of his 'natural son', John Harte, with William Dymning of Pluckley and Robert King of Little Charte, yeomen, also involved in the transaction.[87] This corresponds precisely with Archdeacon Harpsfield's visitation returns for Pluckley in 1557 which recorded that four persons 'suspected of heresy', including one 'henrie Harte', were to be 'secretly apprehended and brought to the King's and Queen's commissioners'.[88] It is clear, then, that Pluckley had served as a centre of radicalism in Kent during the entire mid-Tudor period, and that Henry Harte was implicated in subversive activities at both the

[86] See above, p. 105.
[87] Maidstone, Kent County Record Office, Archdeaconry Act Book, PRC 3/15/22/
[88] Whatmore, p. 120. See also J. F. Davis, 'Heresy and Reformation in the South-east of England, 1520 – 1559' (unpublished D. Phil. dissertation, Oxford University, 1967 – 8), pp. 422 – 3.

beginning and the end. The proof that he was dead before he could be apprehended is established by the remark 'iam mortuus' contained in the returns. Harte's freedom during the Marian years would have permitted him to write a work of the magnitude of *The Confutation* by 1557 – the year of his death and the apparent date of the tract's initial circulation.[89]

Before settling upon Harte as the most likely author of *The Confutation*, however, there is at least one other avenue which is worthy of consideration. For it may be possible to link the author of this treatise with the main figure associated with leadership in the English freewill movement during the early Elizabethan period. This was none other than John Champneys of Middlesex, who had evidently not been heard from since his abjuration before Cranmer in April 1549.[90] Then he had appeared with Joan Bocher and other heretics, especially those deemed guilty of espousing Anabaptist opinions. Champneys, from the parish of Stratford-atte-Bow, had renounced six false tenets before Cranmer, two of which were identical to Cole's flowers.[91] These concerned the impossibility of sinning following regeneration and the necessary distinction between the inner and outer man in order to rationalize such sinfulness when it did actually occur. Furthermore, he had made the claim that men had never been completely free to follow the dictates of the 'Gospel' at any point since the Apostolic period, since the Christian faith had been so severely persecuted. Thus he seemed to be espousing a negative view of history which may have been seen as very much in keeping with the Anabaptist perspective. He also hinted at a form of radical communalism in the Münsterite tradition.[92]

The divines in attendance at these hearings in the spring 1549 must have found Champneys's entire platform repulsive and grossly speculative; they were undoubtedly alarmed at the apparent threat to civil and spiritual stability contained in his opinions (some of which were scarcely comprehensible). It is clear, however, that Champneys had been quite active in writing and disseminating his views prior to his arrest, and he was ordered to desist from such illicit pursuits and recover and destroy as many of his 'books' as possible. It is known that Champneys wrote *The Harvest is at Hand*, a very moderate tract published during the previous year. As Horst has noted, this work

---

[89] Once again, I would stress that it cannot be proved that Harte was actually incarcerated during the Marian proceedings.

[90] Wilkins, IV, 39.

[91] See above, pp. 69 – 73, for Cole's sermon.

[92] Wilkins, IV, 40. Champneys asserted that 'God doth permit to all his elect people their bodily necessities of all worldly things'.

was not at all inflammatory in tone or direction,[93] as it contained a general message of admonishment very similar to Harte's early works. Thus it could not have been the writing for which Champneys stood condemned in 1549, as the latter contained his 'damned opinions' and the 'Anabaptists' errors'.[94] It is certain, then, that Champneys had composed other writings which contained his more radical opinions and precipitated his arrest. Fortunately for Champneys, his punishment on this occasion involved only the bearing of a faggot during the sermon at Paul's Cross on the following Sunday. Little else is known of him until Elizabeth's reign, when, according to Jean Veron, he emerged as the leading protagonist of freewill thought in England.[95]

Following a period of exile Champneys had apparently written yet another treatise in which he had elaborated on the tenets of freewill doctrine. Heylyn described this work as 'a Discourse in the way of a Letter, against the Gospellers.'[96]

Champneys's objective in setting forth his letter was to show that these Gospellers had succeeded in laying 'the blame for all sins, and wickedness, upon God's Divine Decree of Predestination, by which men were compelled into it' − precisely the theme of *The Confutation*. These details harmonize well with the scant information available on the background to the tract, although Heylyn's assertion that Champneys did not publish his work until after his return to England following the death of Mary appears to alter the prospects at first glance. It is, however, possible that Champneys might have sent a copy of his letter back to England before his own arrival, as he may have kept abreast of developments at home by means of underground messengers. Indeed, he may have been involved in the early stages of the prison controversy itself prior to his departure, and thus could have become familiar enough with the disputants to employ a play upon words involving John Careless − although, if so, one would expect some kind of reference to it. The fact that the court of the King's Bench was a court of first instance for crimes committed in Middlesex, the county where Champneys was residing, also raises tantalizing possibilities about Champneys's participation in the

[93] Horst, p. 114.

[94] See immediately above, p. 186, regarding Champneys's alleged errors.

[95] Jean Veron, *A fruteful treatise of predestination and of the divine providence of God, with an apology of the same, against the swynyshe gruntinge of the Epicures and Atheystes of oure time* (London: J. Tisdale, [1561]), fol. 137b (first of two tracts by Veron under RSTC 24681. All future references to this item will be from the second tract in the entry and will be referred to as the *apology*.)

[96] Heylyn, p. 73. Heylyn evidently used the term 'Gospellers' here with reference to the Reformed party. See chapter 1, n 14 above.

episode. Perhaps he had been reapprehended for repeated wrong-doing and placed in the King's Bench prison, although Heylyn's account, which affirms that he 'entered into Holy Orders' following his abjuration, would make his involvement on these terms more difficult to comprehend. It is also possible that Heylyn was simply misinformed about the time of Champneys's return from exile,[97] and that it in fact occurred before Mary's death.

As for the question of Knox's personal acquaintance with the author of *The Confutation*, it is possible that he and Champneys had met in London, since Knox returned to England following his release from detention in the early part of 1549[98] – the very time when Champneys was appearing before Cranmer. Perhaps the Edwardian officials sent Knox to deal with Champneys and may have been convinced of Champneys's orthodoxy following his abjuration. This would account for his subsequent displeasure at the shift in position adopted by the author of *The Confutation*. Furthermore, if Champneys did spend some time in exile during the Marian period, he may have had opportunity to meet Sebastian Castellio, the man who was regarded by Knox as the chief freewill exponent on the continent.[99]

Following his return to England, it is clear that Champneys and Veron tangled at length on the question of predestination, although the exact chronology of their debate is somewhat difficult to reconstruct. Veron published an initial treatise on the Reformed view of predestination in 1561,[100] and Champneys soon took him to task in yet another of his books. According to Veron, Champneys had published his work anonymously and distributed the copies secretly so that 'he myghte in hugger mugger send them unto his privy frends abrode'.[101] His plans had backfired, however, as the printer was discovered when several copies fell into Veron's hands. This had forced Champneys to go even deeper into seclusion, since he had become the 'standard-bearer' and 'stout champion' of 'the free wyll men'.[102]

[97] Heylyn, p. 73.

[98] *NIDCC*, p. 570.

[99] Knox, V, 37, 295. For more on Castellio, see Roland H. Bainton, 'Sebastian Castellio, Champion of Religious Liberty' in *Studies on the Reformation*, pp. 139 – 81, and Stefan Zweig, *The Right to Heresy: Castellio against Calvin*, trans. Eden & Cedar Paul (New York: The Viking Press, 1936).

[100] Horst, p. 114. According to Wallace, Veron actually wrote four tracts dealing with the subject of predestination in this year. See pp. 38 – 9 of his study.

[101] Veron, *apology*, fol. 16b. It is difficult to discern if this is the 'letter' which Heylyn refers to in his chronicle.

[102] *Ibid.*, fols. 40b – 41a. See chapter 8 below for more on Veron's opinion of Champneys.

Since Champneys had attacked him, Veron felt it necessary to issue an apologetic in defence of his views in 1561.[103] From an examination of this work it is clear that Champneys's tenets were still in keeping with the basic themes of *The Confutation*. He was still stressing the universal availability of divine grace and the role of the human will in receiving it, since God had provided all things necessary for man's physical and spiritual well-being.[104] Veron, relying on Augustine for support, argued that the freewill interpretation was nothing short of full-blown universalism, and he continued to uphold the glory of God 'againste all maner of heresies and abhominable erroures bothe of the papistes and of the Anabaptistes'.[105]

It must be admitted that the case in favour of Champneys's authorship of *the Confutation* rests substantially upon the assumption that his letter against the Reformed Gospellers was distinct from his later attack upon Veron's treatise of 1561. Should the two have been one and the same, it would place the writing of *The Confutation* in 1561 or later. This would clearly be impossible, since Knox's reply was probably begun in 1559. It is possible, however, that *The Confutation* was a preliminary draft of Champneys's later work,[106] in which case the possibility of Champneys's authorship remains open. It is also worth remembering that John Careless had been questioned about the identity of one 'master Chamberlain', who had evidently written a 'book' against Careless's 'faith'. Since no one by that name stands out as a likely author, it is quite possible that this Chamberlain was none other than Champneys, whose surname had got somewhat garbled as it passed from an informant to the Marian authorities.[107] This need not conflict with Champneys's alleged exile, since it was not directly stated that Careless's opponent was in England at that time.[108] Moreover, if Champneys were to be accepted as the most likely of all the possible choices for the authorship of *The Confutation*, a link would be established between the late Marian freewill movement

---

[103] Cf. Horst's account, p. 114, with Wallace, pp. 38 – 9. See also chapter 8 below for more on Veron and Champneys.

[104] Veron, *apology*, fols. 17b – 18a.

[105] *Ibid.*, fol. 40b.

[106] On the other hand, the later work may have been a summary of 'The Confutation'.

[107] If so, the situation was far from unique, as is clear from a study of the Privy Council records where in many instances the surnames of offenders appear in various forms. See Burrage, II, 5 – 6. One is also reminded of the case of Robert Seulthroppe, who appeared as Skelthrop as well.

[108] Foxe mentions that Nicholas Chamberlain, a weaver from Coggeshall in Essex, was among the Marian martyrs, but there is no evidence which would suggest that this man played a major role in the King's Bench proceedings. Foxe, VII, 139.

and that of the early Elizabethan period.[109] Unfortunately, the one element lacking in this entire consideration of Champneys is the one which ultimately tips the scales in Harte's favour; namely, a known association with John Careless and a definite, intricate involvement in the King's Bench prison proceedings and the south-eastern freewill movement. As noted, this same point seemed to rule out Robert Cooke as the author of the piece. By way of contrast, there is no good reason why Harte could not have written *The Confutation*. In fact, the evidence suggests that of all the freewillers, Harte had probably the strongest reason and greatest ability for just such a task. To begin with, there was clearly no love lost between Harte and Careless. This much is obvious from Careless's own testimony before the Catholic inquisitor. At the same time, Trewe and Careless appear to have greatly moderated in their attitudes toward one another as the controversy dragged on. The point which all but clinches the argument in favour of Harte's authorship, however, concerns the tonal similarity between his criticisms of the joint communion articles and *The Confutation* itself. In particular, Harte's suspicion that 'a careless man' had instructed the negotiators in 'as careless a faith'[110] agrees perfectly with the repeated references to 'Careless Men' and 'Careless Libertines' in the major tract. This play upon words was obviously a favourite of Harte's, and no other freewiller involved in the dispute was ever known to have employed it. Finally, the theological perspectives presented in *The Confutation* are entirely in accord with Harte's previous remarks upon the subject of election and would indicate that Harte had undergone something of a personal maturation process during the course of the argument. Accordingly, Henry Harte may be said to have been the embodiment of the English freewill movement during the mid-Tudor years. The growing sophistication and intellectual evolution seen in his life and thought was to a great degree mirrored in the freewill campaign as a whole.

[109] Perhaps John Jackson would rank as a possibility if more were known about his involvement in the fray.
[110] See above, p. 165. The fact that Careless died in confinement around 1 July 1556 suggests that the tract must have been authored before that date.

8

Elizabethan Sequel

As the King's Bench controversy continued to fade in importance during the latter stages of Mary's reign, persecution went on unabated in the diocese of Canterbury. Some Kentish Arians were dealt with, and Strype felt that the Marian authorities would gladly have identified the orthodox Protestants with the Arians and Anabaptists in order 'to disgrace and disparage the holy profession'.[1] Accordingly, commissions were set ·up to intensify the search for heretics throughout the nation.[2] Executions continued in Kent, as ten persons suffered at Canterbury in mid-January 1557,[3] and seven more at Maidstone on 18 June.[4] Foxe commented that the prisons of Canterbury diocese were said to have been almost full by the end of the summer.[5]

Numbers were also high in the diocese of London, as ten from Essex, including a fuller from Bocking, were martyred on 2 August.[6] Even Cardinal Pole was upset by Bonner's policies toward the end of August, and sharply criticized the Bishop for condemning men as heretics without his approval.[7] And yet it was Pole who issued a new commission concerning heretics in his own diocese in March 1558.[8]

The final martyrs of the reign of terror came in November, just six days before the death of Mary, as five persons died at Canterbury. No doubt many of these final victims were suspected of holding Anabaptist beliefs. When the nightmare had ended at last, some fifty-four persons had suffered in Kent, with Essex close behind at fifty-one. London and Middlesex had done even worse with approximately fifty-eight victims, probably thanks to the prominence of Smithfield as an execution site.[9] It is, of course, impossible to

---

[1] Strype, *EM*, III, 1, 589.
[2] Canterbury diocese appears to have been the first area designated on 25 April, 1556, while a more sweeping commission was given on 8 February, 1557. See *CPR, Philip and Mary*, III, 24, 281 – 2; cf. Strype, *EM*, III, 476 – 7.
[3] Foxe, VIII, 300.
[4] *Ibid.*, 320.
[5] *Ibid.*, 303.
[6] *Ibid.*, 392.
[7] Strype, *EM*, III, 2, 29 – 30.
[8] *Ibid.*, 120.
[9] *Ibid.*, 554 – 6. As can be seen when all of the totals are carefully studied, over half the

determine how many of these were supporters of Anabaptism, since there is no concrete evidence of actual cases of rebaptism among any of them. It is certain, however, that Kent and Essex provided more than their share of valiant martyrs, and that the King's Bench episode was a most significant indicator of radical activity within these regions.

Whither the disputants?

It might be said with considerable justification that the freewill controversy did not continue into the Elizabethan era in its previous form. This holds true particularly if one defines the contention rather narrowly in terms of the south-eastern radicals and their association with the two-pronged episode in Kent/Essex and the King's Bench prison itself. As will be seen, similar wranglings and disputations regarding freewill and election did indeed occur in the early Elizabethan period, even prior to the full working out of the settlement; and furthermore, to be sure, concern for Anabaptism remained a constant with the ecclesiastical authorities until well on into the 1570s.[10] There is no mistaking a shift in both official attitudes and the participating personalities during these years, however, and the nature and significance of this distinctive change must be analyzed.

To begin, one can say very little with complete confidence regarding the whereabouts of those disputants who actually survived the Marian trauma. The death of Harte in 1557 clearly removed the most notorious of the freewill men from circulation, and it must be remembered that those of his party who did survive would, in all likelihood, not have been overly optimistic regarding their chances of prospering under the new regime. As noted above,[11] some relatively minor players may have lived out the remainder of their time in peace and obscurity in the Bocking and Pluckley areas. Thomas Cole of Maidstone continued in his rather unpredictable ways until his death in 1571 – evidently succeeding for the most part in walking the line between conformity and heterodoxy. On the one hand, we have his impressive list of appointments in the Elizabethan Church (including

Marian martyrs suffered within these localities. The greatest number appear to have died for their faith during the course of 1556.

[10] See below pp. 214 – 5.
[11] See above pp. 67, 76.

that of Archdeacon of Essex), while on the other, the intervention of Matthew Parker in 1566 suggests a continuing proclivity towards eccentricity.[12] Robert Cole, formerly of Faversham, seems to have enjoyed the benefits of the new settlement more than any other participant, as his appointments to St Mary-le-Bow and All Hallows, Bread Street, bear adequate testimony.[13] Then too, Thomas Upcher, the former weaver, served as rector of Fordham under his bishop, Edmund Grindal.[14]

Despite the lack of specific continuity in characters, there is evidence for a continuing tradition of dissent in the communities affected by the freewill debate on the general level. Thus, Patrick Collinson, relying in part on the research of Oxley, asserts that Bocking continued as a site of unrest during the early years of Elizabeth[15] and, along with Braintree, supplied several families bound for settlement in New England prior to the Civil War.[16] Communities such as Cranbrook in the Kentish Wealden region continued to give plenty of evidence of diversity in the 1570s,[17] and Christopher Hill has declared that the 'Weald produced radical heretics' when expounding his interests in the south-east during the seventeenth century.[18] Indeed, 'Kentish radicalism produced a strong Leveller movement, and culminated in a Digger colony and a near-Digger pamphlet'. Even further, it 'was a Muggletonian centre of some significance'.[19] We can thus point with some confidence to an ongoing tradition in these regions encompassing late medieval Lollardy, sixteenth-century heresy, and seventeenth-century radicalism. This sense of continuity is also seized upon by Williams with particular refrence to the subject of English Anabaptism. Hence, between the years '1575 and 1580, English Anabaptism entered a new phase, in which it was virtually succeeded by Brownism and Barrowism. Those very areas where Anabaptism had counted its greatest number of adherents — London, and the southeast and middle-east counties — now witnessed the emergence of Separatist congregations'.[20]

---

[12] See above p. 73.
[13] Garrett, p. 122.
[14] Patrick Collinson, 'The Godly: Aspects of Popular Protestantism' in *Godly People: Essays on English Protestantism and Puritanism* (London: Hambledon Press, 1983), p. 13. Cf. Garrett, p. 317.
[15] Collinson, 'The Godly', p. 12. Cf. Oxley, pp. 3 – 16.
[16] Collinson, 'The Godly', p. 14.
[17] Collinson, 'Cranbrook and the Fletchers: Popular and Unpopular Religion in the Kentish Weald' in *Godly People*, pp. 418 – 19.
[18] Hill, p. 51.
[19] *Ibid.*, p. 52.
[20] Williams, p. 787.

The early Elizabethan freewill debate

Proof of a certain degree of discontinuity between some of the specifics of the Edwardian/Marian controversies and those of Elizabeth's early years can be best obtained by looking at the reemergence of John Champneys; for, although the arguments and issues are necessarily similar in both instances, the cast and the setting are by now distinctively different.

Champneys emerged as something of a nondescript, isolated radical thinker during the Edwardian years[21] — obviously an Anabaptist by the rather imprecise standards of those days. Hargrave tries to establish that Champneys belonged to a 'quite diverse group of churchmen and writers' which participated in the development of 'a distinctively anti-Calvinist tradition of thought' during the early Elizabethan years. Without offering any support, he states that 'some of the figures, and especially John Champneys, are known to have had definite associations with the Freewill movement'.[22] If by 'Freewill movement' we are being asked to think in terms of the Bocking/Faversham circle and the King's Bench dispute (and we almost certainly are), a firm protest must be issued. As indicated above,[23] there is absolutely nothing of substance to link Champneys with these Edwardian and Marian occurrences. What needs to be stressed, therefore, is not the sense of continuity between the characters of the eras, but the striking degree of discontinuity.

Moreover, the role and prominence of Champneys during this later phase is not altogether clear. To Veron, he was certainly the 'valyaunt champion of the free wyll men',[24] especially since he had taken Veron to task for his views on election and predestation. Although reconstructing the precise order of the controversy is nigh unto impossible, it is possible to present a likely scenario. Veron's *A Fruteful treatise of Predestination and of the divine providence of God* was issued in 1561, together with *A Moste Necessary treatise of free will, not onlye against the Papistes, but also against the Anabaptistes*.[25] Since Champneys was known to have been the 'moste pestilent & pernitious sectarie' who issued 'blasphemouse callumnies' against Veron's understanding of 'this most comfortable doctrin of predesti-

---

[21] See above pp. 186 – 7.
[22] O. T. Hargrave, 'The Doctrine of Predestination in the English Reformation' (unpublished Ph.D. thesis, Vanderbilt University, 1966), p. 206.
[23] See discussion above pp. 189 – 90.
[24] Veron, *apology*, fol. 42a or Fiia.
[25] RSTC 24680, 24681 and 24684; Cf. Wallace, pp. 38 – 9.

nation',[26] it is highly probable that 'his rayling and venemous boke'[27] or letter was hastily conceived and distributed later in the same year. A short time afterward, and still in 1561, Veron appears to have countered by reissuing his predestinarian tract, and adding *An Apology or defence of the Doctrine of Predestination*. The *Apology* was required to meet the specific challenges put forth by Champneys in response to Veron's first effort of that year. To complete his position, Veron also published 'The Overthrow of the justification of workes and of the vain doctrine of the merits of men' in 1561.[28]

At this point, specific reference to Champneys comes to an end. Five years later, however, Robert Crowley sought to vindicate himself against an anonymous assailant who had criticized his predestinarian views as laid out in his rebuff directed at Nicholas Shaxton.[29] Fortunately, Crowley reproduced the text of this anonymous work.[30] Unfortunately, he identified its author only as 'Cerberus'. Was this Champneys again? Quite possibly, particularly in the absence of any other known candidates. If so, it would seem plausible that this was a second work by Champneys and not the one issued earlier as a critique of Veron. Veron is never referred to in the text, although Crowley was mentioned by name on more than one occasion.[31] References to John Knox also abound,[32] and the critic seemed conversant with Anthony Gilby's *Briefe Treatyse of Election and Reprobacion*, and William Wittingham's translation of Beza's *Declaration of the Chiefe Poynts of Christian Religion*.[33] Thus the work printed by Crowley could hardly have been the one which Veron claimed as directed at him.[34]

---

[26] Veron, *apology*, fol. 15b or Bviib.

[27] *Ibid.*, fol. 16b.

[28] Wallace, p. 39. Wallace places Champneys's work at an earlier point in the controversy.

[29] See Robert Crowley, *The Confutation of .xiii Articles, wherunto Nicolas Shaxton, late byshop of Salisburye subscribed and caused be set forthe in print* . . . (London; John Day and William Seres, [1548]). RSTC 6083.

[30] Crowley, *An Apologie, or Defence, of those Englishe Writers & Preachers which Cerberus the three headed Dog of Hell, chargeth wyth false doctrine, under the name of Predestination* (London: Henry Binneman, 1566). RSTC 6076; hereafter referred to as *Cerberus*.

[31] *Ibid.*, fols. 28b, 45a.

[32] *Ibid.*, fols. 34a, 73a, 92b.

[33] Hargrave sorted out the various references in his dissertation, p. 210.

[34] Hargrave sees only one work, while Wallace favours the existence of two. Hargrave places Champneys's response after the 'fruteful treatise', Wallace before. See Hargrave, 'Doctrine of Predestination', pp. 189 – 90, 208; Wallace, pp. 38 – 40. Martin seems to see only one tract as well. See 'The First that Made Separation', 288. William Prynne was also in agreement with the one tract theory in *A quench-coale. Or a briefe Disquisition and Inquirie, in what place of the Churche or Chancell the Lords-Table ought to be situated, especially when the Sacrament is administered?* (Amsterdam, 1637), p. 25; RSTC 20474. The editors of the RSTC make some relevant remarks which suggest two separate works. See the comments for RSTC 5742.10 in volume I, p. 258.

Given that the chronology of this early Elizabethan wrangling is difficult, one could hope to find greater profit in examining the tone and content of the freewill argument. Thankfully, this does prove to be the case and serves to establish that, although the players had changed, the discussion continued in the same essential outline. This much is abundantly clear from an examination of both Veron's *Apologye* and the *Apologie of Crowley*.

In the first work, which was addressed to the young Queen, Veron recalled the folly of Champneys during the reign of her 'moste gratious brother good king Edward (the) firtes'.[35] He had then acquired a considerable reputation for himself through inveighing 'against all the godly preachers of that time calling them marked mounsters of Antichrist, and men voyd of the spirit of god'. For his troubles, he was compelled to bear a faggot at St Paul's and listen to the sermonizing of 'father Coverdale'. According to Veron, the experience taught Champneys a vital lesson: that is, one should publish one's opinions anonymously to avoid such handling by authorities. This strategy had since been put into practice by Champneys, although, as noted above,[36] not with total success. Champneys, 'this stoute champion of Palagius', unceremoniously left his unfortunate printer 'in the briars', and proceeded to 'keepe hym self oute of the waye'.[37]

Veron recounted the usual freewill arguments in the course of refuting them. For example, God desires that all men be saved. The fact that some are not bears witness to the role of the human will in the salvation process, and also lends credibility to the task of preaching.[38] Furthermore:

'Sith that god doeth provide for everye manne all those thinges, that do pertayne to the bodilye & corporall life, it is not likely that he wyll fayle in those thinges, that doo pertayne or belonge unto the lyfe of the soule, and unto the healthe and salvation of the same, whiche thinge coulde not bee, onlesse god shoulde offer his grace unto every man, and that sufficientlye unto salvation'[39]

Champneys, as the 'blynde guyde' of 'the free wyll men', was particularly fond of the Apostle Paul's affirmation of the universal salvific desire of God as found in the second chapter of his first epistle to Timothy.[40] For his part, Veron decided to rely on Augustine in

[35] Veron, *apology*, fol. 16a.
[36] See above p. 188.
[37] Veron, *apology*, fol. 16b.
[38] *Ibid.*, fol. 9b.
[39] *Ibid.*, fols. 17b – 18a.
[40] *Ibid.*, fol. 28b. See I Timothy 2: 1 – 6.

refuting the freewill arguments,[41] and took great delight in pointing up the 'absredityes' of his opponent's position.[42]

Before moving on from Veron to Crowley, some final words concerning associations is called for. It is abundantly clear that the Protestantism being espoused at the time by Veron and his colleagues was wary of a two-pronged foe. One prong was sectarianism, which could still collectively be referred to as Anabaptism. The second was the religion of Rome. In the opinions expressed by Champneys and his compatriots, the two appeared to converge as far as Veron was concerned. Thus, he refers joyously to 'the utter overthrowe of the popishpe [sic] pelagisme'.[43] Champneys, in arguing a particular point, proves himself to be 'a verye Pelagian . . . and consequentelye a raunke papyste'.[44] Moreover, Champneys appears to tailor his message to fit his audience 'so that he maye seme to say somewhat to please the free wyll men, and theyr nexte alies the papistes, with all'.[45] And Veron sees himself defending the true church of God 'againste all maner of heretics and abhominable erroures bothe of the papistes and of the Anabaptistes, and of all other sectaryes'.[46] This was the same tack followed by Veron in his earlier *treatise of free wil*, where he apparently viewed the parties as sharing a common commitment to reviving 'the detestable heresies of Pelagius, and of the Luciferians, whiche saye and affirm, that we be able by our own natural strength to fulfil the law and commaundementes of God'.[47] At one point near the beginning of this work, he expressed wonder 'at our pope pelagians and at the viperous broode of the fre wyll men whych do styll to the greate injurye of the gratuite and free grace of God, so set oute boast and advaunce the free wyll and strength of man'.[48]

Here again, what is noteworthy in all these examples is not the obvious and by now familiar polemics, but the association. It is most significant that this form of identification between papist and sectarian should figure so prominently in Veron's thought; for as will be seen shortly,[49] those who framed the Thirty-nine Articles seem to have had similar conceptions and concerns.

Finally, the attitude toward higher learning displayed in this controversy should be noted. Naturally, each side tends to denigrate

[41] See Veron, *apology*, fol. 10a.
[42] *Ibid.*, fol. 30b.
[43] *Ibid.*, fol. 17a.
[44] *Ibid.*, fol. 37b.
[45] *Ibid.*, fols. 41a – 41b.
[46] *Ibid.*, fol. 40b.
[47] See above p. 194 regarding this treatise. This statement is taken from the latter part of the title of that work.
[48] Veron, *free wil*, fol. A5b.
[49] See below p. 207.

the authorities in the opposition's camp. Champneys is regarded as particularly reprehensible because he 'doethe abuse [the] symple and ignoraunt' in his handling of Veron's doctrinal utterances.[50] At the same time, he engages in 'an unlearned fomblynge together of the scryptures, agaynst a doctryn . . . alowed of all the godlye learned men in the world'.[51] To Champneys, Veron's 'learned ministers' were actually 'the divells most obediente children and trusty desciples. Wheras all men may judge hym rather to be an ympe of Sathan'.[52] Yet Champneys continued to harass the godly divines and undermine their efforts to further Christ's 'kingdome', just as he had done during Edward's time. As for motivation, Veron suspected that he knew what 'myght be the chiefest cause why he stomaketh so agaynste the godly learned ministers':

> because that he is hym self voyde bothe of learnynge and also of all true godlynesse. For, ther be non so greate enemies unto learninge, as they (that) be altogether unlerned, & withoute godly knowledge, as this valyaunt champion of the free wyll men is, who is so rude and ignoraunt, that he can not construe 2 lines of Saint Augustine, nor of any other godlye wryter. And yet he alone and none other can declare what be the spyrituall powers that (the) holy ghost doth geve in theese dayes, to all true and perfecte mynisters of the gospell of Chryst.[53]

Obviously, Veron could feel nothing but pity (and considerable contempt) for those who might have the misfortune to be 'scholed at champeneys handes'.[54] Veron was clearly a man of reason, and 'anye reasonable man' could not help being convinced by his arguments.[55]

Enter 'Cerberus'

The anonymous tract which takes Robert Crowley to task is remarkable for several reasons, not the least of which is the support which the author tried to elicit for his position. In the first place, he seems bent on using Augustine for his own purposes, perhaps, as

[50] Veron, *apology*, fol. 17a.
[51] *Ibid.*, fol. 41a.
[52] *Ibid.*, fol. 41b.
[53] *Ibid.*, fols. 41b – 42a.
[54] *Ibid.*, fol. 42a.
[55] See his comments on fol. 38b of this tract.

suggested by Hargrave, to create 'something of a middle position on predestination'.[56] In the process of defending himself against charges of Pelagianism and also repudiating determinism, the author, referred to by Crowley as 'Cerberus', drew on other unlikely sources such as Melanchthon and Bullinger, the latter being reckoned 'the chiefest and most excellent of all the Switcers'.[57] Even Calvin was not spared the indignity of being counted in the writer's camp; he was found useful in countering the Pelagian opinion 'That infantes whiche are not baptised, can not have the Kingdome of God nor eternall lyfe'. Here, for once, Augustine was actually on the wrong side of the fence, opposed to Calvin and 'so many of us, whych are Gospellers'.[58]

Evidently Cerberus (quite probably Champneys), had been accused of Pelagianism and related doctrines such as works' righteousness in the text of a letter. Not only does he thus set out to exonerate himself from such charges, but also to demonstrate where he differs 'from certaine Englishe writers and Preachers, whome he chargeth with the teaching of false doctrine, under the name of Predestination'.[59] For his part, Crowley was sceptical about the existence of such a letter; Cerberus was simply looking for an excuse 'to barke at the Preachers of predestination'. Thus, he trumped up an imaginary charge, taking full advantage of a printer's error in a work by William Samuell as the occasion for the dispute.[60]

Cerberus then proceeded to rehearse eleven Pelagian errors and demonstrate his distance from them through his refutations. Thus, the sixth 'errour is exceeding wicked and execrable, that man by the law, by doctrine, and by free choise, is able to doe any maner of good worke, whatsoever it be, without the grace and helpe of God'. Cerberus also rejects the notion 'that the grace of God is given according to our deserving'.[61] Nor can he accept that divine assistance and 'free choyse' are mutually exclusive in the spiritual drama.[62] In his effort to find the middle path, he actually attempts to turn the tables on his adversaries (undoubtedly the supralapsarians), and to find them guilty of Pelagianism in their extremist posture. Since such a conclusion rests upon a unique approach to logic, it is necessary to quote Cerberus's argument at some length

---

[56] Hargrave, 'Doctrine of Predestination', p. 209. See references to Augustine in Crowley, *Cerberus*, fols. 17a – 18a, 29a – b, 45b, 48b, 87b – 88b.
[57] Crowley, *Cerberus*, fols. 34a, 84a.
[58] *Ibid.*, fol. 24a.
[59] *Ibid.*, fol. 1a.
[60] *Ibid.*, fols. 1a – 3a.
[61] *Ibid.*, fol. 16a.
[62] *Ibid.*, fol. 17a.

And here, yet once againe, I desire thee to marke who they are, which with Pelagius fall into this extremitie to affirme, that if a man have choise, then hath he no nede of Gods helpe, then hath he no choise at all. And who they are, which on the other side, with Austen against Pelagius, do affirme and confesse: that man so hath fredom or choise, that neverthelesse, he hath continually, nede of the helpe & grace of God Who they are, I say, which in this point also, ought worthily to be called Pelagians, let all men judge. The case is so clere, that no lack of knowledge, but onely wilfull blindness, may helpe to cloke the matter.[63]

Similar opinions warranted being classified by Crowley as 'blasphemie intollerable', 'filthy puddle, and sincke moste execrable: full of stinking errours, full of damnable presumption, like to the pride of Lucifer moste abhominable'.[64] Following his recitation, Cerberus began his personal attacks, focussing first on Crowley and then upon John Knox. In both cases, the concern was to avoid the 'Stoicall necessitie' which made God, 'the principal cause', the author of sin and wickedness.[65] Both Crowley and Knox were clearly guilty of maintaining a system which permitted no other conclusion. Even Crowley himself admitted: 'my words might have bene more explained . . . if I had sene that before I wrate that booke'.[66] Naturally, he differed from Cerberus over the interpretation of his words, arguing that while God's predestinating activity was indeed the cause of Adam's fall, it could never be the cause of his sin. Hence the fall was ultimately 'good', since thereby all men were shut up 'under sinne, that the promise which is of the faith of Jesus Christ, might be given to the faithfull'.[67] Cerberus went as far as to claim that 'whatsoever the Ethnickes and ignorant did attribute unto Fortune', his opponents (especially Knox) assigned 'to the providence of God'.[68] Crowley, although asserting that Knox was 'yet living, & able to defend his owne writings', could not resist coming to his defence.[69]

It must be emphasized that Cerberus was deeply impressed with his status as an Englishman. Not only was he setting forth the errors of Pelagius 'in Englyshe',[70] he was also sounding the clarion cry to his fellow countrymen regarding the dire implications of this fatalistic

---

63 *Ibid.*, fols. 17b – 18a.
64 *Ibid.*, fol. 23a.
65 *Ibid.*, fols. 28b – 29a, 34b, 60b.
66 *Ibid.*, fol. 29b.
67 *Ibid.*, fol. 30a.
68 *Ibid.*, fol. 34b.
69 *Ibid.*, fols. 44b – 45a.
70 *Ibid.*, fol. 23b.

doctrine. Although its supporters might try to disguise its meaning, 'yet shall there never the state of a common wealth in England stand, if thys persuasion may once take root among the people'.[71] Indeed, the security of kingdoms everywhere was tied to the rejection of this false doctrine.

> Alas who seeth not the destruction of England to follow this doctrine? who seeth not the confusion of all common weales, to depend hereupon? What Prince may sit safely in the seat of his kingdome? What subject may live quietly possessing hys owne? What man shall be ruled by right of a lawe: if thys opinion may be perfectly placed in the heartes of the people?[72]

Is it not remarkable that one accused of holding sectarian beliefs should demonstrate such concern for his nation's welfare and the maintenance of the social order? Here, Cerberus is reminiscent of the sense of national urgency displayed by the Kentish freewill men during the course of the Edwardian and Marian eras.[73] The contention might be highly theological, but it had ramifications which appeared to be critical for England as a nation. It will be recalled that this struggle for civilization, this modest *kulturkampf*, brought out considerable anxieties in Bradford too as he contemplated with horror the sad state of English religion with the freewill position at the helm.[74] Concern for national welfare would seem to be yet another weapon in the freewillers' arsenal during these years, aimed at disarming their opponents by reversing the tables — although it must also be remembered that Harte had given evidence of this patriotic concern. This strategy included an attempt to set the record straight as to which party was closest to the extremist, unbiblical spirit of Pelagius. It included a direct rebuke aimed at those thus far 'afrayde of freewill' who tended to fall 'out of the lime Kell into the cole pit, from High presumption into depe desperation'.[75]

Another aspect of this freewillers' campaign was the obvious desire to be distanced from both papist and Anabaptist. This, of course, was in addition to the necessity of overthrowing the supralapsarian position. Thus, 'the blinde papistes' may be reckoned genuine 'Pelagians' in their opinions regarding the capacity of men to do good

---

[71] *Ibid.*, fol. 60b.
[72] *Ibid.*, fol. 65b.
[73] See above pp. 81 – 3, 149.
[74] For example, see above pp. 125 – 6.
[75] Crowley, *Cerberus*, fols. 83a, 99a.

apart from grace, 'bicause they hold, eyther al, or some part of hys errours'. Men such as Knox who claim insight into the secret counsels and workings of the Almighty produce 'revelations which . . . are meete for those which delight in the damnable dreames of some doting destinie, and may well be called inspirations of olde Arrians, revelations of blinde Anabaptistes, or unwritten verities of superstitious Papists, rather than the secret counsel of God, revealed unto men of our age'.[76]

The degree to which the anonymous freewiller succeeded in achieving his ends is open to question. No doubt there were many who remained in the ranks of the unconvinced. What seems particularly striking, however, is this attempt at compromise and moderation in the freewill position. His reliance upon Augustine to demonstrate that God's 'predestination is onelye of things that be good'[77] may not be exactly what the divines of 1563 had in mind when they set forth Article XVII and spoke of 'Predestination to Life'.[78] Yet it does demonstrate that a climate for compromise and negotiation was coming into existence when even so-called extremists such as freewill exponents are willing to gravitate toward the middle. It would seem an unavoidable conclusion that the Elizabethan worthies in Convocation would ultimately be the beneficiaries of such moderation, and that their proposals could thus be expected to appeal to an extremely diverse range of Englishmen.[79]

At the same time, Cerberus's distinction between 'prescience and predestination' (again claiming to derive inspiration from Augustine) would undoubtedly be acceptable to both Erasmians and continental Anabaptists; 'For though God doe foresee all things: yet doeth he not predestinate all things'.[80] They would also support his efforts to emphasize the conditional nature of God's dealings with mankind. Again, resort is made to Augustine:

> Thys predestination is of condition and of justice. For God before the fall of man, dyd not by the power of binding so predestinate him to die, that of necessitie he must nedes die, but under that condition, if he sinned. Bicause therefore man did sin, it was a

[76] *Ibid.*, fols. 45a – b, 73a.

[77] *Ibid.*, fol. 48b.

[78] See Charles Hardwick, *A History of the Articles of Religion* (London: George Bell & Sons, 1904), p. 311.

[79] See the discussion below pp. 204 – 6 on Thomas Talbot and his circle.

[80] Crowley, *Cerberus*, fols. 48b – 49a. Potential for confusion exists at this point in the publication owing to two successive folio pages which both bear the number '49'. This can be avoided by using what appears to be the original numbering (i.e. Ni and Nii).

righteous thing, that he should die. If he sinned not, he should not be bound to death by any chayn of Gods predestination.[81]

According to Cerberus, Augustine's perspective on the issue was 'often repeated and commended, by the best learned of the Protestantes' — evidence that he viewed himself as being very much of the emerging mainstream and not party to a minority opinion. Moreover, he remarks in another place that Augustine's comments on the subject of predestination 'do plainely set forth, the full resolution of all this question'.[82]

In summing up his case, the writer returned to a final theme which received much attention from the continental Anabaptists, namely, the primacy of the atonement and the mediatorial function of Christ in the eternal scheme of things. Indeed, his emphasis is purely Christocentric, in opposition to what he considers to be a major oversight on the part of his detractors. While others point to 'a higher cause' for the electing activity of God, that being 'the eternall purpose and predestination of God, which he determined onely in himself', the writer was content to go no further or higher than 'the free mercie of God in Christ'.[83] He could not abide the 'glose' of the Geneva Bible which maintained that God's 'free mercie in Christ is an inferiour cause of salvation'. 'For surelie, that eternall purpose, whych cometh not of Gods free mercie in Christ, is to destroy, and not to save'.[84] Moreover, the coming of Christ would have been made 'in vaine' if 'God the Father is without him alredy reconciled': that is, if we must look to something other than Christ's work of 'reconciliation and mediation' as the basis of man's acceptance before God. To ensure that he would not be taken to task for superficiality, the writer informed his readers that this act of salvation had been performed by Christ 'not only now in tyme, but also everlastingly in the most hygh and eternall purpose of God, before the foundation of the world was layde'.[85]

Perhaps it is not too much to add that the sentiments displayed in the anonymous tract anticipated certain aspects of what might be termed the English compromise as far as the established church is concerned — or, perhaps better, one of the mainstreams of that Anglican tradition which chose to see the world and all that it

---

[81] *Ibid.*, fol. 88b. Cf. the argument of Barry and Lawrence against Bernhere, pp. 160 – 3 above.

[82] *Ibid.*, fol. 48b.

[83] *Ibid.*, fol. 97b.

[84] *Ibid.*, fols. 97b – 98a. Also see Hargrave, 'Doctrine of Predestination', p. 210, regarding the identification of the Geneva Bible.

[85] Crowley, *Cerberus*, fol. 99a.

contained in a relatively optimistic way. Thus one could relate this position to that which Tyacke has enunciated with reference to the ascendancy of Arminianism early in the next century — 'a gospel of hope, in which salvation was the potential lot of everyone'.[86] That our anonymous author is in this line of thought seems clear from the following summary:

> for the Scripture describeth God unto me, wythout Christ as a wrathfull and moste terrible Judge, but in Christ, and for hys sake, as a father whose wrath is pacified, and he well pleased, reconciles, agreed, and at one: and to speak of a hygher cause or purpose, to elect and save only in God, beside or without this free mercie in Christ, or that Christ and Gods free mercie in hym, is not the chiefest cause which worked and obteyneth the decree, and purpose of God, to elect and save, it is plainely nothing else, but to deny the mercy of God in election, reconciliation, redemption and salvation, by Christ, in Christ, and for Christ.[87]

Thomas Talbot and the search for truth

Yet another example of resistance to extreme predestinarian theology is seen in the sentiments of Thomas Talbot, identified by Strype as 'parson of St. Mary Magdalen, Milk-street, London'. In a fluent letter apparently addressed to the bishops during deliberations on the articles of religion, Talbot spoke to the concerns of a moderate group which felt relegated to second-class status in the English Church.[88] Described by Hargrave as evidently 'the leader, or at least the spokesman, of a considerable group of non-Calvinist Anglicans'[89] (again with scant substantiation), Talbot and those in his circle spoke as men fully loyal to the cause of true religion in England. Indeed, it is probable that some may have suffered loss during the Marian reaction. Yet they find that they 'are constrained hitherto to sustain . . . daily the shameful reproach and infamy of free-will men, Pelagians, papists, epicures, anabaptists, and enemies unto God's holy predestination and providence, with other such like opprobrious

---

[86] Nicholas Tyacke, *Anti-Calvinists: The Rise of English Arminianism, c. 1590–1640* (Oxford: Clarendon Press, 1987) p. 246.
[87] Crowley, *Cerberus*, fol. 98b.
[88] Strype, *Annals*, I, 1, p. 494.
[89] Hargrave, 'Doctrine of Predestination', p. 212.

words and threatenings of such like, or as great punishments and corrections, as upon any of the aforesaid errors and sects is meet and due to be executed'.[90] And what of the crime which warranted such persecution?

> they do hold, contrary to a great number of their brethren the protestants, that God's holy predestination is no manner of occasion or cause at all in anywise of the wickedness, iniquity, or sin, that ever was, is, or ever shall be wrought, committed, or done in the world, whereby any part of mankind shall be predestinate, of any unavoidable necessity, to commit and perpetrate the sin and wickedness that mankind, or any part of mankind, from the beginning hath or shall commit or perpetrate; and so to be ordained before all worlds, by force of God's holy predestination, to an unavoidable necessity to be damned eternally.[91]

Talbot's submission went on to reason that God would be the 'author and occasion' of any predestined wrong which had to be performed 'of an inevitable necessity', and pointed out the severity of this state of affairs in serving as 'an example thereof unto the whole world'. Sounding very much like Cerberus, he maintained 'That God doth foreknow and predestinate all good and goodness, but doth only foreknow, and not predestinate, any evil, wickedness, or sin, in any behalf'. This, he claimed, was actually the historic position held by 'all the learned fathers unto this our age', and was still the favoured view of 'a great many of the learned of this our age'.[92]

For these reasons and no other the moderate gospellers were held in contempt by their immoderate brethren — 'the protestants and learned'. They sought earnestly to avoid being classified with 'such heretical names abovenamed', and also to be exempted from such ecclesiastical discipline as might be meted out by the establishment.[93] The exception would be proven cases of heterodoxy, where one might be shown to uphold 'that man of his own natural power is able to think, will, or work of himself any thing, that should in any case help or serve towards his own salvation, or any part thereof'.

Talbot's party also sagaciously recommended that all 'disputation' on the subject of predestination be done 'by writing . . . for the avoiding of all unreverend speaking of God's holy predestination'. It would also serve as a check on 'all contention and brawling, and other

---

[90] Strype, *Annals*, I, 1, p. 496.
[91] *Ibid*., p. 495.
[92] *Ibid*., pp. 495 – 6.
[93] *Ibid*., pp. 496 – 7.

uncharitable behaviour', which is the logical outcome of such careless conversation.

Finally, Talbot and his circle requested equality in freedom of expression. They appear, in fact, to have been asking for nothing less than official sanction to publish and propagate their views as they wished – the same rights held by their more vociferous and weighty opponents. Thus:

> all men may be able to judge and discern the truth betwixt both parties, and brotherly charity be observed and kept among such as do profess God's word, hate all papistry, and be true and obedient subjects unto the queen's majesty, to the good example of all the rest of the people, both within this realm and without.[94]

One gathers from Talbot's lamentations that talk of a 'predestinarian offensive'[95] does not overstate the situation in early Elizabethan England. It is also worth noting that Strype linked the Talbot 'petition' to discussions surrounding the seventeenth article of the Church of England's charter,[96] suggesting the year 1562 as a likely date because of an internal appeal to 'this present parliament'.[97] Strype also inserted a fascinating 'note' pertaining to the tenth article, 'Of Free-will', which he regarded as 'nearly bordering upon the 17th.'[98] This item concerned Richard Taverner's observations on the Reformational free-will discussion as contained in the 'dedication' of his translation of Erasmus Sarcerius' 'common places'. According to Taverner, Sarcerius and Melanchthon were agreed in their determination to avoid going to extremes in such hotly-disputed topics as 'predestination, contingency, and free-will'. These two were not alone, but joined by 'other excellent clerks' in rejecting 'free-will only in spiritual motions'. Even further, this denial of free-will capacity was applicable only to 'such persons as were not yet regenerated and renewed by the Holy Ghost'. In 'the mean season', however, the learned shifted their stance somewhat, so that 'they took it not so away, but they left them also in spiritual motions a certain endeavour, or willing. Which endeavour nevertheless could finish

---

[94] *Ibid.*, pp. 497 – 8.
[95] The expression belongs to O.T. Hargrave. See his article, 'The Predestinarian Offensive of the Marian Exiles at Geneva', *Historical Magazine of the Protestant Episcopal Church*, XLII (1973), 111 – 23.
[96] Strype, *Annals*, I, 1, p. 494.
[97] *Ibid.*, p. 497. There was in fact no parliament sitting in 1562 by current reckoning, but the statement is correct according to the old-style, with New Year's Day falling on 25 March.
[98] *Ibid.*, p. 498.

nothing, unless it were holpen by the Holy Ghost'. Strype concluded the reference abruptly with Taverner's own summation: 'This, after my poor judgement, is the rightest and truest way'.[99]

One wonders if Taverner was speaking for Strype as well as for himself. At any rate, it would seem obvious by now that he spoke for more than a few during this stage of the predestinarian debate. The impression emerges of a pushy, scholasticized minority, endeavouring to railroad its narrow theological programme past all obstacles (including a rather meek majority opinion which tended toward moderation). The immediate result of the struggle, of course, can best be evaluated by referring to the tone of the Thirty-nine Articles themselves, as well as to the overall complexion of religious direction under the Elizabethan settlement.

The intent of the articles of religion

The sensible point of departure for any discussion of the articles of faith pertaining to the English Church is really the Forty-two Articles of 1553. This is particularly true when considering the status of freewill thought in England during the Tudor era, since the predestinarian controversy was gaining steam at this very time. Bicknell has described the Forty-two Articles as 'a doubled-edged weapon, designed to smite two opposite enemies. On the one hand they attack mediaeval teaching and abuses, on the other hand they attack Anabaptist tenets'.[100] According to Bicknell, the concern was actually more for the latter than the former, since 'no party had a good word' for the radicals, and 'there is hardly any error of doctrine or morality that was not proclaimed by some of them'.

This popular conception regarding the intent of the earlier Articles was also very much evident in the writings of Charles Hardwick, who prefaced his examination of the said propositions with a lengthy (though not terribly erudite) discussion of the Anabaptist menace and other troublesome spirits. For example, Hardwick, who sought to identify at least two distinct schools of Anabaptists, maintained that 'some of the original Anabaptists had insisted on the dogma of an

---

[99] *Ibid.* There were three editions of Taverner's work, including one in 1553 when the freewill debate was on the verge of heating up. See *DND*, XIX, p. 395.
[100] E. J. Bicknell, *A Theological Introduction to the Thirty-nine Articles of the Church of England*, revised by H. J. Carpenter, 3rd ed. (London: Longmans, 1955; orig. pub. 1919), p. 11.

absolute necessity',[101] probably derived from Hooper's similarly none-too-astute observations on the same theme.[102] Hardwick then proceeded to find numerous allusions to Anabaptist beliefs in the Articles themselves. Signs of lingering confusion over what Anabaptism really stood for were clear in his treatment of the ninth and tenth articles. The former, 'Of Free Will', 'was meant to disavow all sympathy with Anabaptism on the subject of preventing and co-operating grace'. The latter, ' "Of Grace" was meant as a reply to opposite errors current in a second school of Anabaptism and adopted by a few of the more violent Reformers who were sometimes called the "Gospellers".' To Hardwick, these types appeared 'to have been pushing their belief in absolute predestination to such frightful lengths that human actions were esteemed involuntary, and the evil choice of man ascribed to a necessitating fiat of his Maker'.[103] Similarly, Article seventeen, ' "Of Predestination and Election" was intended to allay the numerous altercations that were stirred in the reforming body, as well as in scholastic and Anabaptist circles by these awful and mysterious topics'. It was further aimed at curbing 'fatalistic errors' which claimed certain victims during these days through 'taking a one-sided view of doctrines then discussed'.[104]

If Hardwick's line may be taken as generally reflecting the official outlook during the mid-Tudor years, one can readily see the value to the authorities of having a convenient scapegoat such as Anabaptism. Anything inexplicable and controversial could easily be attributed to that abysmal, nebulous pestilence which sought to revive the ancient heresies of earlier centuries. Clearly, Hardwick was no friend of extremism of any kind; nor, for that matter, was Bicknell, who proceeded to do with the Thirty-nine Articles what Hardwick had done with the Forty-two. Both men stressed the moderate nature of the various articles of religion, giving full acknowledgement to the debt owed to continental Lutheranism in their formulation. Thus, Hardwick comments that 'it is most important to observe that Parker and his friends, instead of drawing hints from "Swiss" Confessions, which were in high favour with the Marian exiles, had recourse to a series of Articles of "Saxon" origin, particularly distinguished by the moderation of their tone'. Support for the Augsburg Confession was therefore considerable among one 'part of Reformers in this country' soon after 'the accession of Elizabeth'.[105] Bicknell's references to both

---

[101] Hardwick, p. 86.
[102] See Hardwick, pp. 88 – 9, and p. 20 above.
[103] Hardwick, p. 99.
[104] *Ibid.*, pp. 100 – 1.
[105] *Ibid.*, p. 123.

Lutheran confessionalism and the need to refute the Anabaptist errors begins with his treatment of the very first Article, 'Of Faith in the Holy Trinity'.[106] Thus Article X 'asserts the need of grace against Pelagian Anabaptists'.[107] One is almost certainly on safe ground in assuming that little had changed since the sixteenth century, especially when recalling a work such as Thomas Rogers' *Catholic Doctrine of the Church of England*. Speaking about the unregenerate man's inability to perform that which is truly 'good' in the course of dealing with the same Article, Rogers had declared:

> Adversaries unto this truth are all such as hold that naturally there is free-will in us, and that unto the best things. So thought the Pharisees, the Sadducees, the Pelagians, and the Donatists: and the same affirm the Anabaptists and Papists.[108]

Undoubtedly, Rogers and Bicknell would disagree on the extent to which the Articles could be classified as genuinely Calvinistic in tone.[109] They would be at one, however, in seeing Anabaptism as the most outstanding popular enemy of mid-sixteenth century England.

Equally obvious is the conclusion that neither of the sides previously embroiled in the predestinarian controversy of the Edwardian/Marian years could claim full victory in the reign of Elizabeth. This goes without saying as far as the freewillers are concerned, since their close identification with Anabaptism meant an automatic relegation to the dissenting cold, at least initially and officially speaking. The authorities were clearly still very much plagued by Münster-generated phobias regarding the potential for anarchy contained in the radical posture. Defining it precisely did not become a priority. Extreme predestinarians could hardly have been much happier with the 'predestination to life', and no more, assertion, however, especially if the author of *The Confutation* was correct in his claim that predestinarian thought in England had become more extreme than that originally propounded in Geneva. Nevertheless, we have seen attempts made by an array of researchers to portray official theology under Elizabeth as a clear victory for

---

[106] Bicknell, p. 22.
[107] *Ibid.*, p. 172.
[108] Thomas Rogers, *The Catholic Doctrine of the Church of England, An Exposition of the Thirty-nine Articles*, ed. J. J. S. Perowne, Parker Society, No. 40 (Cambridge: University Press, 1854), pp. 105 – 6.
[109] See also the obvious interpretation offered in Richard Laurence, *An Attempt to Illustrate those Articles of the Church of England which the Calvinists Improperly Consider as Calvinistical* (Oxford, 1853).

Calvinism.[110] Here, the issue of the 'Calvinist consensus' and its modifications confront us.[111] Thus, Peter Lake, while wishing to avoid some of the trappings associated with this expression, nonetheless maintains that 'the doctrine of the English church was, by the standards of the mid-sixteenth century, unequivocally reformed' – although he is quick to point out that the 'administrative structure' could not be seen in a similar light.[112] The 'evangelical protestant world-view' which he sees as uniting 'many puritans with the more zealously protestant of the Elizabethan bishops' concerned itself primarily 'with the potentially transforming effects of the gospel on both individuals and on the social order as a whole'. He finds that the 'doctrinal position that lay behind this attitude was uncompromisingly Calvinist'.[113] The enduring strength of this force is seen near the end of the century in the labours of Hooker, whose strategy 'had only been necessary because of the Calvinist dominance of the late Elizabethan church'.[114] Nicholas Tyacke is, if anything, even more forceful on this point, arguing that the 'characteristic theology of English Protestant sainthood was Calvinism, centring on a belief in divine predestination, both double and absolute'.[115] The Thirty-nine Articles are thus seen as having 'clearly favoured the Calvinists' – this much is evidently taken for granted – but 'the Elizabethan Prayer Book needed careful exposition in order not to contradict predestinarian theology'[116] (presumably it still does). Moreover, the Lambeth Articles are depicted as 'unequivocally Calvinist' and as supplying 'an accurate index of received Church of England teaching, although they incurred the displeasure of Queen Elizabeth'. Thus, 'Arminianism before Arminius was for the time being suppressed, and Calvinism remained dominant in England throughout the first two decades of the seventeenth century'.[117]

Despite this apparent unanimity in portraying the Elizabethan and even Jacobean era as the golden age of Calvinism in England, one notes with considerable interest a difference of opinion among these recent writers when it comes to evaluating changes within the English Calvinist world itself at the end of the sixteenth century. Tyacke, for

[110] I am referring specifically to Tyacke in his *Anti-Calvinists: The Rise of English Arminianism, c. 1590 – 1640*, and to Lake's *Anglicans* and *Moderate puritans*. See also Cremeans, p. 60; Wallace, p. 31; cf. Hargrave, 'Doctrine of Predestination', p. 234.
[111] Regarding this term, see Lake, *Anglicans*, p. 6 and p. 12, n 15.
[112] Lake, *Anglicans*, p. 1.
[113] Lake, *Moderate puritans*, p. 279.
[114] Lake, *Anglicans*, p. 238.
[115] Tyacke, p. 1.
[116] *Ibid.*, p. 3.
[117] *Ibid.*, p. 5.

example, considers there was an extremist shift in the 1590s, which brought 'English Calvinist teaching . . . in line with continental religious developments'.[118] Moreover, 'absolute predestination' was still being upheld by the highest worthies in the land during this same period, so that 'it is not an exaggeration to say that by the end of the sixteenth century the Church of England was largely Calvinist in doctrine'. According to Tyacke 'this situation had come about through default of any alternative interpretation of the Elizabethan religious settlement, and its confessional basis remained insecure'[119] in consequence.

In turning to Lake, however, we are encouraged to think in terms of 'the subtle modification of Calvinist orthodoxy' which occurred during these years, made necessary by the task of 'reconciling the demands of experimental predestinarianism with the defence of a genuinely national church'. Calvinism thus came to be softened in its English context in order to make it more palatable. 'Supra-lapsarian Calvinism' was replaced gradually by its gentler counterpart – infralapsarianism or 'sub-lapsarianism'. 'The death of Christ for all men could be asserted and the channels of sacramental grace emphasized, in order to underwrite a generalized style of piety and evangelism and defuse the divisiveness inherent in too bald a distinction between the godly and the ungodly'. Lake describes this accommodation as a 'process of adjustment', 'presided over by men trained in the moderate puritan tradition of the late Elizabethan church'.[120]

Obviously, there are a number of problems inherent in these stances, perhaps owing in part to a lack of familiarity with the details of such things as the King's Bench proceedings. One notes, for instance, a preoccupation with trends and statements dealing with the official level, with relatively little if any consideration of what has come to be termed the popular realm. The apparent defence of a certain perspective by one, or several, high-ranking churchmen does not prove acceptance further down the line. Bishops may rant all they like about accepted doctrine, but ordinary believers in England dating back at least to the time of Wycliffe, displayed an obstinate tendency to believe what they wished. Moreover, the argument which sees the Elizabethan world as a triumph for Calvinism overlooks the presence (and persistence) of a distinctive freewill tradition which came into focus prior to the religious settlement; and this occupied

[118] *Ibid.*, p. 4.
[119] *Ibid.*, p.3.
[120] Lake, *Anglicans*, p. 244.

much of the spiritual ground which, it is claimed, relates to the genius of the Calvinist movement. For example, Lake speaks of 'a certain internal spiritual dynamic' related to the puritan tradition which 'forced the believer into a constant struggle to externalise his sense of his own election through a campaign of works directed against Antichrist, the flesh, sin and the world'. He affirms that it 'is perhaps the basic contention' of his then current investigation 'that if puritanism is to be defined at all it must be in terms of this spiritual dynamic'.[121] Yet can this definition be seen as distinctively, or perhaps better exclusively, puritan in the Calvinist context in the light of the position taken by the freewill party during the mid-Tudor years? Granted, some of the emphases may have differed in the fine points, but it is hard to escape the conclusion that the freewillers exhibited the very same concerns long before puritanism and asceticism came to be seen as bedfellows by the noisy minority of Reformed divines.[122] In addition, 'the puritans' view of themselves as a saving remnant within a still profane nation'[123] seems hardly original or unique when the freewillers' prophetic call to repentance is remembered. And although one might take comfort in the fact that Bancroft later 'did not challenge the objective truth of the Calvinist doctrine of predestination that was still predominant in the English church' during the course of lamenting 'the antinomian consequences of puritan preaching on predestination',[124] one cannot escape the conclusion that the same freewillers did make the connexion a generation earlier and sought to develop a mature theology which seemed more conducive to the question of motivational holiness. The fact that few if any listened at the upper level of the Church does not lessen the reality of the effort. Thus, we approach with some scepticism the assertion that 'before 1604 the challenge to Calvinism never fully escaped from the university confines'.[125] In point of fact, it flourished at the popular level in the south-east before the death of Edward. To be sure, this popular thrust ensured that the mid-Tudor freewill movement would be stamped with a different ecclesiological and sacramental tone than that seen later in the rise of Arminianism, being more akin in most respects to the spirit of Lollardy than to the high churchmanship of the Caroline and Restoration eras.[126] Yet it is not too much to see in the freewillers the development and

---

[121] Lake, *Moderate puritans*, p. 282.
[122] See reference to Knappen's remark, p. 153 above.
[123] Lake, *Anglicans*, p. 242.
[124] Lake, *Moderate puritans*, p. 289.
[125] Tyacke, p. 9.
[126] See *ibid.*, p. 246, regarding the nature of English Arminianism.

popularization of a doctrinal position which is strikingly similar to that later adopted by the English ecclesiastical establishment.

This surely brings us to another question which is fundamental to this inquiry: namely, how much of the official statement of the faith of the English Church would be clearly unacceptable to the freewill men at the end of Mary's reign, especially when the trend toward growing sophistication and moderation in their ranks is taken into account? The answer would almost certainly be, 'not as much as expected'; for, although the continental Anabaptist would find little cause for rejoicing in the Elizabethan religious settlement, the moderating (and by now considerably fractured) freewill forces could live with much of it. Further, one can imagine that even Elizabeth would be sympathetic to the well-intentioned overtures of a Thomas Talbot, or perhaps, a Richard Taverner from another generation. These were not dangerous men, but the very type who could be accommodated by the design of the settlement. This projection would seem to square with the picture which ultimately emerges of the nature of the freewill movement as a whole; for, although the freewill men shared with the genuine Anabaptists the same basic perspectives on the nature of Christian discipleship and the call to radical holiness, they do not appear to have pressed the separatist implications of their stance to their logical conclusions. Perhaps they were never convinced that they had the divine sanction to go that far, since they were still loyal sons of England. In terms of Bainton's acceptable criteria regarding the 'left wing of the Reformation',[127] we find evidence of deep ethical concern (to the point of appearing to genuinely pose a threat to the Reformed establishment in the days of Edward and Mary), a certain degree of Christian primitivism, and an extremely pronounced anti-intellectualism (at least initially). On the other side of the ledger, we do not see excessive apocalyptic expectations, nor a clear-cut, once and for all decision to separate from the ecclesiastical mainstream.

In most cases, then, the actual threat posed by the freewill party to the stability and well being of the realm was surely far more perceived than real. For proof, one need only consider that when Arminianism later triumphed in high places in Laudian England the selfsame Articles remained the official position.[128] Well-stated freewill doctrine could thus be relatively at home with the religious situation in either 1563 or 1660. We must here remember that in the intervening years, the connexion between freewill ideas and sectarian groups such as

---

[127] See above, p. 21 for Bainton's views.
[128] See Tyacke on Laud and Arminianism in England in the seventeenth century (e.g. Appendix II on 'The Arminianism of Archbishop Laud', pp. 266 – 70.

Anabaptists appears to have begun to diminish in the minds of many. Eventually, certain aspects of freewill thought could be said to have become more closely associated with the new establishment than with the radical movement.

A foreshadowing of this trend, which in actuality marked a return to pre-Edwardian days, can be seen in the most outstanding episode involving Anabaptism in the early years of Elizabeth. When the pastor of the Dutch Church meeting in the sanctuary of the Austin Friars is dismissed by the bishop of London in 1560, the principal Anabaptist error which has given offence is once more incarnational.[129] Royal proclamations against Anabaptism during Elizabeth's day are equally notable for their failure to mention freewill ideas.[130] When Sir Francis Knollys attempts to find common ground between the 'free wyll men, or anabaptisticall sectaries' of his day and 'the Famylye of Love', he refers not to their commitment to anti-predestinarian ideas, but to their pursuit of perfectionism (which admittedly has some anti-predestinarian overtures), the one through 'the vertue of love', the other through 'faythe in the belevying that everye man is hable to fulfyll the lawe of God'.[131] A 'form of recantation prescribed to certain Anabaptists' lists numerous 'damnable and detestable heresies', but these reflect concerns on the part of the authorities which are still essentially Henrician in nature: no mention is made of freewill doctrine.[132] Similarly, when a Puritan engages an Anabaptist in debate in 1575, the discussion revolves around predictable topics such as oaths, weapons and magistrates.[133] When a man with a pastoral heart tries to comfort 'a godly and zealous Lady' who is distressed over 'the Annabaptists errouer' in the late 1580s, the focus is the interpretation of 'the sinne against the

---

[129] Heriot, XII, 270.

[130] See the relevant references in Hughes and Larkin above, chapter 2.

[131] *Original Letters Illustrative of English History*, ed. Henry Ellis, Third Series (orig. pub. London, 1846; rep. ed. New York: AMS Press, 1970), IV, 36. See also the proclamation of 1580 'Ordering Prosecution of the Family of Love' in Hughes and Larkin, II, 474 – 5, where the Familists are accused of encouraging 'assemblies of divers simple unlearned people . . . to esteem them to be more holy and perfect men than other are'. Also, see 'The form of abjuration tendered to those of the family of love' from the same time frame, printed in Wilkins, IV, 296, where mystical and eschatological fantasies are condemned. Knollys' concerns also seem to be echoed by John Rogers in the late 1570s, when he appears to see the Familists emerging out of the freewill debate of the late Marian years. See his *The Displaying of an horrible secte of grosse and wicked Heretiques, naming themselves the Familie of Love, with the lives of their Authours, and what doctrine they teach in corners* (London: George Bishop, 1577), fols. B1b, 07b. RSTC 21182. See also Horst, p. 154.

[132] Wilkins, IV, 282.

[133] Albert Peel, ed. 'A Conscientious Objector of 1575', in *Transactions of the Baptist Historical Society*, VII (1920), 71 – 128.

Holye Ghoste' — not 'temptations of election'.[134] And finally, the legacy which radical groups such as Anabaptists bequeathed to later separatist and congregationalist experiments in England was surely in the area of church polity in the first instance and not anti-predestinarian ideology.[135] Thus, one is confronted with the conclusion of Zerger regarding the 'religious soil' of the realm in the early stages of Elizabeth's reign: 'It could and did support an immigrant Dutch Anabaptist movement at the same time that it nourished a native evangelical movement with Anabaptist overtones'. Although this statement might be more appropriately applied to the Edwardian and Marian days (and thus, to the main focus of this study), since it is the present writer's conviction that the programme of the freewill party begins to moderate as it becomes increasingly sophisticated by the end of the Marian purge, he can nevertheless agree that 'the sacramentarian humus of Lollardy' continued to have an influence in the type of harvest being reaped.[136]

England and the freewill tradition

In assessing the place of the freewill movement in its mid-sixteenth-century context, one recalls Hargrave's claim that in the days of the 'early Elizabethan Church' England witnessed 'the development . . . of a distinctly anti-Calvinist tradition of thought'.[137] While we can agree that there was indeed evidence of such a tradition by this period, we must also insist that its specific origins go back at least to Edward's reign, largely in response to the growing extremism of the Calvinist stance in England which, as our evidence suggests, dates not from the last decade of the century (as suggested by Lake), but from the mid-Tudor era itself. Furthermore, in the light of later developments within the English Church, one may well ask whether it is too much to see the English freewill movement of the mid-Tudor years as a genuine part of the tradition of moderation and compromise which came to characterize both the Elizabethan Settlement in religion (as exemplified by the Thirty-nine Articles —

[134] See T[homas] C[ottesford], *Two very Godly and comfortable Letters, written over into England* (London: Edward Allde for Edward White, 1589). RSTC 5841.5.
[135] See White, especially chapters 2 – 5, and Knappen, chapters 10 and 15, for discussions related to this theme.
[136] Fred Zerger, 'Dutch Anabaptism in Elizabethan England', *Mennonite Life*, XXVI (1971), 23.
[137] Hargrave, 'Doctrine of Predestination', p. 206.

surely neither exclusively Catholic nor Calvinist) and the Restoration Church of the next century. As seen above,[138] the term Pelagian cannot be ascribed in a narrow theological sense to the mature freewillers who moved closer to a posture not significantly incompatible with Article X (and its foundational principles) of the English Church. To the best minds of the radical movement, grace was clearly indispensable, and not at all optional.

In another vein, however, a more radical appellation of some sort appears to fit as well if we consider that the freewillers laid great stress upon individual participation and the right of each and every man to develop his own way of looking at life and the world. Moreover, they seem to be intensely nationalistic in the sixteenth-century sense, sharing in a distinct feeling about England's manifest destiny in the divine economy of that day. Above all, Calvinism was for them (as for others since) a 'gloomy creed' indeed,[139] a system which involved 'a closed and programmatic world of language and experience'.[140] Thus they opposed what appeared to be the new order with all of its attendant threats to their way of life, and chose to opt out in some respects, at least temporarily – participants in 'religious voluntarism of a primary sort'.[141] To Collinson, this 'distinct tradition of free will . . . was foreign to protestantism but never lost to sight in the undercurrents of the English Reformation'.[142] Yet, given its ultimate direction and outcome, can one summarily exclude the freewillers and their tradition from the flow of the Protestant world in its peculiarly English context? In this sense, the radicals appear very much a part of the 'Anglican' way – discontented at times, but never fully separatist; absorbing perspectives from the continent (and from closer to home) which strengthened and supported their stance without being engulfed by them and thereby losing their sense of perspective and identity; and finally, remaining true to the grand designs of nationhood and equality. They should thus be permitted to take their place as legitimate members of that diverse body of believers which came to be known as Protestantism.

---

[138] See above, pp. 23 – 4.
[139] J. M. Roberts, *The Pelican History of the World* (Harmondsworth: Penguin Books Ltd., 1980), p. 551.
[140] Collinson, 'Voluntary Religion: Its Forms and Tendencies' in *The Religion of Protestants* (Oxford: Clarendon Press, 1982), p. 252.
[141] *Ibid.*
[142] *Ibid.* For an examination of the continuation of the freewill tradition at the academic level in Elizabethan Cambridge, see H. C. Porter, *Reformation and Reaction in Tudor Cambridge* (Cambridge: University Press, 1958). See especially chapter XVII, 'Peter Baro: Universality of Grace', pp. 376 – 90.

Appendix 1

Further notes on Ridley and the lost tract

The question of Ridley's authorship of a tract on predestination written in response to Bradford's urgings, and its possible identification with the document discussed above,[1] appears to be compounded by the presence of two unidentified and undated letters, written in Latin, among the Emmanuel MSS. The editor of Ridley's letters for the Parker Society provides the following note on these two items:

> These two letters are attributed to Ridley, though bearing neither the name of the writer nor of the person to whom sent, first on account of the internal evidence contained in the former of the two, and secondly on account of their position in the Emmanuel MSS. It appears probable that they were one or both addressed to Bradford. The former alludes to the rumoured treachery of Grimbold, a rumour which proved but too true. It mentions the annotations on Watson's two sermons, which are known to have been the work of Ridley; and it seems likely that one of the 'duo tractatus' referred to in a previous paragraph was the lost and deeply to be regretted treatise on Predestination and Election. If this conjecture be correct, then it is quite certain that the former of the two letters was addressed to Bradford; and a strong ground of probability will be laid for attributing the latter also either to Ridley as the writer, and to Bradford as the person addressed, or to Bradford as the writer, and to Ridley as the person addressed.[2]

The two letters were then printed in both the original Latin and in English translation. In addition, the second letter appeared in another translation in the Society's edition of Bradford's works. Here, it was clearly attributed to Ridley as part of his correspondence with Bradford. The editor's note appeared as follows:

> This letter is translated from the Latin of Bp Ridley, which has been printed in the Supplement to R.'s Works, p. 539, Park. Soc. It would seem likely that the 'Treatise', spoken of in the first

---

[1] See above pp. 130 – 7.
[2] Ridley, *Works*, p. 537.

217

paragraph, may be Ridley's Treatise on election, referred to in Letter LXXXVI., p. 214, above — 'I have in Latin drawn out the places of the scriptures, and upon the same have noted what I can for the time' — but which is not known now to exist. If so, the date of this letter would probably be after the middle of April 1555, which is the supposed date of Letter LXXXVI.[3]

This second letter has been included in Hargrave's discussion of the chronology relating to Bradford's appeal to Ridley at Oxford.[4]

In assessing the letters and the editors' commentaries, one notes instantly the high degree of conjecture regarding the whole affair. While the present writer has little quarrel with the assumption that these are indeed letters forming a part of the Ridley/Bradford correspondence story, there is considerable reluctance in accepting the supposed allusions to the predestinarian tract. For example, it if is assumed that one of the two treatises referred to in the first letter was the piece on predestination, then the fact that they were said to have been 'Anglice scriptos' has evidently been overlooked.[5] As seen above, however (and as the Bradford editor correctly noted), Ridley claimed to have begun the treatise considered by Coverdale to be the piece on predestination by drawing 'out the places of the scriptures . . . in Latin'.[6] Thus, the two hardly seem to fit together naturally.

There is also some difficulty with the reference in the second letter to an 'index' pertaining to the treatise supposedly dealing with predestination. This is said to be 'appended to the conclusion, (fol. 47,)', and to clearly reveal 'the sum of the whole treatise, and of all the matters which are discussed in it'.[7] The document discussed in chapter 5, however, contains no such index and would appear to have been considerably shorter than the work referred to in the anonymous letter which took some forty-seven folio pages. Still, one could put forward numerous possible explanations which would allow the *Responsiones* to be the missing document and the allusion in the letters to be to the same tract as mentioned in the anonymous letter, if it were only a matter of accounting for the index and the apparent discrepancy regarding length. For example, the *Responsiones* could be a draft of what became a much longer work, since Ridley evidently worked on it in stages, or at least intended to do more with it in the future. The index may not have existed in the original form, or may

---

[3] Bradford, II, 220.
[4] Hargrave, 'Marian Predestinarian Controversy'.
[5] Ridley, *Works*, p. 538.
[6] Bradford, II, 220.
[7] Ridley, *Works*, p. 542; cf. Bradford, II, 220.

have been omitted by a copyist. One could even speculate on the difference in paper size, and so on *ad infinitum*.

Further, it should be admitted that there are some aspects of the anonymous correspondence which would suggest, at least initially, that we do in fact have a reference to the Ridley's predestinarian tract. The writer asserts that he wishes to add somewhat to his 'treatise', so that it may be a more solid apology. When this is accomplished, he promises to reread a 'book' which had been 'previously written' by his correspondent (possibly Bradford's work on election), and return the same to him.[8] Even the opening of the letter could possibly seem appropriate to the predestinarian situation as seen in the appeal made by Bradford to the Oxford divines and a possible response from Ridley:

> That I have so long kept silence towards you, has been caused by the somewhat diffuse labour of this my production which I now send you. Although I have been a long time in travail, nevertheless I now bring forth (alas, the folly!) a rough and shapeless lump which needs much polishing. Yet because I know you to be by no means a despiser of my labours, (by which I desire, God is my witness, to benefit as many as possible and to hurt no one,) I have therefore determined to send it you, whatever it is and of whatever sort it may turn out to be.[9]

The tenor of this letter could indeed be accurately placed within the context of the predestinarian debate, and indeed has been so placed by Hargrave (albeit somewhat tentatively).[10] In the end, however, the evidence is unconvincing. In the first place, there is the question of the relationship between the two anonymous letters themselves. As indicated, there is the problem that the first letter mentions the sending of two works in English, when we should expect Latin to be the more appropriate tongue for the predestinarian piece. Further, we are confronted by the fact that in both letters, material is being forwarded from one side to another. The predestinarian tract could certainly not be at one and the same time one of the two English treatises mentioned in the first anonymous letter (as suggested by the Ridley editor) and the item which receives the spotlight in the second letter (favoured by the Bradford editor). Indeed, there are good reasons for assuming it is neither, especially when Ridley's remarks about beginning with scriptural references in the Latin work

[8] Ridley, *Works*, pp. 541 – 2.
[9] *Ibid.*, p. 541.
[10] Hargrave, 'Marian Predestinarian Controversy'. Cf. Laurence, pp. xxxvi – xxxvii.

(assumed by the present writer, Coverdale and Hargrave to be the predestinarian tract) are compared with the circumstances of the second anonymous letter, where the writer still hopes to add scriptures supporting his cause. It would seem unlikely that the tract was to be begun and completed by the same means.

Suffice it to say that the matter is extremely complex. The purpose here, however, has been twofold: first, to demonstrate that the second anonymous letter does not necessarily contain references to the lost tract on predestination as favoured by Hargrave, and thus apparently undermining the present writer's determination to identify Ridley with the authorship of the *Responsiones*; and second, to indicate that even if the second letter is taken as referring to the predestinarian document, it would still not necessarily thwart the present writer's determination to identify Ridley as the most likely author in the mid-Tudor era of the *Responsiones*.

Appendix 2

A note on Symson

Since considerable emphasis has been placed on identifying and clarifying individuals who participated in one or more phases of the Kent-Essex predestinarian controversy, it is necessary to reflect on the recent discussion concerning the involvement of the Symson in the affair. While Horst, Oxley, and possibly, Burrage, appear to have identified the original conventicler bearing the name Symson with the Cutbert Symson of the London congregation, others such as Watts and Martin tend to see John Symson of Great Wigborough as the original offender and thus distinct from the later Cutbert Symson.[1] The initial problem, then, is to decide if the Symson apprehended and detained in 1551 following the discovery of the conventiclers is one and the same with the Symson who played such a prominent role in the King's Bench dispute. A second issue would be to ascertain if this Symson is John or Cutbert Symson.

Let us begin with Cutbert (or Cuthbert) Symson. As seen above,[2] Cutbert Symson was thought to have been a tailor at one point, but became best known during his initial incarceration in the King's Bench and while serving as deacon in the Protestant underground church in London. He was regarded as a man of some wealth and distributed funds to men of the right persuasion in the various prisons during the Marian years.[3] He was apprehended at Islington in December 1557. During his examination, it was stated that he was then 'abiding within the city and diocese of London'.[4] After being subjected to harsh treatment at the hands of his persecutors, he was executed in the spring of 1558.[5] He had evidently spent time in the Tower, Newgate, and the 'Coalhouse' prior to his demise.[6] Visitors at one point seem to have included his wife and one Thomas Symson.

Horst confuses the issues surrounding Cutbert Symson by referring to him in one place as 'a well-known sectary from Essex',[7]

---

[1] Cf. Horst, pp. 125, 150; Oxley, p. 166; Burrage, I, 52; Michael R. Watts, *The Dissenters* (Oxford: Clarendon Press, 1978), I, 12; Martin, 'The First that Made Separation', 310.
[2] See above pp. 64, 172 – 3.
[3] See White, p. 13.
[4] Foxe, VIII, 457.
[5] See above pp. 172 – 3.
[6] Foxe, VIII, 455 – 6, 460.
[7] Horst, p. 125.

and in another, as 'one of the main leaders among the Kentish sectarians'.[8] Indeed, the most likely place of origin for Cutbert Symson is the parish of Elham in Kent, since the will of a 'Cutbertus Symsun' of the said parish was recorded in 1528. Whether this would pertain to the Cutbert of the London congregation is not altogether certain, but it would appear that we have at least found the family.[9] How many other Cutbert Symsons could we expect to find in a nation of some three million inhabitants? It is equally significant that the parson of the church at Elham published his thoughts on the subject of predestination in 1550, thus indicating that some form of pertinent discussion was probably then surfacing in the region — at the formative period of the conventicling movement. Moreover, as already observed,[10] the minister gave evidence of the same spirit of exclusivity and puritanism which was known to have been discussed by the radicals themselves.

Next, we must consider the facts concerning John Simson. According to Foxe, both Simson and one John Ardeley were 'husbandmen in the town of Wigborough in Essex'.[11] These men were condemned to suffer on 25 May 1555, after having been examined in detail by Bonner. It would appear that they had not been in confinement for an overly long period, although Foxe only comments that they 'were brought up both together by the under-sheriff of Essex'.[12] After the trial, at which Simson proved particularly adept at provoking Bonner, they 'were shortly after sent down from London to Essex', and met their respective ends — Ardeley at Rayleigh and Simson at Rochford — around 10 June.[13] While in London, they had been detained for at least a part of the time in Newgate.

According to Watts and Martin, John Simson is a more likely candidate for being the radical conventicler of Edward's day on account of his association not only with Ardeley but also with two men from Maidstone — John Denley, referred to as a 'Gentleman', and John Newman, 'a Pewterer'.[14] These two were apprehended by the infamous Edmund Tirrell while 'travelling upon the way, and going to visit such their godly friends as then they had in the county of Essex'.[15] Denley later wrote to Simson and Ardeley while all were

---

[8] *Ibid.*, p. 150.
[9] See above p. 64.
[10] See above pp. 66 – 7 regarding the parson of Elham and the significance of his remarks for the predestinarian controversy.
[11] Foxe, VII, 86.
[12] *Ibid.*, 86 – 7.
[13] *Ibid.*, 89 – 90.
[14] *Ibid.*, 329, 338; Martin, 'The First that Made Separation', 310; Watts, I, 12.
[15] Foxe, VII, 329.

languishing in prison, reminding them 'that Christ hath promised, to them that continue to the end, everlasting life'.[16] Thus, we have the clear possibility of a continuation of another aspect of the Kent-Essex connexion, although, as Martin has already observed, 'nothing in the trial records as printed by Foxe makes them sound other than orthodox Protestants'.[17] Martin also refers to correspondence of late May 1555 from a 'John Simson condemned for Christe caus' and addressed 'to the congregation dispersed in Suffolk, Norfolk, Essex, Kent, and elsewhere'.[18] Then, too, there is the reference by Doris Witard to a John Simson who, along with a Richard Upchard, witnessed the will of a Robert Cooke. Although the possibilities here would seem to be promising in light of the participants at the time of the initial uncovering of the conventiclers, Witard offers no proof for her rather startling (and otherwise extremely significant) assertion.[19]

In attempting to sort out the complexities of this question of identity, one must at some point ask which of the two possible candidates would have been most likely to have been the Symson of the conventicling movement and the participant in the King's Bench prison dispute, who, according to John Trewe, served in such a crucial capacity on the side of the orthodox reformers.[20] That Cutbert Symson was known to John Bradford is obvious from Bradford's *Farewell to the City of London*, where his name appears.[21] There is no evidence, however, of any such connexion between Bradford (or any other prominent figure in the controversy) and John Simson and his Maidstone friends, so that Cutbert Symson would appear to be the more likely choice in this respect. In addition, his probable origin in East Kent provides an obvious point of departure for speculation on his possible early involvement in the radical movement. Over the course of time, it is probable that Symson joined a growing list of former freewill men who were weaned away from their radical postures and came to embrace orthodoxy. Thus, Symson would be seen as a fit candidate to serve as a deacon in the underground church in London. As for Martin's point on Symson being described as 'a rich man',[22] this need not be seen as an obstacle, since it would be entirely plausible for a single informant to be unaware of Symson's role as bag-man for the reforming circle in London.

---

[16] *Ibid.*, 330−1.
[17] Martin, 'The First that Made Separation', 311.
[18] *Ibid.*, 310; Martyrs, MSS, 260, fol. 47a; cf. fol. 48a. See also fols. 55a−56a; 252b−253b.
[19] Witard, p. 21.
[20] See above pp. 153−4 for Trewe's account of Symson.
[21] Bradford, I, 434 n 2; Martin, 'The First that Made Separation', 310.
[22] Foxe, VIII, 459; cf. Martin, 'The First that Made Separation', 310.

The factor which all but clinches the matter in Cutbert Symson's favour, however, is the chronology of the prison proceedings. To recap, John Simson appears virtually out of nowhere, is condemned by the end of May 1555, and is executed around 10 June of the same year. Cutbert Symson, on the other hand, was known to have been apprehended, along with John Rough, in December 1557 and survived until the spring of 1558. The key to the entire episode is the testimony of John Trewe. According to Trewe, whose narrative of events relating to the prison dispute appears to have carried over into 1556, Symson, along with several colleagues such as Upcher and Richard Woodman, was released from confinement, apparently sometime after January 1555. Although Trewe did not give the date, Foxe did say that Woodman received his reprieve (which later proved to be only temporary) on 18 December of the same year.[23] We clearly cannot be dealing with John Simson for he was already dead. Moreover, our Symson was the agent of a peace proposal carried to the freewill men, probably just before Christmas 1555.[24] In all likelihood, then, he had just been released from a period of confinement and was now free for a time to act as a roving emissary for the predestinarian side and also to serve the underground congregation. The arrest which Foxe describes and which refers to the end of 1557 would thus be Symson's final one, following a recent period of freedom. This deduction is made all the more plausible in the light of Woodman's experience which appears to parallel Symson's. As seen above,[25] Woodman was given the ultimate penalty in June 1557. Cutbert Symson survived him by the better part of a year. This is not to suggest that a John Simson did not enter the Marian scene as described by Foxe, since he undoubtedly was imprisoned as stated. It simply means that if we have only one Symson who attained prominence in the mid-Tudor predestinarian controversy, it would seem at this point that preference must clearly be given to Cutbert Symson, and not to John Simson.[26]

---

[23] Foxe, VIII, 333; cf. above, pp. 264 – 5.
[24] See above, p. 154; Laurence, pp. 57 – 9.
[25] See above p. 153.
[26] Further light on Robert Cooke's will could help resolve more than one dilemma.

Bibliography
Primary Sources

Manuscript material

Cambridge. Emmanuel College Library. Letters of the Martyrs, MSS, 260 – 262.

Cambridge. University Library. MSS, Ee. 2. 34.

Canterbury. Christchurch Cathedral Library. Archdeaconry Visitation Act Books, 1538 – 1555.

Canterbury. Christchurch Cathedral Library. Quarter Sessions Records, 1536 – 1538.

Chelmsford. Essex Record Office. Archdeaconry of Colchester Registers, 1514 – 1564.

London. British Museum. Harleian MSS, 421, fols. 133a – 134b.

London. British Museum. Lansdowne MSS, 980, fol. 82.

London. Lambeth Palace Library. Fairhurst Papers, MS. 2002, fols. 94 – 106; MS. 2006, fols. 250 – 253b.

London. Lambeth Palace Library. The Registers of the Archbishops of Canterbury, Thomas Cranmer, 1532 – 1555; William Warham, I.

Maidstone. Kent County Record Office. Archdeaconry Act Books and Registers, 1495 – 1560.

Oxford. Bodleian Library. Bodleian MSS, 53.

Early printed books and tracts

Baleo, Joanne. *Scriptorum Illustrium maioris Brytannie, quam nunc Angliam & Scotiam vocant: Catalogus*. Basileae,1557, 1559.

Careless, John. *Certeyne godly and comfortable letters*. n.p.: W. Powell, 1566. RSTC 4612.

Champneys, John. *The harvest is at hand*. n.p.: H. Powell, 1548. RSTC 4956.

Church of England. *Visitation Articles: Articles and Injunctions*, Diocese of London, 2 pts. London: R. Wolfe, 1550. RSTC 10247.

Cole, Thomas. *A godly sermon, made at Maydstone the fyrste sonday in Lent*. London: R. Wolfe, 1553. RSTC 5539.

C[ottesford], T[homas]. *Two very Godly and comfortable Letters, written over into England.* London: Edward Allde for Edward White, 1589. RSTC 5841.5.

Coverdale, Miles, ed. *Certain most godly, fruitful, and comfortable letters of such true saintes and holy martyrs as in the late bloodye persecution as gave their lyves.* London: John Day, 1564. RSTC 5886.

Crowley, Robert. *An Apologie, or Defence, of those Englishe Writers & Preachers which Cerberus the three headed Dog of Hell, chargeth wyth false doctrine, under the name of Predestination.* London: Henry Binneman, 1566. RSTC 6076.

—— *The confutation of .xiii. Articles, wherunto Nicolas Shaxton, late byshop of Salisburye subscribed and caused be set forthe in print . . .* London: John Day and William Seres, [1548]. RSTC 6083.

Erasmus, Desiderius. *The Second Tome or volume of the Paraphrases of Erasmus upon the Newe Testament.* n.p., 2 June, 1552.

Foxe, John. *Actes and monuments of these latter and perillous dayes, touching matters of the church.* John Day, 1563. RSTC 11222.

Gardiner, Stephen. *A declaration of such true articles as George Joye hath gone about to confute as false.* London: John Herford, 1546. RSTC 11588.

H[art], H[enry]. *A consultorie for all christians.* Worcester: J. Oswen, 1549. RSTC 12564.

Hart, Henry. *A godlie exhortation to all suche as professe the gospell.* London: John Day and W. Seres, 1549. RSTC 12887.3.

—— *A godly new short treatyse instructying every parson, howe they shulde trade theyr lyves in the imytacyon of vertu.* R. Stoughton, 1548. RSTC 12887.

Lamberd, John. *Of predestinacion & election made by John Lamberd minister of the church of Elham.* Canterbury: J. Mychell, 1550. RSTC 15181.

Lesse, Nicholas, ed. and trans. *A Worke of the predestination of saints wrytten by the famous doctor S. Augustine . . . Item, another worke of the sayde Augustyne, entytuled, Of the vertue of perseveraunce to thend.* London, 1550.

Ochino, Bernardino. Sermons of Barnardine Ochyne, (to the number of .25.) concerning the predestination and election of god, trans. A. Cooke, 'Lady' Bacon, and R. Argentine. John Day, 1570?. RSTC 18768.

Prynne, William. *A quench-coale. Or a briefe Disquisition and Inquirie, in what place of the Church or Chancell the Lords-Table ought to be situated, especially when the Sacrament is administered?* Amsterdam, 1637. RSTC 20474.

Rogers, John. *The Displaying of an horrible secte of grosse and wicked Heretiques, naming themselves the Familie of Love, with the lives of their Authours, and what doctrine they teach in corners.* London: George Bishop, 1577. RSTC 21182.

Scory, John, ed. and trans. Two bokes of the noble Doctor and B.S. Augustine thone entitled of the Predestinacion of saintes, thother of perseveraunce unto thende. The English Experience, No. 32. Amsterdam: Da Capo Press, 1968; orig. pub. 1556.

Stow, John. *The annales of England*. London: G. Bishop & T. Adams, 1605 ed. RSTC 23337.

Turner, William. *A preservative, or triacle, agaynst the poyson of Pelagius, lately renued, & styrred up agayn by the furious secte of the Anabaptistes*. The English Experience. New York: Da Capo Press, 1971; orig. pub. 1551 [by R. Jugge] for A. Hester. RSTC 24368.

Veron, Jean. *A fruteful treatise of predestination and of the divine providence of God, with an apology of the same, against the swynyshe gruntinge of the Epicures and Atheystes of oure time* . . . London: J. Tisdale, [1561]. RSTC 24681.

—— *A moste necessary treatise of free wil, not onlye against the Papistes, but also against the Anabaptists, which in these our daies, go about to renue the detestable heresies of Pelagius, and of the Luciferians, whiche say and affirm, that we be able by our own natural strength to fulfil the law and commaundementes of God*. London: John Tisdale, [1561]. RSTC 24684.

Wilkinson, William. *A Confutation of Certaine Articles Delivered unto the Family of Love*. The English Experience, No. 279. Amsterdam: Da Capo Press, 1970, orig. pub. 1579 by J. Daye. RSTC 25665.

Printed sources: edited

Bradford, John. *The Writings*, ed. Aubrey Townsend. Parker Society, 2 vols. Cambridge: University Press, 1848 – 53.

Burrage, Champlin, ed. *The Early English Dissenters in the Light of Recent Research*. Cambridge: University Press, 1912, II.

Calendar of the Patent Rolls, Edward VI, vols. I, III. London, 1925, 1925; Philip and Mary, vol. III. London, 1938.

Cranmer, Thomas. *Works*, ed. John Cox. Parker Society, 2 vols. Cambridge: University Press, 1844 – 6.

Dasent, J.R., ed. *Acts of the Privy Council of England*, New Series. London, 1890 – 92, I – V.

English Wycliffite Writings, ed. Anne Hudson. London: Cambridge Univ. Press, 1978.

Erasmus, Desiderius. *The First Tome or Volume of the Paraphrases of Erasmus upon the Newe Testament*, ed. John Wall. Delmar, N.Y.: Scholars' Facsimiles & Reprints, 1975, orig. pub. 1548.

—— 'The Free Will' in *Erasmus-Luther: Discourse on Free Will*, trans. and ed. E. F. Winter. New York, N.Y.: Frederick Ungar Publishing Co., 1961, 3 – 94.

—— 'On the Freedom of the Will' in *Luther and Erasmus: Free Will and Salvation*, trans. and eds. E. G. Rupp and A. N. Marlow. *LCC*, No. 17. Philadelphia: The Westminster Press, 1969, pp. 35 – 97.

—— 'De Libero arbitrio Diatribe seu collatio' in *Opera Omnia*, Tomus Nonus. Repub. London: The Gregg Press, 1962, pp. 1215 – 1248.

Gairdner, J. and R. H. Brodie, eds. *Letters and Papers, Foreign and Domestic of the reign of Henry VIII*. London, 1862 – 1932, XV, XVI, XVIII, XIX, XX.

Gilbert, Walter, ed. *The Accounts of the Corpus Christi Fraternity, and papers relating to the Antiquities of Maidstone*. Maidstone, 1865.

Goodwin, James, ed. *The First Register of St. Mary's Church, Bocking, Essex, England*. n.p., 1903.

Hooper, John. *Early Writings*, ed. Samuel Carr. Parker Society, No. 20. Cambridge: University Press, 1843.

Houlbrooke, R. A., ed. *The Letter Book of John Parkhurst Bishop of Norwich Compiled During the Years 1571 – 75*. n.p.: Norfolk Record Society, 1974 – 5.

Hughes, P. L. and J. F. Larkin, eds. *Tudor Royal Proclamations*. New Haven: Yale University Press, 1964, 1969, I, II.

Hume, M. A. S. and R. Tyler, eds. *Calendar of State Papers-Spanish*. London: His Majesty's Stationery Office, 1912, IX.

Kirk, R. E. G. and E. F. Kirk, eds. 'Returns of Aliens in London', *Hugenot Society of London Publications*. Aberdeen, 1900 – 7, rep. 1969, Kraus Reprint, X, 3 pts.

Knox, John. *The Works*, ed. David Laing. Edinburgh: Woodrow Society, 1846 – 64, V.

Laurence, Richard, ed. *Authentic Documents Relative to the Predestinarian Controversy*. Oxford, 1819.

Lemon, R. and M. A. E. Green, eds. *Calendar of State Papers, Domestic Series, of the reigns of Edward VI, Mary, Elizabeth*. London, 1856 – 71, I.

The Lisle Letters, ed. Muriel St. Clare Byrne. Chicago & London: University of Chicago Press, 1981, II, V.

Luther, Martin. 'De servo arbitrio' in *D. Martin Luthers Werke. Kritische Gesamtausgabe* (Weimar Ausgabe), 18 Band. Orig. pub. Weimar, 1883; 1908; 1964, 551 – 787.

—— *The Works*, gen. eds. J. Pelikan and H. T. Lehmann, trans. and ed. P. S. Watson. Philadelphia: Fortress Press, 1972, XXXIII.

Melling, Elizabeth, ed. *Kentish Sources: The Poor*. Maidstone: Kent County Council, 1964, IV.

Original Letters Illustrative of English History, ed. Henry Ellis, Third Series. Orig. pub. London, 1846; rep. ed. New York: AMS Press, 1970, IV.

Peel, Albert, ed. 'A Conscientious Objector of 1575', *Transactions of the Baptist Historical Society*, VII (1920), 71 – 128.

Philpot, John. *The Examinations and Writings*, ed. Robert Eden. Parker Society, No. 34. Cambridge: University Press, 1842.

Ridley, Nicholas. *Treatises and Letters of Dr. Nicholas Ridley*. London: The Religious Tract Society, n.d.

—— *The Works*, ed. Henry Christmas. Parker Society, No. 39. Cambridge: University Press, 1843.

Robinson, Hastings, ed. *Original Letters Relative to the English Reformation*. Parker Society, 2 vols. Cambridge: University Press, 1846 – 47.

—— ed. *The Zurich Letters*. Parker Society, Second Series, No. 54, 2 vols. Cambridge: University Press, 1842, 1845.

Rogers, Thomas. *The Catholic Doctrine of the Church of England, An Exposition of the Thirty-nine Articles*, ed. J. J. S. Perowne. Parker Society, No. 40. Cambridge: University Press, 1854.

Selected Writings of Hans Denck, ed. F. L. Battles et al. Pittsburgh: Pickwick Press, 1976.

Simons, Menno. *The Complete Writings*, ed. J. C. Wenger, trans. Leonard Verduin. Scottdale, Pa.: Herald Press, 1956.

Smit, H. J., ed. *Bronnen Tot De Geschiedenis Van Den Handel Met Engeland, Schotland en Ierland*. Rijks Geschiedkundige Publicatien, Tweede Deel, 1485 – 1585, Eerst Stuke, 1485 – 1558. 'S-Gravenhage: Martinus Nijhoff, 1942.

'Speculum de Antichristo' in *The English Works of Wyclif*, ed. F. D. Matthew. London: Trubner & Co. for The Early English Text Society, 1880.

Tyndale, William, trans. *The New Testament* (1534 ed.), ed. N. Hardy Wallis. Cambridge: University Press, 1938.

Virgoe, R., ed. 'Some Ancient Indictments in the King's Bench Referring to Kent, 1450 – 1452', in *Kent Records: Documents Illustrative of Medieval Kentish Society*, ed. F. R. H. Du Boulay. Kent Records, No. 18. Ashford: Kent Archaeological Society, 1964, XVIII, 214 – 65.

Whatmore, L. E., ed. *Archdeacon Harpsfield's Visitation, 1557*. London: Catholic Record Society, 1951, XLV.

Whitely, W. D., ed. 'The Confutation of the Errors of the Careless by Necessity', *Transactions of the Baptist Historical Society*, IV (1914), 88 – 123.

Wilkins, David, ed. *Concilia Magnae Britanniae et Hiberniae*. Tomus III, IV. London, 1737; reprint Brussels, 1964.

Williams, G. H. and A. M. Mergal, eds. *Spiritual and Anabaptist Writers*. LCC, No. 25. Philadelphia: Westminster Press, 1957.

The Work of William Tyndale, ed. G. E. Duffield. The Courtenay

Library of Reformation Classics, I. Appleford: Sutton Courtenay Press, 1964.

Contemporary and later accounts and chronicles

Barclay, Robert. *The Inner Life of the Religious Societies of the Commonwealth*. London: Hodder and Stoughton, 1876,

Braght, Thieleman J. van. *The Bloody Theater or Martyrs' Mirror of the Defenseless Christians*, trans. J.F. Sohm. Scottdale, Pa.: Herald Press, 1968; orig. pub. 1660.

Brandt, Gerard. *The History of the Reformation and other Ecclesiastical Transactions in and about the Low-Countries*. London: Timothy Childe, 1720, I.

Burnet, Gilbert. *The History of the Reformation of the Church of England*. New York, N.Y.: D. Appleton & Company, 1843; orig. pub. 1714, III.

Chronicle of the Grey Friars of London, ed. John G. Nichols. Camden Society Publications, No. 53, Old Series. London, 1842.

Cramp, J. M. *Baptist History*. London: Elliot Stock, 1868.

Crosby, Thomas. *The History of the English Baptists*. London, 1738,

Davids, T. W. *Annals of Evangelical Nonconformity in the County of Essex*. London: Jackson, Walford, and Hodder, 1863.

Foxe, John. *The Acts and Monuments*, ed. Josiah Pratt. 8 vols. London: Religious Tract Society, 1877.

Hasted, Edward. *The History and Topographical Survey of the County of Kent*. 12 vols. Canterbury, 1797 – 1801; rep. 1972, E P Publishing Ltd in collaboration with Kent County Library.

Hey, John. *Lectures in Divinity*. Cambridge, 1798, IV.

Heylyn, Peter. *Ecclesia restaurata: or, the history of the reformation of the Church of England*. London, 1661.

Ireland, W. H. *A New and Complete History of the County of Kent*. London, 1829, II – III.

Jacob, Edward. *History of Faversham*. n.p.: The Faversham Society, 1974; orig. pub. 1774.

Lambarde, William. *A Preambulation of Kent*. London: Chatham, Baldwin, Cradock, and Joy, 1826 rep.; orig. pub. 1576.

Lewis, John. *A Brief History of the Rise and Progress of Anabaptism in England*. London, 1738.

—— *The History and Antiquities of the Abbey and Church of Faversham in Kent*. n.p., 1727.

Morant, Philip. *The History and Antiquities of the County of Essex*. Chelmsford, 1816 rep.; orig. pub. 1768, II.

Petreius, Theodorus. *Catalogus Haereticorum*. Cologne, 1629.

Pocock, Nicholas, ed. *Troubles Connected with the Prayer Book of 1549*.

Camden Society, New Series, No. 37. New York: Johnson Reprint Corporation, 1884.

Stow, Thomas Quinton. *Memoirs of Rowland Taylor, LLD*. London, 1833.

Strype, John. *Annals of the Reformation and Establishment of Religion*, New ed. Oxford: Clarendon Press, 1824.

—— *Ecclesiastical Memorials*. Oxford: Clarendon Press, 1822.

—— *The History of the Life and Acts of . . . Edmund Grindal*. Oxford: Clarendon Press, 1821.

—— *The Life and Acts of Matthew Parker*. Oxford: Clarendon Press, 1821.

—— *The Life of the learned Sir Thomas Smith*. Oxford: Clarendon Press, 1820.

—— *Memorials of . . . Thomas Cranmer*. Oxford: Clarendon Press, 1812.

Whittingham, William. *A Brief Discourse of the Troubles at Frankfort, 1554 – 1558 A.D*. London: Elliot Stock, 1908; orig. pub. 1575.

Winchester, Thomas. *A Dissertation on the XVIIth Article, of the Church of England*. Oxford, 1773.

Wriothesley, Charles. A Chronicle of England During the Reigns of the Tudors, ed. W. D. Hamilton. Camden Society Publications, New Series, vol. XI. New York: Johnson Reprint Corporation, 1965; orig. pub. 1875, I.

Secondary Sources

Monographs

Bax, E. Belfort. *The Rise and Fall of the Anabaptists*. London: Swan Sonnenschein and Co., 1903.

Bergston, Torsten. *Balthasar Hubmaier: Anabaptist Theologian and Martyr*, ed. W. R. Estep, trans. I. J. Barnes and W. R. Estep. Valley Forge, Pa.: Judson Press, 1978.

Bicknell, E. J. *A Theological Introduction to the Thirty-nine Articles of the Church of England*, revised by H. J. Carpenter, 3rd. ed. London: Longmans, 1955; orig. pub. 1919.

Bindoff, S. T. *Tudor England*. The Pelican History of England, No. 5. Harmondsworth: Penguin Books Ltd., 1950.

Bowden, Peter. *The Wool Trade in Tudor and Stuart England*. London: Macmillan, 1962.

Brailsford, H. N. *The Levellers and the English Revolution*, ed. Christopher Hill. London: The Cresset Press, 1961.

Burns, Norman. *Christian Mortalism from Tyndale to Milton.* Cambridge, Mass.: Harvard University Press, 1972.

Burrage, Champlin. *The Early English Dissenters in the Light of Recent Research.* Cambridge: University Press, 1912, I.

Cantor, Norman. *Perspectives on the European Past: Conversations with Historians.* New York: Macmillan Company, 1971.

Chalklin, C. W. *Seventeenth-century Kent: A Social and Economic History.* London: Longmans Green and Co. Ltd., 1965.

Churchill, Irene. *Canterbury Administration.* London: Church Historical Society, 1933.

Clark, Henry. *History of English Nonconformity.* New York: Russell & Russell, 1965; orig. pub. 1913, I.

Clark, Peter. *English Provincial Society from the Reformation to the Revolution.* Sussex: The Harvester Press, 1977.

―――― and Paul Slack, eds. *Crisis and Order in English Towns, 1500 – 1700.* London: Routledge & Kegan Paul, 1972.

Clarkson, Leslie. *The Pre-Industrial Economy in England, 1500 – 1750.* London: B. T. Batsford Ltd., 1971.

Clifford, John, ed. *The English Baptists.* London: E. Marlborough & Co., 1881.

Cohn, Norman. *The Pursuit of the Millenium.* London: Secker & Warburg, 1957.

Collinson, Patrick. *The Elizabethan Puritan Movement.* London: Jonathan Cape, 1967.

―――― *Godly People: Essays on English Protestantism and Puritanism.* London: Hambledon Press, 1983.

Cooke, G. A. *Topographical and Statistical Description of the County of Kent.* London: Sherwood, Neely, and Jones, n.d.

Coutts, Alfred. *Hans Denck, 1495 – 1527: Humanist and Heretic.* Edinburgh: Macniven & Wallace, 1927.

Cox, J. C. *Kent*, rev. ed. P. M. Johnston. London: Methuen & Co. Ltd., 1935.

Cremeans, Charles D. *The Reception of Calvinistic Thought in England.* Urbana: Univ. of Illinois Press, 1949.

Cross, Claire. *Church and People, 1450 – 1660.* Atlantic Highlands, N.J.: Humanities Press, 1976.

Davis, J. F. *Heresy and Reformation in the South-East of England, 1520 – 1559.* London: The Royal Historical Society, 1983.

Davis, Kenneth R. *Anabaptism and Asceticism.* Scottdale, Pa.: Herald Press, 1974.

Dickens, A. G. *The English Reformation.* New York: Schocken Books, 1964.

―――― *Lollards and Protestants in the Diocese of York, 1509 – 1558.* London: Oxford University Press, 1959. Contains quotations from C. Jenkins. *Studies Presented to A. F. Pollard.*

—— *Reformation Studies.* London: The Hambledon Press, 1982.

—— and John Tonkin. *The Reformation in Historical Thought.* Cambridge, Mass.: Harvard Univ. Press, 1985.

Dixon, R. W. *History of the Church of England.* London: George Routledge and Sons, Ltd., 1891, IV.

Elton, G. R. *Policy and Police.* Cambridge: University Press, 1972.

—— *Reform and Reformation: England, 1509 – 1558.* Cambridge, Mass.: Harvard Univ. Press, 1977.

Evans, Benjamin. *The Early English Baptists*, I. London: J. Heaton & Son, 1862.

Evans, Robert. *Pelagius: Inquiries and Reappraisals.* New York: The Seabury Press, 1968.

Ferguson, John. *Pelagius.* Cambridge: W. Heffer, 1956.

Field, C. W. *The Province of Canterbury and the Elizabethan Settlement of Religion.* n.p., n.d.

Fuller, Thomas. *The Church History of Britain.* Oxford: University Press, 1845, IV.

Furley, Robert. *A History of the Weald of Kent.* Ashford, 1874, II.

Gairdner, James. *Lollardy and the Reformation in England.* London Macmillan and Co., 1913, IV.

Garrett, Christina. *The Marian Exiles.* London: Cambridge University Press, 1966.

Haigh, Christopher. *Reformation and Resistance in Tudor Lancashire.* Cambridge: University Press, 1975.

Haller, William. *Foxe's Book of Martyrs and the Elect Nation.* London: Jonathan Cape, 1963.

Hardwick, Charles. *A History of the Articles of Religion.* London: George Bell & Sons, 1904.

Haslewood, Francis. *The Antiquities of Smarden, Kent.* London, 1866.

Heer, Friedrich. *The Intellectual History of Europe*, trans. Jonathan Steinberg. London: Weidenfeld and Nicolson, 1966.

Higham, Roger. *Kent.* London: B. T. Batsford Ltd., 1974.

Horst, Irvin B. *The Radical Brethren: Anabaptism and the English Reformation to 1558.* Nieuwkoop: B. de Graaf, 1972.

Hussey, Arthur. *Notes on the Churches in the Counties of Kent, Sussex, and Surrey.* London: John Russell Smith, 1852.

Jessup, Frank. *A History of Kent.* n.p.: Kent Archaeological Society, 1974.

—— and Ronald Jessup. *The Cinque Ports.* London: B. T. Batsford Ltd., 1952.

Johnson, David. *Southwark and the City.* Oxford: University Press for the Corporation of London, 1969.

Johnson, Paul. *A History of the English People.* London: Weidenfeld and

Nicolson, 1985.

Johnston, P. M. and H. A. Piehler. *Essex*, 6th ed. n.p., 1938.

Jones, Whitney. *The Tudor Commonwealth, 1529 – 1559*. London: The Athlone Press, 1970.

Jordan, W. K. *Edward VI: The Threshold of Power*. London: George Allen & Unwin Ltd., 1970.

—— *Edward VI: The Young King*. Cambridge, Mass.: The Belknap Press of Harvard University Press, 1968.

—— *Social Institutions in Kent, 1480 – 1660*. Ashford: Kent Archaeological Society, 1961.

Kendall, R. T. *Calvin and English Calvinism to 1649*. Oxford: University Press, 1979.

Knappen, Marshall. *Tudor Puritanism*. Gloucester, Mass.: Peter Smith, 1963; orig. pub. 1939.

Kramer, Stella. *The English Craft Gilds*. New York: Columbia University Press, 1927.

Lake, Peter. *Anglicans and Puritans?: Presbyterianism and English Conformist thought from Whitgift to Hooker*. London: Unwin Hyman Ltd, 1988.

—— *Moderate puritans and the Elizabethan church*. Cambridge: Cambridge University Press, 1982.

Laurence, Richard. *An Attempt to Illustrate those Articles of the Church of England which the Calvinists Improperly Consider as Calvinistical*. Oxford, 1853.

Lechler, G. V. *John Wycliffe and His English Precursors*. London: Religious Tract Society, 1904.

Lipson, Ephraim. *The Economic History of England*. London: A. & C. Black, Ltd. 1929, I.

Loades, D. M. *The Oxford Martyrs*. London: B. T. Batsford, 1970.

—— *Two Tudor Conspiracies*. Cambridge: University Press, 1965.

Lorimer, Peter. *John Knox and the Church of England*. London: Henry S. King & Co., 1875.

Marius, Richard. *Thomas More: A Biography*. New York: Alfred A. Knopf, 1984.

McConica, James. *English Humanists and Reformation Politics*. Oxford: Clarendon Press, 1965.

Miller, G. A. *Noble Martyrs of Kent*. London: Morgan & Scott Ltd., n.d.

New, John F. H. *Anglican and Puritan: The Basis of Their Opposition, 1558 – 1640*. Stanford: Stanford University Press, 1964.

Newman, A. H. *A History of Anti-Pedobaptism from: the Rise of Pedobaptism to A.D. 1609*. Philadelphia: American Baptist Publication Society, 1897.

Oxley, James. *The Reformation in Essex to the Death of Mary*.

Manchester: University Press, 1965.

Page, William, ed. *The Victoria History of the County of Kent.* London: The St. Catherine Press, 1926, 1932, II – III.

—— and H. A. Doubleday, eds. *The Victoria History of the County of Essex.* Oxford: University Press for the London Institute of Historical Research, 1907, II.

Pike, Edward. *The Story of the Anabaptists.* London: National Council of Evangelical Free Churches, 1904.

Pinnock, Clark, ed. *Grace Unlimited.* Minneapolis: Bethany Fellowship, Inc., 1975.

Pollard, A. F. *Thomas Cranmer and the English Reformation, 1489 – 1556.* London: Putnam, 1926.

Porter, H. C. *Reformation and Reaction in Tudor Cambridge.* Cambridge: University Press, 1958.

Ramsey, Peter. *Tudor Economic Problems.* London: Victor Gollancz Ltd., 1968.

Reid, W. Stanford. *Trumpeter of God: A Biography of John Knox.* New York: Charles Scribner's Sons, 1974.

Ridley, Jasper. *John Knox.* Oxford: University Press, 1968.

—— *Nicholas Ridley: A Biography.* London: Longmans, Green & Co., 1957.

—— *Thomas Cranmer.* Oxford: Clarendon Press, 1962.

Roberts, J. M. *The Pelican History of the World.* Harmondsworth: Penguin Books Ltd., 1980.

Rupp, E. G. *Studies in the Making of the English Protestant Tradition.* Cambridge: University Press, 1966.

Russell, J. M. *The History of Maidstone.* Maidstone: William S. Vivish, 1881.

Smithson, R. J. *The Anabaptists: Their Contribution to our Protestant Heritage.* London: J. Clarke, 1935.

Streatfield, Frank. *Account of the Grammar School . . . of Maidstone.* Oxford: Rogers & Broome, 1915.

Tawney, R. H. *The Agrarian Problem in the Sixteenth Century.* New York: Harper & Row, 1967.

Thomson, John A. F. *The Later Lollards, 1414 – 1520.* London: Oxford University Press, 1965.

Trinterud, Leonard J., ed. *Elizabethan Puritanism.* New York: Oxford University Press, 1971.

Tyacke, Nicholas. *Anti-Calvinists: The Rise of English Arminianism, c. 1590 – 1640.* Oxford: Clarendon Press, 1987.

Usher, R. G. *The Rise and Fall of High Commission.* Oxford: Clarendon Press, 1913.

Vaughan, Robert. *The Life and Opinions of John de Wycliffe, D.D.* London: Holdsworth and Ball, 1831; rep. AMS Press, 1973.

Vedder, Henry. *Balthasar Hubmaier*. New York: AMS Press, rep. 1971; orig. pub. 1905.

Wallace, Dewey D., Jr. *Puritans and Predestination: Grace in English Protestant Theology, 1525 – 1695*. Chapel Hill, N. C.: University of North Carolina Press, 1982.

Watts, Michael R. *The Dissenters*. vol. 1. Oxford : Clarendon Press, 1978.

White, B. R. *The Engish Separatist Tradition*. Oxford: University Press, 1971.

Wilbur, E. M. *A History of Unitarianism in Transylvania, England, and America*. Cambridge, Mass.: Harvard University Press, 1952.

Williams, G. H. *The Radical Reformation*. Philadelphia: The Westminster Press, 1962.

Witard, Doris. *Bibles in Barrels: A History of Essex Baptists*. n.p.: Essex Baptist Assoc., n.d.

Woodcock, Brian. *Medieval Ecclesiastical Courts in the Diocese of Canterbury*. London: Oxford University Press, 1952.

Young, C. R. *The English Borough and Royal Administration, 1130 – 1307*. Durham, N.C.: Duke University Press, 1961.

Zweig, Stefan. *The Right to Heresy: Castellio against Calvin*. Trans. Eden and Cedar Paul. New York: The Viking Press, 1936.

Articles

Aston, Margaret. 'Lollardy and the Reformation: Survival or Revival?' in *Lollards and Reformers: Images and Literacy in Late Medieval Religion*. London: The Hambledon Press, 1984, pp. 219 – 42.

Bainton, Roland H. 'The Left Wing of the Reformation' in *Studies on the Reformation*. Boston: Beacon Press, 1963, pp. 119 – 29.

—— 'The Paraphrases of Erasmus', *Archiv für Reformationsgeschichte*, LVII (1966), 67 – 76.

Cave-Browne, J. 'Cranbrook Church', *AC*, XXII (1897), 221 – 31.

Clark, Peter. 'The Ecclesiastical Commission at Canterbury: 1572 – 1603', *AC*, LXXXIX (1974), 183 – 97.

—— 'The Prophesying Movement During the 1570s', *AC*, XCIII (1977), 81 – 90.

Collinson, Patrick. 'Voluntary Religion: Its Forms and Tendencies' in *The Religion of Protestants: The Church in English Society, 1559 – 1625*. Oxford: Clarendon Press, 1982.

Cooper, W. D. 'John Cade's Followers in Kent', *AC*, VII (1868), 233 – 71.

Davis, J. F. 'Joan of Kent, Lollardy and the English Reformation', *Journal of Ecclesiastical History*, XXXIII (1982), 225 – 33.

—— 'Lollard Survival and the Textile Industry in the South-east of England' in *Studies in Church History*, ed. G. J. Cuming. Leiden: E.J. Brill, 1966, III, pp. 191 – 201.

—— 'Lollardy and the Reformation in England', *Archiv fur Reformationsgeschichte*, LXXIII (1982), 217 – 36.

Davis, Kenneth R. 'Erasmus as a Progenitor of Anabaptist Theology and Piety', *MQR*,XLVII (1973), 163 – 78.

Devereux, E. J. 'The Publication of the English *Paraphrases* of Erasmus', *Bulletin of the John Rylands Library*, LI (1969), 348 – 67.

Dickens, A. G. 'The Radical Reformation', *Past and Present*, XXVII (1964), 123 – 5.

Elton, G.R. 'England and the Continent in the Sixteenth Century' in *Reform and Reformation: England and the Continent, c1500 – c1750*, ed. Derek Baker. Oxford: The Ecclesiastical History Society, 1979, pp. 1 – 16.

Farrer, A. J. D. 'The Relation between English Baptists and the Anabaptists of the Continent', *Baptist Quarterly*, New Series, II (1924), 30 – 6.

Frampton, T. S. 'List of Incumbents of St. Peter's, Seal', *AC*, xx (1893), 258 – 75.

Furley, Robert. 'The Early History of Tenterden', *AC*, XIV (1882), 37 – 60.

Garrett, C.H. 'The Legatine Register of Cardinal Pole, 1554 – 57', *Journal of Modern History*, XIII (1941), 189 – 94.

Giraud, F. F. 'Expenses of the Corporation of Faversham, Temp. Hen. VIII', *AC*, x (1876), 233 – 41.

—— 'Faversham Town Charters', *AC*, IX (1874), lxii – lxx.

—— 'On the Parish Clerks and Sexton of Faversham, A.D. 1506 – 1593', *AC*, xx (1893), 203 – 10.

—— 'The Service of Shipping of the Barons of Faversham', *AC*, XXI (1895), 273 – 82.

Haas, Martin. 'The Path of the Anabaptists into Separation: The Interdependence of Theology and Social Behaviour' in *The Anabaptists and Thomas Muntzer*, eds. James M. Stayer and Werner O. Packull. Dubuque, Iowa: Kendall/Hunt Publishing Co., 1980, pp. 72 – 84.

Hall, Thor. 'Possibilities of Erasmian Influence on Denck and Hubmaier in their Views on the Freedom of the Will', *MQR*, XXXV (1961), 149 – 70.

Hargrave, O.T. 'The Freewillers in the English Reformation', *Church History*, XXXVII (1968), 271 – 80.

—— 'The Predestinarian Controversy Among the Marian Protestant Prisoners', *Historical Magazine of the Protestant Episcopal Church*, XLVII (1978), 131 – 51. Includes quotation from Gordon Rupp,

'John Bradford, Martyr, Ob. 1 July, 1555', *The London Quarterly and Holborn Review*, CLXXXVIII, 1(1963), 52.

—— 'The Predestinarian Offensive of the Marian Exiles at Geneva', *Historical Magazine of the Protestant Episcopal Church*, XLII (1973), 111 – 23.

Haslewood, Francis. 'Notes from the Records of Smarden Church', *AC*, IX (1874), 224 – 35.

—— 'The Rectors of Pluckley, Kent, For Upwards of Six Hundred Years', *AC*, XXII (1897), 85 – 101.

Heriot, Duncan. 'Anabaptism in England during the 16th and 17th Centuries', *Transactions of the Congregational Historical Society*, XII (1933 – 6), 256 – 71, 312 – 20; XIII (1937 – 9), 22 – 40.

Hill, Christopher. 'From Lollards to Levellers' in *Rebels and Their Causes: Essays in Honour of A. L. Morton*, ed. Maurice Cornforth. London: Lawrence and Wishart, 1978, pp. 49 – 67.

—— 'Occasional Conformity' in *Reformation Conformity and Dissent*, ed. R. Buick Knox. London: Epworth Press, 1977, pp. 199 – 220.

Horst, Irvin B. 'England' in *Mennonite Encyclopedia*, ed. H. S. Bender et al. Scottdale, Pa.: Herald Press, 1955 – 9, II, 215 – 21.

Kendall, R. T. 'The Puritan Modification of Calvin's Theology' in *John Calvin: His Influence in the Modern World*, ed. W. Stanford Reid. Grand Rapids: Zondervan Publishing House, 1982, pp. 199 – 214; 382 – 5 (notes).

Kershaw, S. W. 'On Manuscripts and Rare Books in the Maidstone Museum', *AC*, XI (1877), 189 – 98.

—— 'The Weald and its Refugee Annals', *AC*, XX (1897), 209 – 20.

Knecht, R. J. 'The Early Reformation in England and France: A Comparison', *History*, LVII, 189 (1972), 1 – 16.

Kreider, Alan, ed. 'An English Episcopal Draft Article Against the Anabaptists, 1536', *MQR*, XLIX (1975), 38 – 42.

Loades, David. 'Anabaptism and English Sectarianism in the Mid-Sixteenth Century' in *Reform and Reformation: England and the Continent, c1500 – c1750*, ed. Derek Baker. Oxford: Basil Blackwell, 1979, pp. 59 – 70.

Martin, J. W. 'Christopher Vitel: an Elizabethan Mechanick Preacher', *The Sixteenth-Century Journal*, X (1979), 15 – 22.

—— 'English Protestant Separatism at its Beginnings: Henry Hart and the Free-Will Men', *The Sixteenth-Century Journal*, VII (1976), 55 – 74.

—— 'The First that Made Separation from the Reformed Church of England', *Archiv für Reformationsgeschichte*, LXXVII (1986), 281 – 312.

Nippold, Friedrich. 'David Joris von Delft' in *Zeitschrift für die Historische Theologie*, ed. Christian W. Riedner. Gotha, 1863, pp. 3 – 168.

Parker, T. M. 'Arminianism and Laudianism in Seventeenth-Century England' in *Studies in Church History*, eds. C. W. Dugmore and Charles Duggan, vol. 1. London: Thos. Nelson and Sons Ltd., 1964, pp. 20 – 34.

Reid, E. J. B. 'Lollards at Colchester in 1414', *English Historical Review*, XXIX (1914), 101 – 3.

Robertson, Scott. 'Rectors and Vicars of Preston-by-Faversham', *AC*, XXI (1895), 135 – 56.

Rye, W. B. 'The Ancient Episcopal Palace at Rochester, and Bishop Fisher', *AC*, XVII (1887), 66 – 76.

Stayer, James. 'Reublin and Brotli: The Revolutionary Beginnings of Swiss Anabaptism' in *The Origins and Characteristics of Anabaptism*, ed. Marc Lienhard. The Hague: Martinus Nijhoff, 1977.

Tarbutt, W. 'The Ancient Cloth Trade of Cranbrook', *AC*, IX (1874), xcvi – civ.

Tate, W. E. 'A Hand-list of English Enclosure Acts and Awards: Open Fields, Commons and Enclosures in Kent', *AC*, LVI (1943), 54 – 67.

Taylor, A. H. 'The Church of St. John the Baptist, Smallhythe', *AC*, XXX (1914), 133 – 91.

Thirsk, Joan. 'Industries in the Countryside' in *Essays in the Economic and Social History of Tudor and Stuart England*, ed. F. J. Fisher. Cambridge: University Press, 1961, 70 – 88.

Thorp, Malcolm. 'Religion and the Wyatt Rebellion of 1554', *Church History*, XLVII (1978), 363 – 80.

Trinterud, Leonard J. 'The Origins of Puritanism', *Church History*, XX (1951), 37 – 57.

Walcott, Mackenzie and Scott Robertson, eds. 'Inventories of Parish Church Goods in Kent, A.D. 1552', *AC*, VIII (1872), 74 – 163; IX (1874), 266 – 84; X (1876), 282 – 97; XIV (1882), 290 – 312.

Wallis, Jerry L. 'The Free Will Defense, Calvinism, Wesley, and the Goodness of God', *Christian Scholar's Review*, XIII, 1(1983), 19 – 33.

Whitely, W. T. 'Continental Anabaptists and Early English Baptists', *Baptist Quarterly*, New Series, II (1924), 24 – 30.

Woodruff, C. E. 'Extracts from Original Documents Illustrating the Progress of the Reformation in Kent', *AC*, XXXI (1915), 92 – 120.

Zerger, Fred. 'Dutch Anabaptism in Elizabethan England', *Mennonite Life*, XXVI (1971), 19 – 24.

Reference works

Bill, E. G. W., ed. *A Catalogue of Manuscripts in Lambeth Palace Library*. 2 vols. Oxford: Clarendon Press, 1972, 1976.

Brauer, Jerald, ed. *The Westminster Dictionary of Church History*.

Philadelphia: Westminster Press, 1971.

Devereux, E. J. *A Checklist of English Translations of Erasmus to 1700.* Oxford Bibliographical Society, Bodleian Library, Occasional Publications, No. 3. Oxford, 1968.

Douglas, J. D., gen. ed. *The New International Dictionary of the Christian Church.* Grand Rapids: Zondervan Publishing House, 1974.

Emmison, F. G., ed. *Wills at Chelmsford (Essex and Hertfordshire).* London, 1958, I.

Plomer, Henry R., ed. *Index of Wills and Administrations now preserved in the Probate Registry at Canterbury, 1396 – 1558 and 1640 – 1650.* London: Kent Archaeological Society, 1920.

Pollard, A. W. and G. R. Redgrave. *A Short-Title Catalogue of Books Printed in England, Scotland, & Ireland and of English Books Printed Abroad, 1475 – 1640.* 2nd ed. revised and enlarged by W. A. Jackson, F. S. Ferguson, and Katharine F. Pantzer. 2 vols. London: Bibliographical Society, 1976, 1986.

Richardson, Alan, ed. *A Dictionary of Christian Theology.* London: SCM Press, 1969.

Stephen, Leslie and Sidney Lee, eds. *Dictionary of National Biography.* 21 vols. Oxford: University Press, 1963 – 4.

Theses

Bacher, John R. 'The Prosecution of Heretics in Mediaeval England'. An Essential Portion of a Dissertation in History. Ph.D. thesis. University of Pennsylvania, 1942.

Barchard, Frank V., Jr. 'Reginald, Cardinal Pole, 1553 – 1558'. Ph.D. thesis. Tulane University, 1971.

Davis, J. F. 'Heresy and Reformation in the South-east of England, 1520 – 1559'. D.Phil. thesis. Oxford University, 1967 – 8.

Hargrave, O. T. 'The Doctrine of Predestination in the English Reformation'. Unpublished Ph.D. thesis. Vanderbilt University, 1966.

Penny, D. Andrew. 'The Freewill Movement in the Southeast of England, 1550 – 1558: Its Relationship to English Anabaptism and the English Reformation'. Unpublished Ph.D. thesis. University of Guelph, 1980.

St John, Wallace. 'The Contest for Liberty of Conscience in England'. Ph.D. thesis. University of Chicago, 1900.

Other unpublished works

Lambeth Palace Library. Index to the Vicar-General Records.

Index

Adam, 42, 78, 92, 97-8 n268, 114, 118, 122 n91, 134, 151, 156, 161-3, 174, 180-1, 200

Adisham (Kent), 43, 75, 113 n51

Ambrose, George, 165, 167

Anabaptism, 12, 26, 45, 84, 145, 197, 208-9; continental, 18-20, 26, 39, 74, 85, 87, 99, 102, 104 n6, 111, 155-6, 202; English, 3-5, 19-22, 29-32, 38-9, 102 n287, 139 n62, 192-3, 209; Kentish, 49, 131, 146 n43

Andrews, James, 157

Antwerp, 157

Ardeley, John, 222

Arden, Thomas, 58-9

Ardingly (Sussex), 157

Arianism, 171

Aristotle, 34

Arminianism, 5, 22-4, 163, 210, 212 n126, 213

Arminius, James, 24

Articles, Forty-two, 18, 105, 207-8

Articles, Lambeth, 210

Articles, Six, 182

Articles, Thirty-nine, 18, 197, 207-10

Ashford (Kent), 38, 41, 44, 52, 59-60, 68, 75-6, 104, 111, 131, 144

Aston, Margaret, 7, 22

Atonement (of Christ), 84, 99, 120, 133-4, 151-2, 155, 161 n110, 163, 171 n11, 203

Augustine, St, 35, 64, 134, 138, 189, 196, 198-200, 202-3

Avington (or Abyngton), Thomas, 141, 157-8, 166, 173

Bagge, Richard, 52

Bainton, Roland, 21, 95 n254, 188 n99, 213

Bancroft, Richard, 212

Baptism, 3, 11, 26, 30, 50, 63, 72, 82-3, 89, 95, 147, 152, 153 n81, 158 n102, 183-4; rebaptism, 19-20, 26, 192

Barnehall (Essex), 159

Barnes (Essex), 159 n105

Barnes, Robert, 14, 29-30, 32, 34

Baro, Peter, 216 n142

Barrett, John, 52, 68 n94, 143 n20

Barrowism, 193

Barry, John, 68 n94, 143, 159-63, 203 n81

Basel, 97

Becon, Thomas, 23

Bedfordshire, 74

Bentham, Thomas, 112, 172 n17

Bernhere, Augustine, 18, 125-30, 145, 159-63, 172, 175, 181 n64, 203 n81

Beza, Theodore, 195

Bible (English), 2, 4, 10-11, 26, 42-3, 45-6, 84, 86, 91, 102

Bicknell, E. J., v, 207-9

Biddenden (Kent), 46

Bland, John, 43, 75-6, 113 n51

Bocher, Joan, 32, 43, 75-6, 101, 139 n62, 179, 186

Bocholt, 47, 160 n109

Bocking (Essex), 1, 14, 51-7, 62-3, 67, 69 n102, 75, 77-8, 103, 153, 157 n95, 159, 165, 182, 191-4

Boleyn, Anne, 31

Bonaventure, 64

Bonner, Edmund, bishop of London, 105-6, 110, 113, 117, 142, 147-8, 153, 166 n132

Boughtell, --, 52

Boxley (Kent), 68

241

Cottesford, Thomas, 131 n23, 215 n134
Council, Privy, 52, 54, 69, 76, 109, 113, 169, 189 n107
Coventry (Warw.), 106, 140, 147
Coverdale, Miles, 51, 109, 128, 130, 137, 142, 183, 196, 218, 220
Cranbrook (Kent), 44, 46, 59-60, 157, 193
Cranmer, Thomas, archbishop of Canterbury, 29, 31, 33, 39-46, 51, 72, 75, 102 n287, 103-6, 108, 117, 125, 127-8, 139 n62, 144, 186, 188
Crome, Edward, 29, 109
Cromwell, Thomas, 29-31, 44-5
Cross, Claire, 22
Crowhurste, Robert, 173
Crowley, Robert, 195-204, *passim*
Curle, --, 117

Dagenham (London area), 165
Davis, John F., 9, 12, 23
Davis, Kenneth R., 26 n116
Davy, Thomas, 157
Dawby, Thomas, 41, 43
Day, John, 77
Dedham (Essex), 56
Delft, 32
Denck, Hans, 96-9, 134 n42
Denley, John, 222
Dering, John, 47
Dering, Richard, 46
Devereux, E. J., 86 n208
Dickens, A. G., 1, 4, 6, 10, 13, 23
Dinestake, Richard, 53, 75-6
Dodman, John, 159-60 n108
Dodmer, Thomas, 123
Dort, Synod of, 26
Dover (Kent), 44, 57, 143; Suffragan Bishop of, 113, 145; Strait of, 74
Drakes, Robert, 165, 167
Dudley, John, duke of Northumberland, 104
Dunslake, Richard, see Dinestake, Richard

Dymning, William, 185

Ealner, Nicolas, 47
Edward VI, 19, 32, 105, 156, 181-3, 196, 212-13
Egerton (Kent), 76
Eglins, John, 52, 67
Election, v, 2, 14, 76, 158 n102, 184, 192, 204; relationship to predestination, 28, 35; Gardiner on, 36-7; Robert Cooke and, 63; Erasmus on, 92-4; Hoffmann on, 100; Bradford and, 114, 116-22, 125, 128; Ridley (?) and, 131, 135-6, appendix 1; Trewe and, 149-50, 156; Bernhere, Barry and Lawrence and, 159-61, 163; Trewe and Careless and, 170; Reformed view of, 173; anonymous writer and Knox and, 174-6, 178-81; Harte and, 190; Champneys and Veron and, 194
Elham (Kent), 64, 66, 222
Elizabeth I, v, 76, 101 n285, 102 n287, 141, 143, 208-10
Elton, G. R., 8, 11, 13, 31
Erasmus, Desiderius, 4, 17-18, 26, 32, 83 n190, 84, 86-100, 102, 123, 135 n43, 183 n81
Erastianism, 23
Essex, 10, 12, 21, 51-7, 108, 131, 143, 159, 160 n108, 191-2, 223
Eucharist, 8-9, 85, 145
Evans, Benjamin, 164 n123
Eynsford (Kent), 91

Familists, 23, 160 n109, 214
Farnborough (Kent), 91
Faversham (Kent), 1, 44, 52-5, 57-9, 68, 74-7, 85, 90, 101, 104, 110-11, 143, 148, 157, 193-4
Ferrar, Robert, 109, 126, 144
Fisher, John, 88-9
Fitz-Williams, Sir William, 112, 136 n53
Fleet (prison), 109, 157-8

DATE DUE

DEC 1 0 1993			
JUL 10 '96			
OCT 2 2 2001			